THE POCKET ENCYCLOPEDIA OF

California Wines

Revised Edition

BOB THOMPSON

Simon and Schuster
New York

 Published by Simon and Schuster. A Division of Simon & Schuster, Inc., Simon & Schuster Building, Rockefeller Center, 1230 Avenue of the Americas, New York, New York 10020.

Designed by Barbara M. Marks
Manufactured in the United States of America

10 9 8 7 6 5 4 3 2 1

Library of Congress Cataloging in Publication Data

Thompson, Bob, DATE
The pocket encyclopedia of California wines.

1. Wines and wine making—California. I. Title.
TP557.T49 1985 641.2'22'09794 85-10742
ISBN: 0-671-52324-4

Contents

Acknowledgments

The mass of facts in this volume comes principally from direct questioning, the tasting notes from serious drinking, but I owe much to many for help kindly and freely given. Winery owners and winemakers have given of their time and knowledge without exception; to them a blanket thanks. I particularly wish to thank the following people for special contributions to my knowledge of the subject:

Dr. Maynard A. Amerine
Dan Berger
William Bonetti
Don Carano
Nathan Chroman
Darrell Corti
Narsai David
Jack Davies
Greg Doerschlag
Bob Foster
Greg Fowler
Joe Heitz
Hugh Johnson
Nancy Johnston
Tor Kenward
Michael Mondavi
Robert Mondavi
Tim Mondavi
Nick Ponamareff
Phillip Posson
Belle Rhodes
Dr. Bernard Rhodes
Shirley Sarvis
Peter M. F. Sichel
Dr. Vernon L. Singleton
Margaret Smith
Harvey Steiman
Rich Thomas
Dr. A. D. Webb

and, most of all,
Harolyn Thompson

Foreword

When my publishers asked me to write a book on California wines as a companion volume to my *Pocket Encyclopedia of Wine* I had to answer that it could not be done from England. Far too much is going on in California for anyone to follow it in detail from a distance.

There was only one person whom I believed could do the job perfectly: my friend Bob Thompson, who from his home in the Napa Valley has kept a cool, appraising eye on the frenetic California wine scene since many of its present protagonists were under age for tasting.

The following pages speak for themselves. Rely on them and you will not be disappointed. In using them you will pick up a thorough working knowledge of the most exciting wine region in the world.

Hugh Johnson
Essex, England

Introduction

When Hugh Johnson wrote the first *Pocket Encyclopedia of Wine* he called it an exercise in crowding angels on a pinhead, or students into a telephone box. When I added the first *Pocket Encyclopedia of California Wine* to the series in 1980, my effort seemed more like taking a census in a rabbit warren. Rabbits, I have learned since, are not prolific enough to convey a clear picture of how fast vineyards and wineries are springing up in California.

The membership of the Wine Institute, the trade association of California wineries, has shot from fewer than 320 then to more than 490 now. (The "more than" is there because the institute has had time to send out at least two more quarterly lists of new members since this manuscript went to the printers.)

Though it is being said in an era of flat markets that new wineries are desperate responses to surplus grapes, the picture is more mixed than that. A good many of them are in places where both vine and cellar are newcomers to the landscape; a fair number of new cellars in old districts belong to brand-new faces in the business. More to the point, vineyards continue to expand. "Chardonnay" acreage has shot from 1,600 in 1970 to 12,250 in 1980 to 22,000 in 1985. "Cabernet Sauvignon" is the same story. So are "Sauvignon Blanc," "Gewürztraminer," and others.

Be the economics what they might, conscientious wine merchants present us year after year with shelf after shelf of new bewilderment.

Little wonder that many people react by clinging to any old favorite. There is, after all, a good deal of sense in remaining loyal to a proven friend. Wineries stay in business by offering wines that taste good. On no few nights each year I hurry past the new labels in my cellar in favor of an old favorite I know is going to fit my mood and the meal. Even so, this book is an express invitation to split the ticket, to haunt the frontier, because it is on the other nights, when my courage is up, that I earn the stunning rewards of discovery. Sometimes they come in the form of novelty—a Sauternes-sweet Chardonnay from Mendocino. Sometimes they come in the form of a classic—a subtle, claretish Napa Valley Cabernet Sauvignon from a name unknown.

All of the chances are here. The listings take no pity on those who do not live where the mainstream flows. The newest, tiniest, and most obscure join with the oldest, largest, and most famous. (Well, almost all the chances are here. In the tumult, a few cellars no doubt have slipped through the net. Also, regional and local merchant labels do not appear.)

This guide is as bereft of generalities as I can make it, because generalities are not worth much when it comes to wine, except here. A few generalities here will help explain the underpinnings of details in the body of the text.

• On average, I taste and note between 2,000 and 3,000 California wines a year at dinner, at informal tastings, and at formal competitions. Wines that have made consistent impressions are described; wines that have not, are not. The descriptions are, I hope, simple and consistent enough so that other tasters can identify wines of kindred character. No description is meant to be the last word. Winemakers change their minds, or their sources of grapes, or their employment too often for that.

• In these changing times, a willful winemaker often matters more than a vineyard does. When an opinionated man leaves one cellar and vineyard behind for another, he is apt to continue making very similar wine in his new surroundings while his replacement may do something entirely different with the original property.

• The avalanche of new cellars and vineyards has begotten the beginnings of an appellation system, a new development in California (and the rest of the United States) since the original edition of this book. These appellations are paid close heed throughout the text, though little or nothing is known about many of them. The simple fact is, what comes to be known will be defined by them, so they might as well be learned. These appellations (dubbed "American Viticultural Areas" by their inventor, the Bureau of Alcohol, Tobacco, and Firearms) are outlined on maps, pages 30–58.

• In thinking about appellations, one grand generality needs to be remembered: Europe is no place to look for a geographic and climatic model for California. A persistent range of mountains runs parallel to the California coast, shutting off the flow of sea air to the interior in all but a few places. These corridors mark the finest growing conditions for fine varieties whether they are north or south of any reference points. In other words, the cool spots where "Pinot noir" might turn out well are dotted here and there from Mendocino County almost all the way south to Los Angeles, and these are cheek-by-jowl with warmer spots better left to "Cabernet Sauvignon." Put still another way, there is no such thing as a Burgundy or Bordeaux in California. The climatic and thus vinous fragmentation caused by its coastal mountains will last a long while yet, especially in districts where the oldest vines are barely mature now.

How to Read an Entry

KEY TO SYMBOLS

D	Dessert wine
S	Sparkling wine
T	Table wine
*	Ordinary wine
**	Average or above among its peers
***	Among the finest or most famed
****	Grand, prestigious, expensive
*/**	Wines in both classes
□	Consistent good value in its class
nyr	Not yet ranked; fewer than 5 vintages to assess
'80 '81 etc.	Recommended years which may be currently available
esp.	especially
n., e., s., w.	north, east, south, west
r. s.	residual sugar
t. a.	total acidity
v. a.	volatile acidity

"**Cabernet Sauvignon**" refers to a grape variety
Cabernet Sauvignon refers to a varietal wine

Although wine is unalterably a subjective experience (and all the better for it) the * to **** rankings are made somewhat objective by tempering my odder enthusiasms and distastes with the results from well-established annual competitions.

Winery names are printed in red to separate their entries from other categories of information such as merchant brands and technical or tasting terms.

In addition to the rating, the top line of each winery entry shows location within California, usually by county but sometimes by a larger or smaller unit where that is more telling.

Within the body of each winery entry are several other consistent points which require explanation.

Price Range. Each winery entry shows a price range, low to high, for wines in 750ml (or 24 oz.) bottles available at the cellar door as of autumn 1984. The purpose is to provide a single scale from inexpensive to extremely expensive bottlings. Elsewhere, prices may vary enormously, but relative positions should hold.

Availability. Suggested in terms of annual volume. For all but a handful of wineries that did not wish to reveal the information, there is a rounded figure for current sales in cases of 12 standard bottles. For those whose memories do not go back so far, when the federal government repealed Prohibition, it gave the individual states the power to govern commerce in beverages containing alcohol. In these circumstances, each state is a separate market. One winery will claim "national distribution" by sending a case here and a case there, while another makes no such claim in spite of having more wine in more places. Using cases for sale as an index, assume:

- 1,000 cases or less. It is best to live within 50 miles of the cellar or to know its owner.
- 5,000 cases or less. It helps to live in California, but a handful of stores in active urban wine markets are likely to have small rations.
- 10,000 cases or less. Most major urban centers in states without severe impediments to wine sales will have at least one stellar merchant with supplies.
- 20,000 cases or less. In states with active wine audiences, a few skilled merchants beyond the major urban markets may be expected to stock at least some types from a winery's list.
- 40,000 cases or less. Most states with active wine audiences will have limited to good supplies in most cities and some outlying areas.
- 100,000 to 500,000 cases. Wines are almost sure to be available even in the most regressive government monopoly states, and surely will be available in all the rest.
- 1 million cases or more. There is enough for everybody.

Vintages. Vintages noted in descriptions of individual wines point toward better than average efforts by the winery. (The general quality of vintages is described on pp. 25–27, but exceptions to these generalities are abundant.) Owing to a lack of older stocks in the retail trade, vintage references are mostly a service to those with well-developed cellars, but it never hurts to keep an eye open in well-stocked shops.

Learning from the Label

United States law demands that labels carry a useful minimum of information about the wine in the bottle; voluntary disclosure by wineries often tells a great deal more. The model labels are of the latter school.

1. Brand Mandatory. The single most important piece of identification on any label, though in cases of wineries with several brands it sometimes needs to be compared with the bottler's name (see 7).

2. Wine-type Mandatory. Basic possibilities are varietal and generic. By law varietal wine must be a minimum 75% of the grape variety giving it its name (51% for wines bottled before 1983). Though most fine bottlings use a higher proportion, it is a mistake to assume that 100% automatically makes the best wine. Most varieties can gain by discreet blending. Generic names impose no requirements as to grape variety and only very dim ones as to character. Though this does not stop excellent wines being offered under generic names, it does make useful generalizations difficult. Related to generics are proprietaries—wines with coined names. Most echo generic names (Rhineskeller rather than Rhine) but some are completely fanciful (Eshcol, Spiceling) or geographic (Healdsburger).

3. Specific character Optional. Several label terms modify types to indicate color, degree of sweetness, or other qualities. Definitions are in the A–Z section.
For table wines: Late-harvest, dry, off-dry.
For sparkling wines: Natural, Brut, Extra Dry, Sec.
For sherry-types: Dry, Cocktail, Golden, Cream.
For Port-types: Ruby, Tawny, Tinta, Vintage.

4. Region of origin Mandatory. Several layers of names are in current use. Most general is California; to use it, state law requires 100% of the grapes to come from within the state. Traditionally, counties have been the most common smaller unit; federal law requires a minimum 75% of the grapes in a wine to have been grown within the county named. Increasingly, federally approved American Viticultural Areas are supplanting county appellations; to use one of these, federal law requires 85% of the grapes in a wine to come from within boundaries drawn according to climate and soil factors rather than political boundaries. Most fall within the larger boundaries of a single county; some overlap the boundary between two counties. Approved areas are noted with the maps on pages 30–58, and also are cross-referenced in the A–Z.

5. Individual vineyard Optional. A rapidly developing practice, especially among small wineries, is to identify a specific property as the source of a wine. Properties may be owned by the winery or an independent grower. Federal law requires that 95% of the grapes in a wine come from the named property. Vineyard names may not stand alone, but must be used in conjunction with an American Viticultural Area (see 4). A less precise alternative is Estate Bottled, which may be used for all vineyards owned or controlled by a winery and lying within the same American Viticultural Area as the winery itself.

6. Vintage Optional. States the year in which the grapes were grown and the wine fermented. If used, by federal law 95% of the wine must come from the year stated. (The allowance permits practical topping of casks during aging.)

7. Bottler Mandatory. The small type at the bottom of a label must give the name of the bottler and the bottler's business (not necessarily winery) address. The line may say "Bottled by," in which case the firm could buy the wine one day and bottle it the next. "Cellared and bottled by" (or similar) indicates that the bottler has done work, often invaluable, to put his stamp on the wine. "Made and bottled by" can be used only if the bottler fermented a minimum 10% of the wine in the bottle. "Produced and bottled by" may be used only if the named bottler fermented a minimum 75% of the wine. "Grown, produced and bottled by" guarantees complete control of 100% of the wine from vineyard to bottling line.

8. Alcohol content Mandatory. The legal limits for table wine are 7% to 14%. The alcohol content can be stated, with a permitted allowance of 1.5% above or below the actual content, or the words "Table wine" or "Light wine" can appear

instead. If the alcohol content exceeds 14%, it must be stated accurately. For sherry-types, the alcohol limits are 17% to 20%, and for Port-types 18% to 20%, with a permitted allowance of 1% from actual.

9. **Sparkling wines** If the word "Champagne" appears on a label, it must be accompanied somewhere on the package by a statement noting the technique used to produce the wine. These include *méthode champenoise* ("*méthode champenoise*" or "fermented in this bottle"), transfer process ("Bottle fermented" or "fermented in the bottle"), and bulk process ("bulk process" or "Charmat process"). Descriptions of the processes are in the A–Z section.

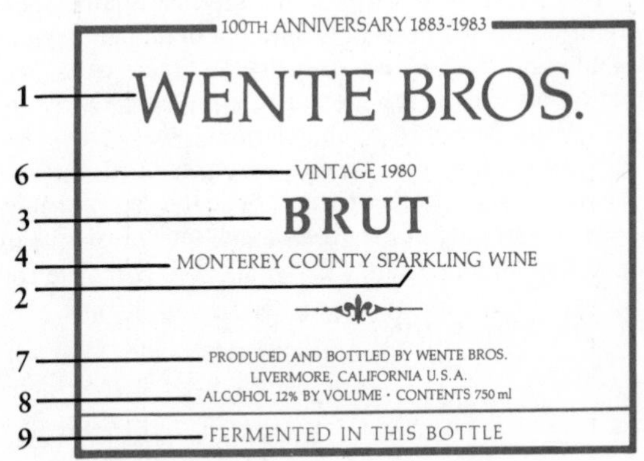

Grape Varieties

Everywhere in the world grape varieties give wines their fundamental characteristics. Growing regions add important shadings and winemakers add still other colorings, but Cabernet Sauvignon remains itself whether it grows in its ancestral home in Bordeaux, in the Napa Valley, or in almost any suitable part of the world.

In much of Europe these distinctions exist but go unstated because long experience within a region of homogenous climate has pared the roster of grapes to a very few; regions and varieties go together in unbreakable alliance.

In California, with its checkered pattern of climate, any one grape variety is likely to do well in a dozen geographic districts, and any one district is likely to do well by a dozen varieties. This condition accounts for the Californian habit of naming wine types after a dominant variety rather than a place.

As a means of linking districts with kindred weathers, the University of California devised the system of climate regions noted on page 28. The school also made climate-based recommendations of where each grape will grow best. One word of caution about these recommendations: they are based mainly on wine quality, but also on economics. Also, they are only a rough first try. Excellent wines belie the recommendations, sometimes in spite of the economics, sometimes because the study missed a point.

GRAPES FOR WHITE WINE

Chardonnay (alias Pinot Chardonnay)
California's greatest age-worthy dry whites come from Bur-

gundy's greatest white grape. U. C.-Davis's (University of California at Davis) varietal association is apple-like, but oak aging often revolutionizes its aromas to richer ones more remindful of peach, or, in wines from extra-ripe fruit, even pineapple. The best wines from Napa and Sonoma stay in top form for 10 years and more; durability of wines from other districts remains to be proven. Highly recommended for Region I, recommended for Region II. Total acreage in the state is 22,076. Napa has all the edge going back in history, but splendid examples are being made in Sonoma, Mendocino, and Santa Barbara counties, and very good ones in almost every coastal county.

Chauche Gris
See: Gray Riesling.

Chenin Blanc (alias Pineau de la Loire)
Makes gentle wine of pleasing though indistinct flavors—serviceable rather than great. Widely made as varietal, though much of a large tonnage goes into generic whites. Styles range from all-steel aging to barrel-fermented, and from bone-dry to moderately sweet (2% r. s.), with most at 1% to 1.5% r. s. For early drinking in every case. The vine is a prolific bearer. Recommended for Region I; qualified recommendation for Regions II and III. Total state acreage is 43,496, with a huge proportion of that in the San Joaquin Valley. The finest examples have come from Napa, Sonoma, Mendocino. San Luis Obispo, and an area along the Sacramento River in Yolo County.

Emerald Riesling
To date the most successful white cross ("White Riesling" x "Muscat") by Dr. Harold Olmo at U. C.-Davis. It was designed to yield quality counterparts in warm regions to wines from "Johannisberg Riesling" grown in cool areas; its results are not quite that fine, but more than competitive with Sylvaners. In coastal vineyards (esp. Monterey), it has made its best wines. They can be attractive dry, but seem more appealing at 1% r. s. and bottled as soon as possible. 2,740 acres bearing, of which the great majority are in the San Joaquin Valley.

Flora
Another of Olmo's U. C.-Davis hybrids ("Gewürztraminer" x "Sémillon"), it resembles "Gewürztraminer" more in cool conditions, "Sémillon" more in warmer ones. Very little is planted (416 acres bearing). Only Parducci Wine Cellars is consistently producing varietal wine from it in commercial volumes. Schramsberg's Crémant is based in "Flora."

Folle Blanche
The variety's historic role in France is in Cognacs. In California it can be useful in sparkling wines for its subdued varietal flavors and tartness. All 351 bearing acres are in the coastal counties. Only Louis M. Martini makes it as a varietal table wine.

Franken Riesling
See: Sylvaner.

French Colombard
Well ripened, it has distinct perfumey aromas—sometimes dimestore, sometimes finer. Long a tart blending grape for generics, it came into its own in varietal wines with cold fermentation and the ability to control sweetness. Now in considerable favor as a modestly priced sipper of 1 to 2% r. s., much in the vein of Liebfraumilchs or Moselblümchens, though more specific in varietal flavors. U. C. has recommended it for Regions III and IV. 29,985 acres are in bearing in the state, 90% of them in the San Joaquin Valley, but the finest wines come from plantings in Mendocino and northern Sonoma County. All of them should be drunk young.

Fumé Blanc
See: Sauvignon Blanc.

Gewürztraminer
In German, *gewürz* means spicy (the variety is Italo-Austrian in origin, mainly Alsatian in recent times), and was added to Traminer in an attempt to describe the flavor. In California spicy is a minority report; most examples are flowery, hinting at the grape's family ties to the Muscats, but keep the faint hint of bitterness that marks fine examples from Alsace. U. C. recommends it for Region I, gives it a qualified recommendation for II. In practice II and cool III have yielded the most admired wines, especially Russian River Valley and Alexander Valley. The variety has yielded excellent wines from other parts of Sonoma, Napa, Monterey, Mendocino, and Santa Barbara, though most have been only serviceable. All of 2,795 bearing acres are in coastal counties. A majority of Gewürztraminer wines are made just off-dry (.6 to 1.5% r. s.); a handful are bone-dry, another handful extra-sweet (4 to 30% r. s.) owing to *Botrytis*. The finest in all styles benefit from 3 years in bottle.

Gray Riesling
No Riesling, but the surprisingly bright offshoot of a meager French grape, "Trousseau." Pleasant fruit flavors mark modest but well-balanced wines, a few of which may show a hint

of color from faintly pink grapes. U. C. does not recommend planting it, but the wine's followers lap up everything that can be made from 2,031 acres, half of that shared among Alameda, Monterey, and Napa counties. The wines almost inevitably are off-dry, at .6 to 1.5% r. s.

Green Hungarian
Dull grape of uncertain origin, in spite of which typically bland varietal wines from it enjoy a certain vogue. U. C. does not recommend it. The 325 acres, most in coastal counties, yield apparently inexhaustible crops judging by the floods of off-dry to outright sweet Green Hungarian wines on the market.

Johannisberg Riesling
See: White Riesling.

Muscat Blanc
(alias Moscato Canelli, Muscat Canelli,
Muscat de Frontignan)
Adaptable variety has enough finesse of flavor to make a lighter, simpler alternative to Gewürztraminer (most frequently under the name Canelli), and enough strength to make fortified varietal dessert wine (almost always under the name of Muscat Frontignan). It also does well in sparklers styled after Asti Spumantes. 977 acres are widely scattered about the state. As off-dry, drink-it-up table wine, it usually comes from Regions II and III; as age-worthy dessert wine it tends to come from III and IV, but exceptions exist in both directions. Several wineries vary the name a bit (Moscato Amabile, Moscato d'Oro, etc.).

Pinot Blanc
Much in the shade of Chardonnay, perhaps as much because of the fashion for Chardonnay as any inherent shortcomings. Indeed, the finest bottlings sometimes win blind tastings of Chardonnay because they are subtler, yet can be firmer. The grape is recommended for Region I by U. C., and given qualified recommendations for II and III. Of 2,220 acres, all but a handful are in the coastal counties, where their crops go as much to sparkling as still wine. Napa, Sonoma, and Monterey contend for honors with wines made in the same oak-aged fashion as Chardonnay. A few cellars offer the wine without a smack of oak.

Pinot Chardonnay
See: Chardonnay.

Sauvignon Blanc (alias Fumé Blanc)
The white cousin to "Cabernet Sauvignon" steadily produces

strongly flavored wines in several districts, much as it does in its original vineyards in Bordeaux and along the Loire. Its character is readily defined as herbaceous to grassy. The grape is highly recommended for Region I, recommended for II and III. Of 11,640 acres, 70% are in coastal counties from Mendocino to Santa Barbara. Livermore Valley has grown it best for long-lived, truly grand wines, but so slow-developing a style is not in current favor there or elsewhere. Santa Ynez Valley shows signs of possible greatness, but, for the moment, Napa and Sonoma yield excellent wines from the variety most consistently. Styles vary from no wood age to 2 years in oak, from bone-dry to distinctly sweet. Some are labelled Sauvignon Blanc, others Fumé Blanc, without any apparent thought to style.

Scheurebe
A German-bred variety based in "White Riesling," and much similar to it, has yet to be planted to enough acres to appear in vineyard surveys, but two wineries offer it as a varietal, Balverne in an off-dry style, Joseph Phelps in a *Botrytis*-affected late-harvest style.

Sémillon
Often described as tasting fig-like, the traditional Bordeaux variety in fact ranges from outright blandness to figgy to very nearly identical to "Sauvignon Blanc." The grape is recommended for Regions II and III, where it can become distinctive enough to make varietal wine, but is more likely to be valued as a blend grape to tone down "Sauvignon Blanc." It has enough virtues in the San Joaquin Valley to have almost half of its 3,230 acres there for blending into generics and varietals. As a varietal wine, it has been made dry with only modest hopes, but several winemakers have begun to work seriously with it. Sémillon's finest hours have been as a *Botrytis*-affected or sun-dried sweet wine.

Sylvaner
A secondary grape to "White Riesling" in Germany, it hardly ranks that high in California, but does decent service in off-dry, drink-it-up style wines sometimes as a varietal, sometimes as a major partner in proprietaries where it is called "Monterey Riesling," "Sonoma Riesling," or something similar. It is recommended for Region II by U. C., and given qualified recommendations for I and III. Most of the 1,455 acres are in coastal counties.

White Riesling
(alias Johannisberg Riesling)
Germany's greatest grape transplanted to sunny California

with surprising success, especially after stylistic revolution in the late 1960s shifted away from dry to off-dry table wines; a taming of *Botrytis* then added super-sweet nectars to its range in the early 1970s. U. C. highly recommends the variety for Region I, and recommends it with qualification for II. Virtually all of the state's 8,273 acres are in coastal counties, with more than half the total in Napa, Sonoma, and Monterey. These same counties, plus Mendocino and Santa Barbara, have yielded most of the treasurable bottlings of both off-dry and dessert-sweet styles . . . in areas as warm as Region III. The dessert-sweet ones have run even higher in r. s. (to 54% to date) than German Trockenbeerenausleses and French Sauternes.

GRAPES FOR RED WINE

Alicante Bouschet
Common blending variety much planted during Prohibition because its tough skin allowed it to ship well to home winemakers. Plantings have declined to 3,800 acres, most in the interior valleys, where it has some value because of its deep color. It is rarely made as a varietal table wine; Papagni Vineyards is the steady supplier.

Barbera
A secondary grape in Italy's Piedmont has been that region's most successful export to California. It makes an agreeably fruity red wine in the interior, a surprisingly complex and ageworthy one in the coastal counties (especially if blended with Petite Sirah for tannic backbone). U. C. recommends it for Regions III and IV, recommends it with qualifications for II and V. Acreage is 17,420, nearly all in the San Joaquin Valley.

Cabernet Sauvignon
The great grape of the Médoc also makes coastal California's greatest red wines. Its tastes are the austere ones of herbs, tea, or olives, and wines from it tend to be tannic as well. The grape is highly recommended for Region I, recommended for II, and recommended with reservations for III (where it has made some of its finest wines). Most of its 22,040 acres are in the coastal counties, especially Napa, Sonoma, and Monterey. Nearly all truly famous bottlings from the 1930s through the mid-1970s came from Napa, but Sonoma and Mendocino have raised some challenges. Sparse plantings in the Santa Cruz Mountains demonstrate why that region was famous before 1919. Monterey, San Luis Obispo, and Santa Barbara Cabernet Sauvignons have tended to have exaggerated herbaceous or vegetative flavors to date.

Carignane
A common blending grape with some flavor kinships to "Cabernet Sauvignon." It is recommended for Regions III–V. A great majority of its 21,165 acres are in the San Joaquin. A few coastal wineries bottle it as a varietal.

Carnelian
Developed by Dr. H. P. Olmo at U. C.-Davis from the same family tree that earlier yielded "Ruby Cabernet." It was meant to produce Cabernet-like wines in warm growing regions. The proof is not yet in; most early varietal wines have been made as Nouveau-types. Acreage is 1,767, nearly all in the San Joaquin.

Charbono
Originally Italian, it makes in California a paler, softer cousin of Barbera. Of the state total of 85 acres, 80 are in Napa, where Franciscan and Inglenook make it as a varietal.

Gamay (alias Napa Gamay)
A heavy-bearing grape thought to be the "Gamay" grown in Beaujolais, but perhaps only a kin to it. It makes a sturdy, straightforward wine if handled conventionally, and responds well to carbonic maceration. It gets only a qualified recommendation for Regions I and II. Napa and Monterey have about 1,000 acres each, of a state total of 4,150.

Gamay Beaujolais
Long held to be the true "Gamay" of Beaujolais, it finally turned out to be a frail clone of "Pinot Noir."

Grenache
A curiously perfumey (U. C.-Davis says "estery") character marks this variety from the Rhône districts of France. In California, its best roles have been in off-dry rosés and tawny Port-types, but it is made as a red varietal from time to time. Though recommended for Region II, it has proven hard to ripen in the warmest coastal regions. The majority of its 17,060 acres are in the San Joaquin Valley and in southern California.

Grignolino
U. C.-Davis thinks at least 2 varieties are identified and sold as "Grignolino." The taste of the wines bears this out. Some are tart and pungently spicy, almost orange liqueur–like in flavor. Others are just tart. It may be at its finest as a dry rosé. Heitz Cellars demonstrates the possibilities yearly. Only 52 acres are planted, 18 in Napa, 34 in Santa Clara.

Merlot
Very similar in flavor to "Cabernet Sauvignon," but almost

its antithesis in tactile sensations, its wines being fleshy, lacking in tannic astringency. Its resurgence in California vineyards began because it was sought as a softener of Cabernet Sauvignons. It has succeeded in becoming a substantial varietal in its own right. U. C.-Davis has made no recommendation. Only 2,161 acres are in the state. The coastal counties, mainly Napa and Sonoma, have by far the largest plantings. The trick is to achieve a little tannic spine. Most do so by blending a small proportion of Cabernet Sauvignon with it.

Mission
Ancient variety that came to California from Spain via South America, carried in the 1770s by Franciscan missionaries. Then and since, purple grapes as big as musket balls have yielded dessert wines that begin without distinction but live long enough to gain it. U. C. recommends it for Region V, but its finest results have come from Amador County in the Sierra Foothills. Most of the state's 3,220 acres are in the San Joaquin and southern California.

Napa Gamay
See: Gamay.

Petite Sirah
Not the "Sirah" of the Rhône, but most probably an offshoot of a lesser Rhônish grape, "Duriff." It carries flavor hints of black pepper and broadsides of tannin. For years a backbone in generic reds, it began to emerge as a varietal in the 1960s. U. C. recommends it for Region II, qualifies the recommendation for III. Of a state acreage of 8,345, more than half is in the San Joaquin, but the most rewarding plantings are in Napa, Sonoma, Mendocino, and Monterey. It is hard to make into a stylish wine unless given long aging in oak, a softening dollop of a blend grape ("Pinot Noir" does well), or both. Some of these have been fine, especially after 4 or 5 years in bottle.

Pinot Noir
The great black grape of Burgundy shows all manner of faces in California: sometimes deplorable, sometimes outstanding, but mostly a tease. The best wines from it show a minty flavor against a meaty texture. A faintly raisiny note marks many of the best of these. U. C. recommends it in Region I, qualifies the recommendation in II. Of 8,900 acres, 80% are in Napa, Sonoma, and Monterey. The coolest parts of these counties—Mendocino and, perhaps, Santa Barbara—are where most hope rests. At its best, it has yielded extraordinary red wines capable of aging 15 years. But its frequent shortcomings have

led to most of it being used in *méthode champenoise* sparkling wines and still Blanc de Noirs, where it is reliably attractive.

Ruby Cabernet
The earliest and now most widely planted of the varieties developed at U. C.-Davis by Dr. H. P. Olmo was meant to capture the flavors of "Cabernet Sauvignon" in a variety that would grow well in San Joaquin Valley heat. It got much of the way there, but fell far enough short that it has not become popular as a varietal wine. Still, the crop from 13,200 acres is much valued in the San Joaquin for the quality it gives red table wines and the occasional varietal. The best are dry, and aged in oak.

Syrah
Only a handful of acres (87) have been planted to the true "Sirah" of the Rhône, mainly in Napa, Sonoma, and San Luis Obispo (the latter from an Australian clone). Its true worth in California is only beginning to be seen, but the handful of wines at hand show promise.

Tinta Madeira
One of the classic varieties of the Douro Valley in Portugal, it has lent its curiously dusty, almost oaky character to several Port-types of quality. The shaky market for such wines has meant that its 335 acres are more than needed just now, but it deserves to survive. U. C. recommends it highly for Region V, recommends it for IV, and qualifies the recommendation for III. The plantings follow faithfully.

Zinfandel
Purely Californian now, though it appears to have remote ancestry in one of the Primitivos of southern Italy. The flavor associated is almost always given as berry-like, especially blackberry-like. Recommended for Region I, and given qualified recommendation for II and III, it is among the most planted black varieties in the state, with 28,045 acres scattered throughout every district. It can be very fine from cooler parts of Mendocino (Anderson Valley), Sonoma, Napa, and the Santa Cruz Mountains. It is less fine, headier, but still engaging, from warmer zones such as Amador, San Luis Obispo, and the warmer parts of Sonoma and Mendocino. Unhappily for its current reputation, it can be made in every style from Nouveau to dry Port, and has been—but without much notice on the labels. Confused consumers have turned instead to "blush" wines from it. Called White Zinfandel, these have become a fad since 1982, proving that there is nothing wrong with the basic flavor of the variety.

Vintage Chart

With the profusion of new wineries has come new awareness of variation among vintages in California. Distinctions once lost in multiple vineyard blends now stand out, especially in reds, but also in whites.

To date, only Napa and Sonoma have enough wineries and enough history to allow generalizations worth making. The following summaries apply mainly to those regions. Supplementary notes follow for other districts that need separate explanation.

Cabernet Sauvignon

1984 Hot. Earliest harvest in memory. Wines powerfully scented in the fermentors. (More normal year for Central Coast.)

1983 Favorable weather. Room for optimism. (Early rains made Central Coast miserable.)

1982 Summer heat led to early harvest. No easy generalities as wines go to bottle in 1984.

1981 In spite of a warm growing season, some subtlety and delicacy in wines of at least fair balance. Pleasing now; may mature well.

1980 Big, richly scented wines, perhaps akin to '78s. Some seem forward; some seem ready to endure for longer than average.

1979 Cool year yielded austere, deeply flavored wines. Some of the restrained ones should age for years yet. Tannic monsters may never be anything else.

1978 Lovely fruit flavors from warm year. Many at or past peak.

1977 Many struggled to ripen, but some subtle, delicate treasures. (Central Coast had easier weather.)
1976 Heavy, dull after hot drought year.
1975 Early rains caught some, but finesse in the best after a cool season. Not a vintage for fanciers of the bold.
1974 Showy early. Holding surprisingly well.
1973 Overlooked early. Not as aromatic as 1974, but sturdier.
1972 Rainy year. Mostly a washout.
1971 Poorest year of the decade.
1970 Touted as vintage of century. Good, but never quite lived up to the promise.

Pinot Noir

1984 Too warm for best showing. (Central Coast is better hope.)
1983 Favorable weather. Room for optimism. (Central Coast fared less well.)
1982 Only moderate hopes as wines go to bottle, but some stars emerging.
1981 Escaped late heat; seem to be developing well. Should be given 5 years in bottle.
1980 Middling.
1979 One of the decade's finest vintages. Complex, balanced wine with prospects of aging well to 10 years, perhaps more.
1978 Middling.
1977 Above average. Soft, rounded. At or past peak.
1976 Hot, dry year yielded little of interest.
1975 Challenges 1979 as outstanding year of decade. Intriguing combination of delicacy, longevity.

Zinfandel

1984 Maybe overripe, but smelled fine in fermentors.
1983 Have a chance.
1982 Warm, early year made many overripe, but some show some promise.
1981 If picked early enough, well above average. Rest are merely heady.
1980 Warm growing conditions led to many overripe, soft wines.
1979 Only a few ripened well, but those are splendid.
1978 Superior vintage. At top form now, and easing onto downslope.

Chardonnay

1984 Like other varieties, lovely in the fermentors.
1983 Just coming to market. Outstanding prospects among the ripe, rich school.
1982 Overall, not much, but in particular instances, spectacular. Handicapper's nightmare.
1981 Splendid wines. Firm, durable, enticingly scented.
1980 Neck and neck with '81s. Napa especially good.
1979 Some aging well. Started as austere wines.
1978 Showy early. Most faded now, but a few of the subtler ones were still gaining in 1984.

Sauvignon Blanc

1984 The usual hopes.
1983 Well above average. Showing well early.
1982 Sound, steady. Some are superb.
1981 Most splendid. The best still gaining in bottle.
1980 Good, steady. At or past the peak now.

Late-Harvest Johannisberg Riesling

1982 A few tried, but autumn was warm and dry.
1983 Not completely favorable, but a handful could try, especially in Mendocino and Lake counties.
1982 Superb year. Many powerfully scented, richly concentrated late-harvest wines in all districts, but few exaggerated monsters. Easily best season since '73 in the North Coast.
1981 Very good year. Sugars reached 30° Brix in wide area, 40° Brix in favored spots.
1980 Much like '81, good in spots.
1979 Excellent year for wines in medium range (to 30° Brix).

California Wine Districts

California has relied on counties as its main vinous dividing lines. This begins to change in favor of finer shadings shown on more detailed maps in the following pages. Meanwhile, counties are a convenient way to locate individual wineries.

Groups of counties are useful general keys to climate, thus wine character. The main division is interior and coast, with the interior (San Joaquin to Kern) much warmer and drier—climate Regions IV and V (see below). The coast, in turn, divides into three areas: North Coast (Napa, Sonoma, Mendocino, Lake, with more extremes of weather than the others); Central Coast (Alameda to Santa Barbara, usually mild); and South Coast (Riverside and San Diego, forever mild). All are Regions I–III. Two remaining distinctive areas are the Sierra Foothills (El Dorado, Amador, Calaveras, all hot in summer, cold in winter), and the Sacramento Delta (Sacramento and Yolo, tempered by the Sacramento River).

CLIMATE REGIONS

A rough scale developed at the University of California-Davis, divides the state into 5 climate Regions:

Region I—less than 2,500 degree days
Region II—2,501–3,000 degree days
Region III—3,001–3,500 degree days
Region IV—3,501–4,000 degree days
Region V—4,001 or more degree days

Degree days measure average daily temperatures above

50°F. The Regions summarize total degree days between April 1 and October 30.

Generally, the school recommends fine wine varieties for Regions I–III, heavy bearers and varieties for dessert wines for Regions IV–V. Notes on individual varieties (immediately following) list specific recommendations.

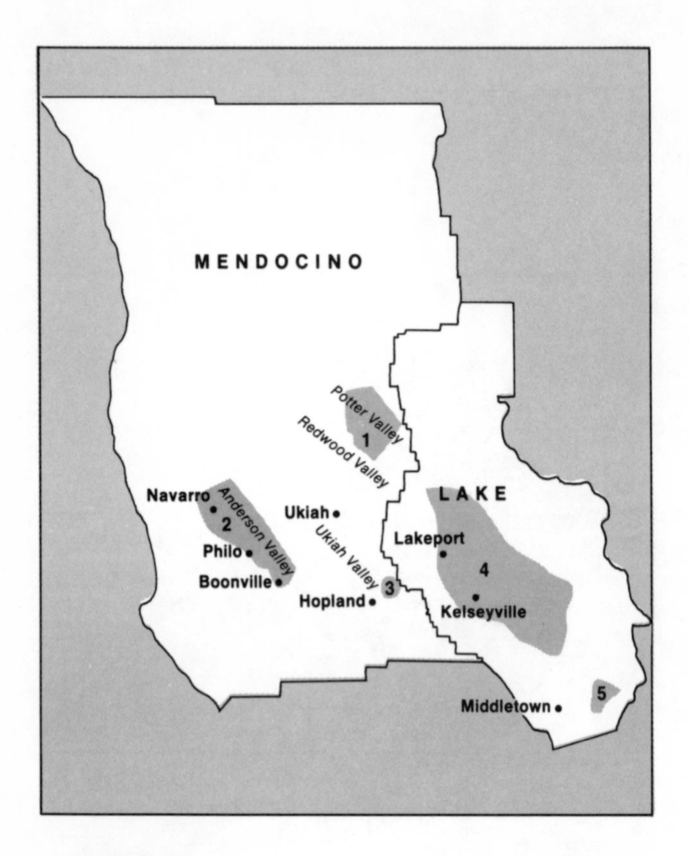

1. Potter Valley
2. Anderson Valley
3. McDowell Valley
4. Clear Lake
5. Guenoc Valley

Mendocino and Lake

MENDOCINO COUNTY

Northernmost of the coastal counties, Mendocino has 24 wineries and 10,000 acres in vines in several sub-districts with diverse climates and soils. Its principal varieties (in acres) are "Carignane" (1,921), "Zinfandel" (1,322), "French Colombard" (1,111), "Cabernet Sauvignon" (927), and "Chardonnay" (898).

SUB-DISTRICTS:

Anderson Valley AVA. A small, shallow valley of the Navarro River planted only since the 1960s, mostly between Philo and Navarro. Climate Regions I and II, it has yielded fine White Rieslings, Gewürztraminers, and Chardonnays, and begins to loom as a source of *méthode champenoise* sparkling wines. Has 582 acres in vines and is growing.

Hopland. Not an AVA. Downstream along the Russian River from Ukiah, the area has 2,200 acres in vines, but has made few identifiable wines. McDowell Valley falls within it.

McDowell Valley AVA. A small, one-winery area e. of Hopland. Climate Region III, and an apparent good location for making Zinfandel, Syrah, and French Colombard.

Potter Valley AVA. An upland valley n.e. of Ukiah, it has about 1,000 acres of vines. White Rieslings and Sauvignon Blancs have been the most interesting wines to date. Climate Region III.

Redwood Valley Not an AVA, but a well-defined area n. of Ukiah. Region III, it has turned out some fine Cabernet Sauvignons from its hilly w. side. Planted acreage is about 2,200.

Ukiah Valley Not an AVA, but the largest district in the county in plantings (4,500 acres). Its historic reputation is for French Colombards and Zinfandels; it has done well by Chardonnays. Within it is a single-vineyard AVA, Cole Ranch.

The catchall Mendocino AVA encompasses all of these.

LAKE COUNTY

Well known for grapes before Prohibition, the county has only recently replanted vines after a long hiatus. The county has 7 wineries. Current acreage is about 3,000. Cabernet Sauvignon accounts for at least half of that total. There are two districts, neither with a clear track record to date, though Cabernet, Sauvignon Blanc, and White Riesling appear suited. Climate Region III.

SUB-DISTRICTS:

Clear Lake AVA. Encircles the lake, and has most of the acreage.

Guenoc Valley AVA. A one-winery, 275-acre area s. of Middletown.

WINERIES

Lake County
Cobb Mountain
Guenoc Winery
Kendall-Jackson Winery
Konocti Winery
Lower Lake Winery
Rudd Cellars, Channing

Mendocino County
Baccala Winery, William
Blanc Vineyards
Braren-Pauli Winery
Cresta Blanca Winery
Dolan Vineyards
Edmeades Vineyards
Fetzer Vineyard
Frey Vineyards
Greenwood Ridge
Handley Cellars
Hidden Cellars
Husch Vineyards
Lazy Creek Vineyards
McDowell Valley Vineyards
Milano Winery
Mountain House Winery
Navarro Vineyards
Olson Vineyards
Parducci Wine Cellars
Parsons Creek Winery
Pepperwood Springs Vineyards
Roederer
Scharffenberger Cellars
Tijsseling Vineyard
Whaler Vineyard

Sonoma

The most sizable of the vinegrowing continues n. of San Francisco also is the most diverse in climate and soils, and has the largest number of AVAs within it. Sonoma has 100 wineries and 30,200 acres in vineyard. Its principal varieties (in acres) are "Chardonnay" (6,460), "Cabernet Sauvignon" (4,715), "Zinfandel" (4,635), "Pinot Noir" (2,841), "Sauvignon Blanc" (1,767), "French Colombard" (1,388), "White Riesling" (1,367), "Gewürztraminer" (1,260), and "Chenin Blanc" (1,102).

SUB-DISTRICTS:

Alexander Valley AVA. A sprawling length of the Russian River watershed reaching from Healdsburg n. to the Mendocino County line. Regions II and III, it is versatile. Some of its most memorable wines are Chardonnays, Gewürztraminers, and Zinfandels.

Carneros AVA. The southern tip of Sonoma Valley, overlooking San Pablo Bay, has a reputation for fine Chardonnay and Pinot Noir. It also has turned out some excellent Cabernet Sauvignon, but the grape is hard to ripen in the foggy, Region I climate. The AVA laps over into the Napa Valley.

Chalk Hill AVA. The area reaches into hilly country e. of Windsor and s. of Healdsburg. Its Sauvignon Blancs have intense character, its Chardonnays subtle ones. It is climate Region II. Vineyard acreage approaches 1,600.

Dry Creek Valley AVA. A narrow, snaking valley w. and n. of Healdsburg, it has a long reputation for flavorful Zinfandels and a more recent one for Sauvignon Blancs and Cabernet Sauvignons.

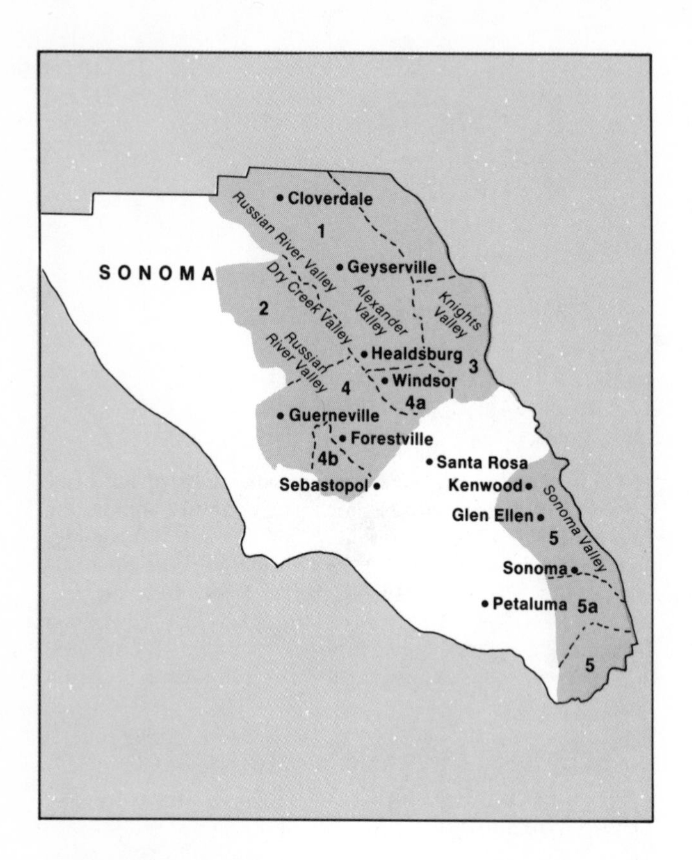

1. Alexander Valley
2. Dry Creek Valley
3. Knights Valley
4. Russian River Valley
   4a. Chalk Hill
   4b. Sonoma-Green Valley
5. Sonoma Valley
   5a. Carneros

Knights Valley AVA. An upland valley at the s.e. tip of the county, just across the line from the upper Napa Valley, it has made outstanding late-harvest White Rieslings and subtle Sauvignon Blancs. Cabernet Sauvignon shows promise, also. Vineyard acreage is 1,000; climate is Region III.

Russian River Valley AVA. The plains and low hills w. of Windsor and Santa Rosa, Regions I and II, are the source of some extraordinary Chardonnays and Gewürztraminers, and some fine Pinot Noirs. The region begins to have a reputation for fine *méthode champenoise* sparkling wines.

Sonoma-Green Valley AVA. South and w. of Forestville, just within the w. boundary of the larger Russian River Valley AVA, it is known for Chardonnays and sparkling wines. Vineyard acreage is 800.

Sonoma Valley AVA. The southern (Carneros) end of the only Sonoma region draining into San Francisco Bay is Region I. It warms almost to Region III to the n. at Kenwood, where Sauvignon Blanc replaces Chardonnay, and Cabernet Sauvignon and Zinfandel have been striking. Total acreage is 5,900.

WINERIES

Sonoma County
Adler-Fels
Alderbrook Vineyards
Alexander Valley Vineyards
Balverne Vineyards
Bellerose Vineyard
Belvedere Wine Co.
Buena Vista
Bynum Winery, Davis
California Wine Co.
Cambiaso
Carmenet
Caswell Vineyards
Charis Vineyards
Chateau St. Jean
Clos du Bois
Cordtz Brothers
Coturri & Sons, H.
Dehlinger Winery
DeLoach Vineyards
Diamond Oaks Vineyard
Domaine Laurier
Domaine Michel
Donna Maria Vineyards
Dry Creek Vineyard
Duboeuf & Son, Georges
Duxoup Wine Works
Ferrer, Gloria
Field Stone Winery
Fisher Vineyards
Foppiano Wine Co., Louis
Fritz Cellars
Geyser Peak
Glen Ellen Winery
Grand Cru
Gundlach-Bundschu Vineyard Co.
Hacienda del Rio
Hacienda Wine Cellars
Hafner Vineyard
Hanzell
Haywood Winery
Hop Kiln Winery
Hultgren & Samperton

Wineries (*cont.*)

Hunter Vineyard, Robert
Iron Horse Ranch & Vineyards
Italian Swiss Colony
Jimark Winery
Johnson's of Alexander Valley
Jordan Vineyard and Winery
Kenwood Winery
Kistler Vineyards
Korbel & Bros., F.
La Crema Vinera
Lambert Bridge
Landmark Vineyards
Las Montanas
Laurel Glen
Lyeth Vineyard & Winery
Lytton Springs Winery
Marietta Cellars
Mark West Vineyards
Martini & Prati
Matanzas Creek
Merry Vintners
Mill Creek Vineyards
Morris Winery, J. W.
Pastori
Paulsen Vineyards, Pat
Pedroncelli Winery, J.
Piper-Sonoma
Pommeraie Vineyards
Preston Vineyards & Winery
Rafanelli Winery, A.
Ravenswood
Richardson Vineyards
River Oaks Vineyards
River Road Vineyards
Rochioli Vineyards
Rose Family Vineyard
St. Francis
Sausal Winery
Searidge Winery
Sebastiani Vineyards
Seghesio Winery
Sellards Winery, Thomas
Simi Winery
Soda Rock Winery
Sonoma-Cutrer Vineyards
Sonoma Hills Winery
Sotoyome
Souverain Cellars
Stemmler Winery, Robert
Strong Vineyards, Rodney
Swan Vineyards, Joseph
Taft Street
Topolos at Russian River Vineyards
Toyon Winery & Vineyards
Trentadue Winery
Valley of the Moon
Warnelius Vineyards
Wheeler Winery, William
White Oak Vineyards
Zellerbach Vineyard, Steven

Napa

Climates and soils are more homogenous in this small county n. across the bay from San Francisco than in most others, because it is dominated by the Napa Valley. Within its narrow confines are more than 130 wineries, and 28,400 acres of vineyards. Principal varieties (in acres) are "Cabernet Sauvignon" (5,901), "Chardonnay" (5,662), "Sauvignon Blanc" (2,733), "Pinot Noir" (2,330), "Chenin Blanc" (2,274), "Zinfandel" (2,095), and "White Riesling" (1,332).

SUB-DISTRICTS:

Carneros AVA. At the southern tip of the valley, looking into San Pablo Bay, it is climate Region I, and much favored for Chardonnay. It has made some fine Pinot Noirs, and a few excellent Cabernets, though the variety is hard to ripen. Acreage is about 2,000.

Chiles Valley Not an AVA, but a small upland valley parallel to and just e. of the main Napa Valley. Few identifiable wines have come from it, but there is promise for Cabernet Sauvignon.

Howell Mountain AVA. A small area ranging around the 1,400-ft. elevation mark in hills e. of St. Helena, its best wines have been Cabernet Sauvignons and Zinfandels.

Pope Valley Not an AVA, but probably should be separated from Napa Valley as an appellation. Few identifiable wines have come from it. Several varieties show promise.

Napa Valley AVA. The name takes in nearly the whole county, including both of the smaller AVAs noted above. Climate Regions I through III, it is in nearly all of its areas best

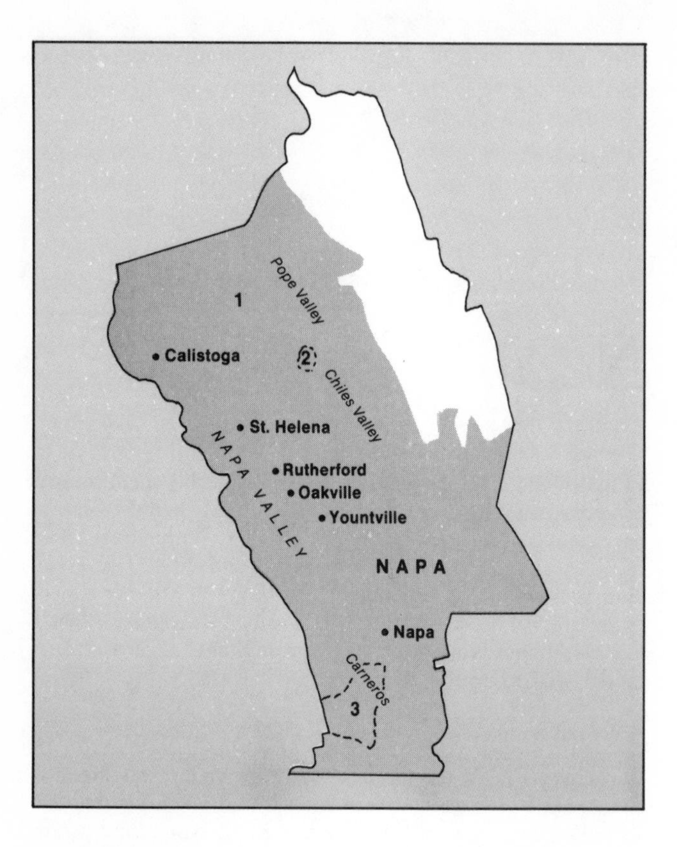

1. Napa Valley
2. Howell Mountain
3. Carneros

suited to make Cabernet Sauvignon, but is versatile, capable of outstanding Chardonnays, Sauvignon Blancs, White Rieslings, Gewürztraminers, and, more rarely, Zinfandels.

WINERIES

Napa Valley
Acacia
Acacia-Cafaro
Alatera Vineyards
Alta Vineyard
Anderson Vineyard, S.
Beaulieu Vineyard
Beringer Vineyard
Buehler Vineyards
Burgess Cellars
Cain Cellars
Cakebread Cellars
Calafia Cellars
Carneros Creek
Casa Nuestra
Cassayre-Forni
Caymus Vineyard
Chappellet Vineyard
Château Boswell
Chateau Bouchaine
Chateau Chevalier
Chateau Chêvre
Chateau Montelena
Christian Brothers Winery
Clos du Val Wine Co.
Conn Creek
Costello
Cuvaison, Inc.
Daniel Society, John
Deer Park Winery
Diamond Creek Vineyards
Domaine Chandon
Domaine Marville
Domaine Mumm
Duckhorn Vineyards
Dunn Vineyards
Ehlers Lane Winery
Evensen Winery
Fairmont
Far Niente
Flora Springs Wine Co.
Folie à Deux
Forman Winery
Franciscan Vineyards
Freemark Abbey
Frog's Leap Wine Cellars
Girard Winery
Green & Red Vineyard
Grgich-Hills
Groth Vineyards & Winery
Hagafen
Heitz Cellars
Hill Winery, William
Honig Cellars, Louis
Inglenook Vineyards
Jaeger Vineyard
Johnson-Turnbull Vineyards
Keenan Winery, Robert
Kornell Champagne Cellars, Hanns
Krug Winery, Charles
La Jota Vineyard Co.
La Vieille Montagne
Laird Vineyards
Lakespring Winery
Llords & Elwood Winery
Long Vineyards
Manzanita
Markham Winery
Martini, Louis M.
Mayacamas
Merryvale Vineyards
Mihaly Winery, Louis
Mondavi Winery, Robert
Mont St. John Cellars
Monticello Cellars
Mt. Veeder Vineyard
Napa Cellars
Napa Creek Winery
Newlan Vineyards & Winery
Newton Vineyards

WINERIES (*cont.*)

Neyers
Nichelini Vineyards
Niebaum-Coppola Estates
Opus One
Pecota Winery, Robert
Peju Province
Pepi Winery, Robert
Perret Vineyards
Phelps Vineyards, Joseph
Piña Cellars
Pine Ridge
Prager Winery
Quail Ridge
Raymond Vineyard & Cellar
Ritchie Creek
Roddis Cellars
Rombauer Vineyards
Ross Winery, Donald C.
Round Hill
Rutherford Hill Winery
Rutherford Vintners
Saddleback Cellars
Sage Canyon Winery
St. Andrews Winery
St. Clement Vineyard
Saintsbury
Sattui Winery, V.
Schramsberg
Schug Cellars
Sequoia Grove
Shafer Vineyards
Shaw Vineyards & Winery, Charles F.
Shown & Sons
Silver Oak Cellars
Silverado Vineyards
Sky Vineyard
Smith-Madrone
Spottswoode Vineyard & Winery
Spring Mountain Vineyards
Stag's Leap Wine Cellars
Stags' Leap Winery
Steltzner Vineyard
Sterling Vineyards
Stonegate Winery
Stony Hill Vineyards
Storybook Mountain Vineyards
Stratford
Sullivan Vineyard & Winery
Sutter Home
Traulsen Vineyards
Trefethen Vineyards
Tudal Winery
Tulocay Vineyards
Vichon
Villa Mt. Eden
Vose Vineyards
Wermuth Winery
Whitehall Lane Winery
Yverdon Vineyards
ZD

Alameda, Santa Clara, and Santa Cruz

Three counties have scant acreage among them—1,700 in Alameda, 1,700 in Santa Clara, and only 87 in Santa Cruz. But two regions in the area—Livermore Valley and Santa Cruz Mountains (where most of its 64 wineries are found)—are justly famed. "Gray Riesling" has the largest acreage of any one variety, 444 (all in Alameda). "Cabernet Sauvignon" has 201 acres in Santa Clara, 57 in Alameda, 12 in Santa Cruz. "Chardonnay" has 191 in Alameda, 92 in Santa Clara, 19 in Santa Cruz.

SUB-DISTRICTS:

Livermore Valley AVA. Historic area in eastern Alameda County has made its greatest wines from "Sauvignon Blanc" (125 acres) grown in its rockiest soils. Acreage is 1,200.

Hecker Pass Not an AVA. Rolling country reaching w. from Gilroy has been a focal point of country jug wineries for most of its history; its sparse remaining acreage reflects this ("Carignane," "Petite Sirah," and "Zinfandel" dominate plantings). As local acreage dwindles, its wineries are buying fruit of finer varieties from elsewhere.

Santa Cruz Mountains AVA. A sprawling territory extending from Santa Cruz County on the s. through Santa Clara and into San Mateo County. It has some legendary patches of "Cabernet Sauvignon," some well-regarded ones of "Chardonnay" and "Pinot Noir," but few acres of any one grape.

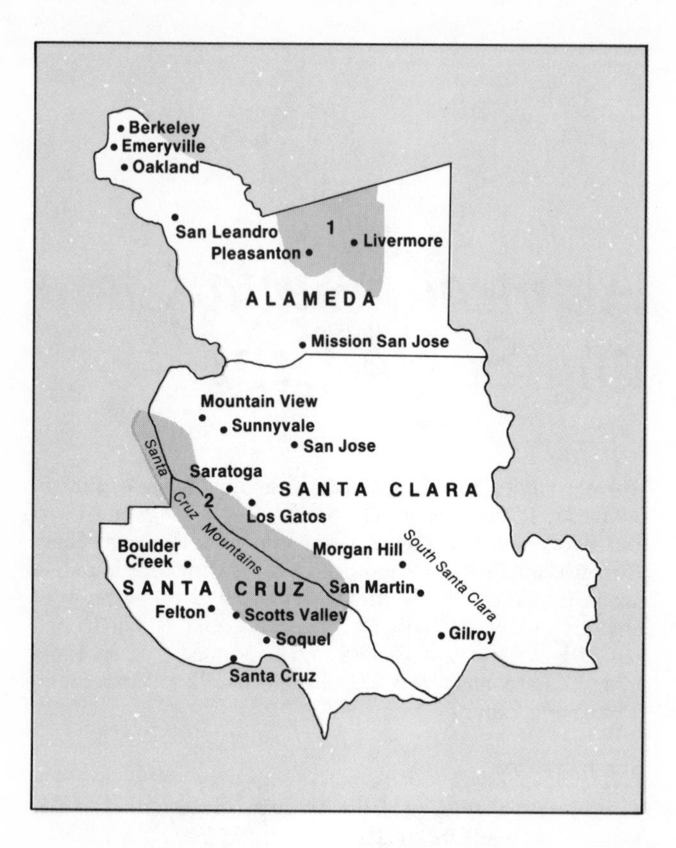

1. Livermore Valley
2. Santa Cruz Mountains

WINERIES

Alameda County
Bay Cellars
Concannon Vineyards
Elliston Vineyards
Fenestra
Fretter Wine Cellars
Livermore Valley Cellars
Montali Winery, R.
Montclair Winery
Rosenblum Cellars
Stony Ridge
Villa Armando
Weibel
Wente Bros.

Santa Clara (and San Mateo) County
Almaden Vineyards
Cloudstone Vineyard
Congress Springs Vineyard
Conrotto Winery, A.
Cronin Vineyards
Fogarty Winery, Thomas
Fortino Winery
Gemello Winery
Gentili Wines, J. H.
Guglielmo Winery, Emilio
Hecker Pass Winery
Kennedy Winery, Kathryn
Kirigin Cellars
Kruse Winery, Thomas
Lamb Winery, Ronald
Live Oaks Winery
Lohr, J.
Mirassou Vineyards
Mount Eden Vineyards
Mountain View Winery
Novitiate Wines
Obester Winery
Page Mill Winery
Pedrizzetti Winery
Pendleton Winery
Rapazzini Winery
Ray Vineyards, Martin
Ridge Vineyards
San Martin
Sarah's Vineyard
Sherrill Cellars
Silver Mountain Vineyards
Summerhill Vineyards
Sunrise Winery
Sycamore Creek
Villa Paradiso
Woodside Vineyards

Santa Cruz County
Bargetto's Santa Cruz Winery
Bonny Doon Vineyards
David Bruce
Cook-Ellis
Crescini
Devlin Wine Cellars
Felton-Empire
Frick Winery
McHenry Vineyard
River Run Vintners
Roudon-Smith Vineyards
Santa Cruz Mountain Vineyard
Smothers
Staiger, P. & M.
Walker Winery

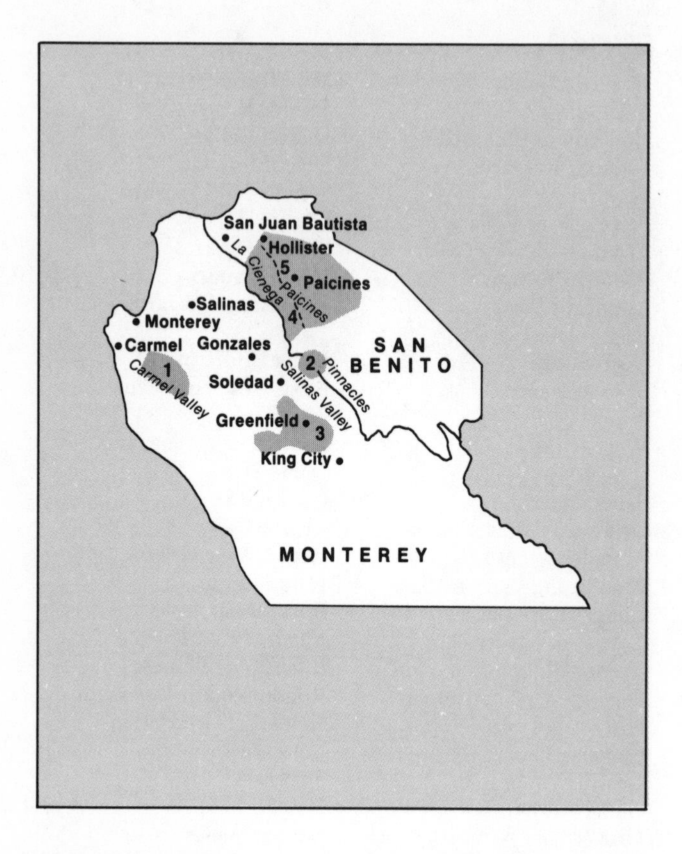

1. Carmel Valley
2. Chalone
3. Arroyo Seco
4. La Cienega
5. Paicines

Monterey and San Benito

MONTEREY COUNTY

Since the 1960s, Monterey has grown from one winery to a dozen, and from fewer than 100 acres to more than 30,000. Current acreage is 33,000. Leading varieties (in acres) are "Cabernet Sauvignon" (3,853), "Chenin Blanc" (3,662), "Pinot Noir" (3,088), "White Riesling" (3,062), "Chardonnay" (2,296), "Zinfandel" (2,195), "Petite Sirah" (1,666), and "Sauvignon Blanc" (1,577). Riesling has been the most impressive single variety.

SUB-DISTRICTS:

Arroyo Seco AVA. Encompasses the Salinas Valley floor and benchlands from Greenfield n. to Gonzales. It includes 8,500 acres of vineyard. Fine Rieslings have come from here. Some Chardonnays have been agreeable, if light and quick to age. Red varieties have dwindled to a few small plantings, except at the s. boundary.

Carmel Valley AVA. Not quite 200 acres of vineyard have been planted in the long. e.–w. valley of the Carmel River. Cabernet Sauvignon has been the most impressive wine.

Chalone AVA. A one-winery, 125-acre appellation at present, known equally for Chardonnay and Pinot Noir. It is on a long slope in hills e. of Soledad.

King City has been proposed as an AVA. A hefty proportion of the county's grapes are in it, s. of Greenfield to the San Luis Obispo County line.

Monterey AVA. A catchall district encompassing all plantings.

SAN BENITO COUNTY

Though the county has 4 wineries, nearly all of 4,580 acres of vineyard belongs to Almaden, which has acquired AVA status for Cienega on the w. side of the San Benito River valley and Paicines on the e. side. A one-winery AVA called Lime Kiln is within the larger Cienega one. One vineyard in the w. hills of Cienega has produced some powerful Pinot Noirs, but few identifiable wines of quality have come from the county. Principal varieties: "Chardonnay" (1,019), "Pinot Noir" (764), "Cabernet Sauvignon" (508).

WINERIES

Monterey County

Carmel Bay Winery
Chalone Vineyards
Château Julien
Durney Vineyards
Jekel Vineyard
Masson Vineyards, Paul
Monterey Peninsula Winery
Monterey Vineyard, The
Morgan Winery
Smith & Hook
Taylor California Cellars
Ventana Vineyards

San Benito County

Calera Wine Co.
Casa de Fruta
Cygnet Cellars
Enz

San Luis Obispo and Santa Barbara

SAN LUIS OBISPO COUNTY

Climates and soils both are diverse in the county, which has 20 wineries and 5,200 acres of vineyard unevenly divided between two main growing districts. The leading varieties (in acres) are "Zinfandel" (1,061), "Cabernet Sauvignon" (916), "Sauvignon Blanc" (837), "Chenin Blanc" (662), and "Chardonnay" (604).

SUB-DISTRICTS:

Edna Valley AVA. Much the smaller of the two main districts with 650 acres of vines, it has won quick fame for fine Chardonnays since pioneer plantings went in during the 1970s. It lies directly s. of the city of San Luis Obispo. The climate is Regions I to II.

Paso Robles AVA. Zinfandels have been its mainstay since pre-Prohibition times. Sauvignon Blancs have shown promise in the surge of plantings that took acreage from 900 in the late 1970s to their current level. Chenin Blancs may prove even better. The region is mostly rolling grasslands stretching away e. from the town of Paso Robles, but has forested hills w. of that town. The climate is mostly Region III.

York Mountain AVA. A small, hilly patch on the w. boundary of Paso Robles is at present close to a one-winery appellation.

SANTA BARBARA COUNTY

To the surprise of most who do not know California in detail, this is one of the state's coolest growing regions, because e.–w. river valleys leave large expanses open to incursions of foggy sea air. The county has 24 wineries. Total acreage has shot from virtually none in the early 1970s to 10,000. Princi-

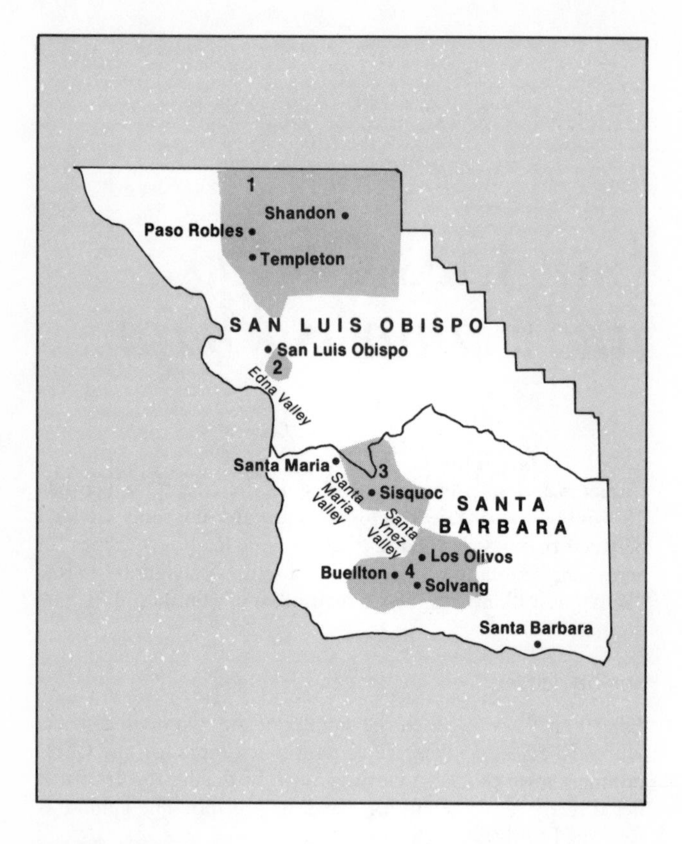

1. Paso Robles
2. Edna Valley
3. Santa Maria Valley
4. Santa Ynez Valley

pal varieties (in acres) are "White Riesling" (2,195), "Chardonnay" (2,081), "Gewürztraminer" (1,010), "Chenin Blanc" (897), and "Cabernet Sauvignon" (843). "Pinot Noir" has 628 acres, "Sauvignon Blanc" 391.

SUB-DISTRICTS:

Santa Maria Valley AVA. The largest district, it has only begun to have identifiable wines from vines that date back no further than the early 1970s. No clear trend has appeared; several varieties are doing quite well, including "Chardonnay," "White Riesling," "Gewürztraminer," and "Pinot Noir." The region runs inland from the town of Santa Maria. The climate is Region I.

Santa Ynez Valley AVA. About 1,200 acres have been planted, mostly e. of Solvang, but to some degree in the cooler territory w. of it. Climate is mainly Region II, with a bit of I. The finest wines to date have been Sauvignon Blancs, with White Rieslings and Chardonnays not far off the pace. A few Pinot Noirs have clamored for attention.

WINERIES

San Luis Obispo County
Adelaida Cellars
Arciero Winery
Belli & Sauret
Caparone
Castoro Cellars
Chamisal Vineyard
Claiborne & Churchill
Corbett Canyon Vineyards
Creston Manor Vineyards & Winery
Deutz
Eberle
Edna Valley Vineyards
Estrella River
Farview Farm
HMR Ltd.
Las Tablas
Martin Bros.
Mastantuono
Pesenti
Ranchita Oaks
Rolling Ridge Winery
Ross Keller
Saucelito Canyon Vineyard
Watson
York Mountain

Santa Barbara County
Au Bon Climat
Austin Cellars
Babcock Vineyards
Ballard Canyon Winery
Brander Vineyard, The
Carey Cellars, J.
Firestone Vineyards
Gainey Vineyard
Houtz Vineyards
Longoria Wine Cellars
Los Viñeros Winery
Qupé
Rancho Sisquoc
Sanford & Benedict
Sanford Wines
Santa Barbara Winery
Santa Ynez Valley Winery
Stearns Wharf Vintners
Vega Vineyards & Winery
Zaca Mesa

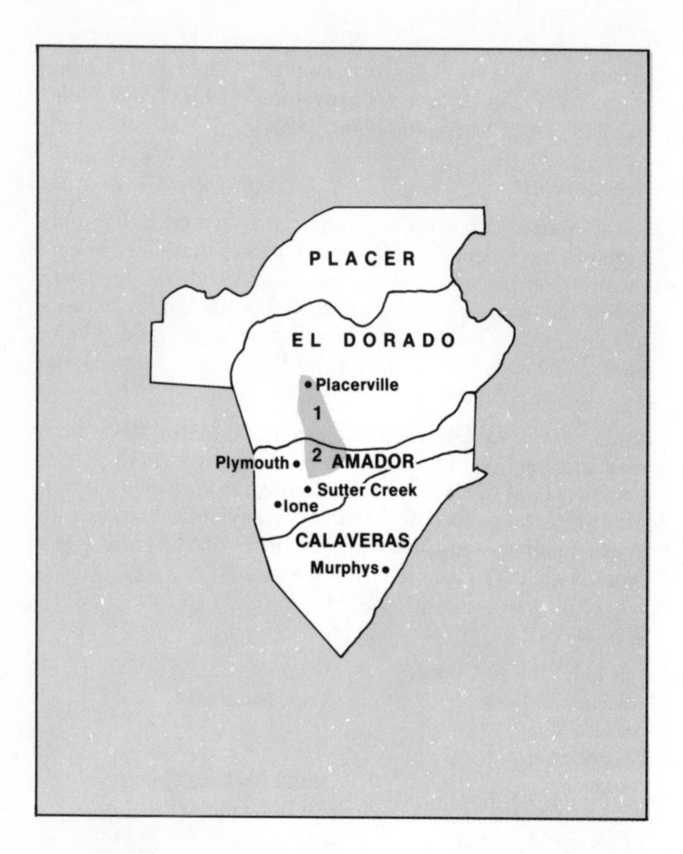

1. El Dorado
2. California-Shenandoah Valley

Sierra Foothills

Three counties—Amador, Calaveras, and El Dorado—share a long tradition of making heady Zinfandels from grapes grown at elevations from 800 to 1,800 feet. In recent times, growers have pushed to make something of their Sauvignon Blancs and Cabernet Sauvignons. Combined acreages are modest: "Zinfandel" is far and away the leader with 1,086 in Amador, 139 in El Dorado, and 37 in Calaveras. "Sauvignon Blanc" has 282 acres in Amador, 92 in El Dorado, and 21 in Calaveras. Total acreage for the three counties is 2,169. There are 27 wineries.

SUB-DISTRICTS:

El Dorado AVA. Centered on Placerville and extending s. to touch Amador County, it covers all of the vines in its county.

Fiddletown AVA. It is a small eastward extension of Shenandoah Valley.

Shenandoah Valley AVA. In Amador, the largest district runs e. from Plymouth. Zinfandels are its stock in trade. Sauvignon Blanc is the new hope in table wine, and Port is beginning to be an attractive possibility.

WINERIES

Amador County
Amador Foothill Winery
Argonaut Winery
Baldinelli Vineyard
Beau Val Wines
d'Agostini
Greenstone Winery
Karly Wines
Kenworthy Vineyards
Monteviña
Santino Winery
Shenandoah Vineyards
Sierra Vista
Stoneridge

WINERIES (*cont.*)

Story Vineyard
TKC
Winterbrook Vineyards

Calaveras County
Chispa Cellars
Stevenot Vineyards

El Dorado County
Boeger Vineyards
El Dorado Vineyards
Fitzpatrick Winery
Gerwer Winery
Granite Springs
Herbert Vineyards
Madrona Vineyards

Placer County
Nevada City Winery

San Joaquin Valley

A gigantic and fertile trough running 300 miles down the center of California from Lodi to Bakersfield, the Great Valley provides most of America's everyday drinking wine, dessert wine, and brandy. Except for the immediate area around Lodi, cooled by sea air sweeping up the Sacramento River, the climate is homogenous from end to end, warming steadily from Region IV at the n. to Region V at the s. Because of this and the fact that most of the San Joaquin's major wineries draw grapes from all of the valley's counties, only Lodi has historic identity as a sub-district. About 30 companies make wine in the valley, which has 210,000 acres of wine grapes and a quarter of a million of "Thompson Seedless." The principal counties are Fresno, Kern, Madera, Merced, San Joaquin, Stanislaus, and Tulare. The principal wine varieties (combined acreages) are "French Colombard" (65,109), "Chenin Blanc" (30,393), "Barbera" (18,015), "Carignane" (17,250), "Grenache" (14,800), "Ruby Cabernet" (12,812), and "Zinfandel" (11,656). All but Zinfandel are fairly evenly distributed; of the latter's acreage, 10,587 is in San Joaquin County, nearly all in Lodi, where the variety can make a wine deserving of more fame than it has now. Lodi has been proposed as an AVA, as has "Madera," an area overlapping the Madera-Fresno county line.

Wineries

San Joaquin Valley
Anderson Wine Cellars (T)
Bella Napoli (SJ)
Bogle (Y)
Borelli Winery, Ciriaco (SJ)
Borra's Cellar (SJ)
Caché Cellars (Sol)
Cadenasso (Sol)
California Growers (F)
Chateau de Leu (Sol)

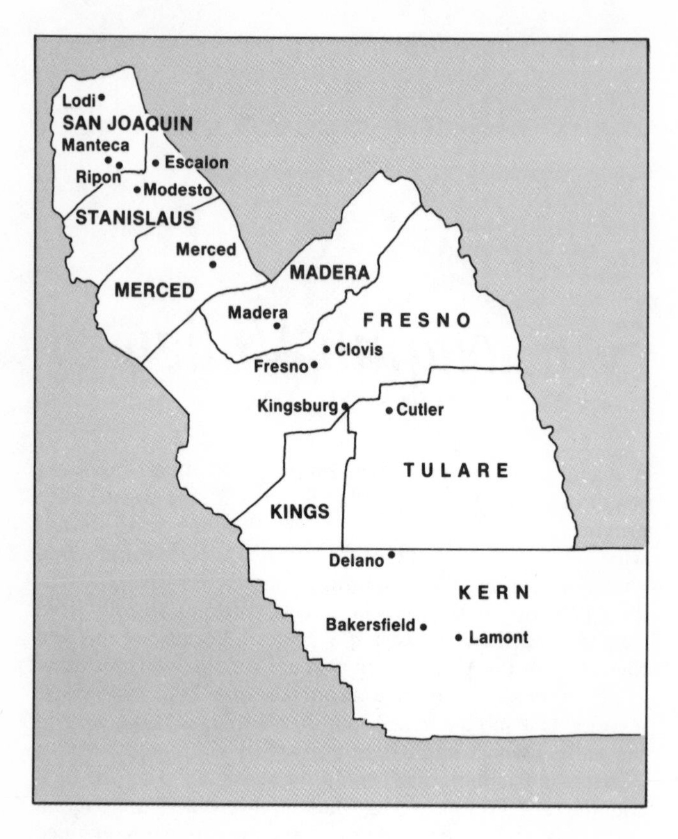
Lodi
SAN JOAQUIN
Manteca
Ripon
Escalon
Modesto
STANISLAUS
Merced
MERCED
MADERA
Madera
FRESNO
Clovis
Fresno
Kingsburg
Cutler
TULARE
KINGS
Delano
KERN
Bakersfield
Lamont

Wineries (*cont.*)

Coloma Wine Cellars (SJ)
Cook Winery, R&J (Y)
Cosentino Wine Co. (Stan)
Delicato Vineyards (SJ)
East-Side Winery (SJ)
Farnesi (F)
Ficklin Vineyard (M)
Franzia Brothers (SJ)
Gallo Winery, E&J
Gibson Vineyards (F)
Giumarra Vineyards (K)
Guild Wineries (SJ)
Harbor Winery (Sac)
JFJ Bronco (Stan)
LaMont Winery, M (K)
Lost Hills Winery (SJ)
Lucas Winery, The (SJ)
Nonini Winery, A. (F)
Orleans Hill Vinicultural Soc. (Y)
Papagni Vineyards (M)
Phillips Vineyards, R.H. (Y)
Quady Winery (M)
Sierra Wine Corp. (T)
Susiné (Sol)
Turner Winery (SJ)
Wooden Valley (Sol)

Code:
K (Kern)
M (Madera)
SJ (San Joaquin)
Sac (Sacramento)
Sol (Solano)
Stan (Stanislaus)
T (Tulare)
Y (Yolo)

1. Temecula
2. San Pasqual Valley

Southern California

California s. of the Tehachapi Mountains has two main districts, one dying, the other aborning. Total acreage is modest in both. Other than that, they have almost nothing in common. A few more than half of the 27 wineries are in the emerging area.

SUB-DISTRICTS:

Cucamonga Not an AVA, it is the dying district, disappearing in face of relentless urbanization. The hottest Region V in the state, it was (and remains) best suited to dessert wines. Most of it is in the s. w. tip of San Bernardino County, but some spills into adjoining Riverside County. Total acreage is about 5,000, mostly of "Zinfandel" and "Mission."

San Pasqual AVA. A tiny, one-winery district in San Diego County at the town of Escondido, it is in many ways an extension of Temecula.

Temecula AVA. Most of Riverside County's 3,000 acres of vines are in the region, practically at the San Diego County line. Plantings date to the 1960s. To date, whites have fared better than reds, but no one variety seems clearly best. The main plantings (in acres): "Sauvignon Blanc" (638), "White Riesling" (494), "Chardonnay" (458), and "Chenin Blanc" (316).

WINERIES

Cucamonga District
Filippi Vintage Co., J.
Galleano
Opici Winery
Rancho de Philo

Los Angeles County
Ahern Winery
Donatoni Winery
McLester Winery
San Antonio Winery

WINERIES (*cont.*)

San Diego County
Culbertson Winery, John
Ferrara Winery
Menghini Winery
Point Loma Winery
San Pasqual Vineyards

Temecula District
Callaway Vineyards and Winery
Cilurzo Vineyard and Winery
Filsinger Vineyards & Winery
Hart Vineyards
Mesa Verde Winery
Mount Palomar Winery

A–Z *of* *California Wine*

Acacia Napa T ***
Built on a Burgundian model, it produces only Chardonnay and Pinot Noir, most marked with the names of individual Carneros district vineyards. First crush was '79. Partners Mike Richmond and Jerry Goldstein limit production to 22,000 cases. Prices $12.50–$17.

• Chardonnay. Rich in varietal flavors, firm, well marked by aging in French oak. '81 '83

• Pinot Noir. Five separate wines show a startling range of textures from pillow-soft Madonna Vineyard to steely St. Clair Vineyard. Between the extremes come Iund, Lee, and Winery Lake. Wood notes always definite, never dominant. '79 '81

Acacia-Cafaro Napa T nyr
Owners of Acacia in partnership with Joe Cafaro (ex-Chappellet, ex-Robert Keenan) plan for this label to produce Bordeaux equivalents to Burgundian varietals of Acacia. First vintage, '84, was made in leased space.

Adelaida Cellars San Luis Obispo T nyr
John and Andrée Munch's first vintage in their 4,500-case winery toward the w. edge of the Paso Robles district was '81. The wines are Chardonnay and Cabernet Sauvignon, both from locally purchased grapes. Both were well received in their first outings. Prices $7.27–$7.75.

Adler-Fels Sonoma T, S nyr
In cellars on a lofty slope at the top end of the Sonoma Valley, a small partnership produces 5,000 cases of wine from grapes purchased in Sonoma and Napa. The major wines are Pinot Noir (from old vines, just beginning to replace an earlier,

extra-oaky Cabernet Sauvignon) and Mélange à Deux (a *méthode champenoise* sparkler from "Gewürztraminer" and "White Riesling"). Also on the list: Fumé Blanc (perfumey with oak), Chardonnay, White Riesling, and Gewürztraminer. The first full vintage was '81. Prices $6.50–$15.

Ahern Winery Los Angeles T **/***
Owner-winemaker James Ahern's 5,000-case production is dominated by Chardonnay. Bottlings are identified by vineyard. The first vintage was '78. All grapes are purchased. Prices $6.50–$12.
• Chardonnay. The bottlings that have made the name come from Edna Valley's MacGregor and Paragon vineyards (the latter richer in varietal). A third entry from Santa Maria Valley's Bien Nacido Vineyards joined the list with '82. The style is toasty-oaky, but subtly so.
Also: Central Coast Sauvignon Blanc, Napa Cabernet Sauvignon, Amador Zinfandel.

Ahlgren Vineyards Santa Cruz T **
Family-owned winery-in-a-basement in Boulder Creek produces a variety of small lots (to 300 cases each) of handcrafted Cabernet Sauvignon (local and Napa bottlings), Chardonnay (local and Monterey), Sémillon (local), and Zinfandel (local or Livermore), all from purchased grapes. Exaggerated boldness has been the style. The first vintage was '76. Prices $6.75–$13.

Alatera Vineyards Napa T nyr
Grower Holbrook Mitchell uses leased space to make small lots of dry Gewürztraminer from his 14-acre Yountville vineyard only in favorable years. Sales are mostly at the proprietor's door.

Alderbrook Vineyards Sonoma T nyr
A trio of partners make only white wines—Chardonnay (firm, full-bodied, heaped with varietal character), Sauvignon Blanc (richly fruity rather than grassy), and Sémillon—at a cellar w. of Healdsburg. The wines come increasingly from grapes grown by one of the owners on 63 nearby acres. The volume in '84 was 10,000 cases, on the way to a planned 20,000. Prices $6–$8.75. The first wines, '82s, were pleasing and gave excellent value.

Alexander Valley
An AVA with versatile growing conditions extending n. from Healdsburg in Sonoma County. See maps.

Alexander Valley Vineyards Sonoma T **/***
The Wetzel family winery produces a steady 26,000 cases per year of well-made wines from their 240-acre vineyard on roll-

ing benchland in the Alexander Valley e. of Healdsburg. The first crush was '75. Prices $6–$10.

• Chardonnay. Authoritative fruit, bone-dry, often with a Burgundian whiff of SO_2 as a complication in aroma. It consistently appeals to European-oriented palates. '80 '81

• Cabernet Sauvignon. From '78 on, ripe, almost plummy fruit, and increasingly flavorful of that characteristic. Seems to peak early. '79 '81

Also: Chenin Blanc (dry, oak aged), Johannisberg Riesling (1.5% r. s.), Gewürztraminer (picked early, finished off-dry), Pinot Noir (the most successful one from its district).

Alicante Bouschet

A black grape and, infrequently, its wine (see p. 21).

Almadén Vineyards Central Coast/San Joaquin
T, S, D */**

The statistically staggering winery and vineyard enterprise of National Distillers, Inc., includes 6,385 acres of vines (San Benito, Monterey) and five wineries (San Benito, Santa Clara, Kings, Kern) with a grand total of 40.3 million gallons in cooperage, including 2.3 million in barrels. Sales are in the neighborhood of 8.5 million cases per year. The list includes one of everything. Prices $2.85–$9.50. Table winemaster Klaus Mathes finds means to bottle vintage-dated varietals with specific appellations under both the Almadén name and a costlier Charles Lefranc label. Almadén also produces LeDomaine sparkling wines. The Almadén label is best regarded for Cabernet Sauvignon-Monterey, a steady winner of awards at fairs (straightforwardly varietal, approachable in youth). Also: Gewürztraminer, sparkling Blanc de Noirs.

Alta Vineyard Napa T **

The neighbor to Schramsberg near Calistoga has specialized in North Coast Chardonnay since its founding in '79, but owner Ben Falk is adding Sauvignon Blanc and Gamay to the roster with '84. Annual production is about 2,000 cases. The Chardonnay, soft, well marked by oak and other bouquets, has seemed on its best form in the first year or two in bottle. Price $14.50.

Amador Foothill Amador T */**

Near Plymouth in the Shenandoah Valley, the 7,500-case winery of Ben Zeitman explores several avenues opened by Zinfandel, esp. White Zinfandel (distinct blush, some r. s.) and Zinfandel (straight-ahead, sound varietal, less husky than many from this region). First vintage was '80. Also: Amador Fumé, Cabernet Sauvignon (initial vintage was '84). Prices $5.50–$8.

Ambassador
Label belonging to M. LaMont is used for low-priced San Joaquin Valley wines sold mainly in jugs.

American oak
Domestic wood much used for barrels. Flavors it imparts to wine are described variously as dill, pickle barrel, coconut, and, at full tilt, bourbon, which latter indeed gets its main flavor from this wood.

Anderson Valley
AVA near the coast in Mendocino County is well regarded for Chardonnay and Gewürztraminer, and appears ready to become a focal point of *méthode champenoise* sparkling wine production. See maps.

Anderson Vineyard, S. Napa T, S nyr
Stanley and Carole Anderson use only "Chardonnay" grown on their 32-acre vineyard e. of Oakville to make a still Chardonnay (soft, distinctly oaky) and a sparkling Brut. They buy "Pinot Noir" from four nearby growers for a sparkling "Blanc de Noirs" (subtle flavors, rich textures in a highly promising '81). The label first appeared on '80s. Annual production nears 3,000 cases each of still and *méthode champenoise* sparkling wine. Prices $13.50–$15.50

Anderson Wine Cellars Tulare T nyr
Donald Anderson makes an annual 2,400 cases of Chenin Blanc, French Colombard, and Ruby Cabernet from his 20-acre vineyard near the town of Exeter. The first vintage was '80. The wines are sold in local trade.

André
Label of E. & J. Gallo for fruity, off-dry, and sweet Charmat sparkling wines.

Angelica
Generic dessert wine-type named in honor of Los Angeles. Originally it was a blend (now illegal) of brandy and grape juice. Current wine by the name is made much in the manner of Cream Sherry.

Arciero Winery San Luis Obispo T nyr
In 1984 the owners, the Arciero family, and winemaker Greg Bruni made 9,000 cases of wine as a sort of fanfare for the real event: beginning with the vintage of '85, the plan is to make 100,000 cases of Chardonnay, Sauvignon Blanc, Zinfandel, and Cabernet Sauvignon from their own 260 acres plus other vineyards in the Paso Robles district. The cellar, set in one of the family vineyards, is east of the town of Paso Robles, and has been designed for expansion.

Argonaut Winery Amador T *
In the Sierra Foothill town of Ione, a 2,000-case cellar is devoted (typically of its region) to Zinfandels of heroic proportion. The owning partners also offer a spiritually kindred Barbera. The first crush was '76. Prices $5–$6; sales are mostly local.

Arroyo Seco
An AVA within Monterey's Salinas Valley ranges across the valley floor between the towns of Soledad and Greenfield. See maps.

Arroyo Sonoma
One of several labels in use by California Wine Co.

Ascension
Label belonging to York Mountain Winery.

Au Bon Climat Santa Barbara T nyr
Jim Clendenen and Adam Tolmach leased space in a small cellar on a large vineyard w. of Alamos to begin making wine in '81. Their first wines include Chardonnay, Pinot Noir, and a Nouveau-style red called Primeur. Production is 3,500 cases. Prices $5–$12.

Austin Cellars Santa Barbara T nyr
One of several cellars recently opened by a winemaker gone independent, Austin makes an annual 12,000 cases of Chardonnay (two or more per season, all lean, with a nice earthy smack), Sauvignon Blanc (regular bottlings well off-dry and redolent of the regional asparagus aroma; special *Botrytis*-affected ones rich and engaging), Gewürztraminer (straightforward varietal), Johannisberg Riesling (sipper), and Pinot Noir (distinct wood flavors). Prices $7–$10, and to $25 for special Sauvignon Blanc. Tony Austin (ex-Firestone) first crushed for his own label in '81. A vineyard is coming to fill part of the need. Meanwhile, all grapes are purchased, their vineyards often identified on the labels.

AVA American Viticultural Area
Grape growing region with boundaries approved by the Bureau of Alcohol, Tobacco, and Firearms, a nascent system of appellations of origin for American wines. See maps.

Babcock Santa Barbara T nyr
After one successful Johannisberg Riesling made in leased space, a vineyardist built his own cellar and expanded his roster to seven wines, including Chardonnay, Pinot Noir, Gewürztraminer, and Sauvignon Blanc, all from his 40 acres toward the w. limits of the Santa Ynez Valley. There were 4,000 cases of '84s. Prices not established in late '84.

Baccala Winery, William   Mendocino   T   nyr
A winery just n. of Hopland in inland Mendocino County first crushed in '81, but was just finding its true identity in 1984. Estate-grown '83 Chardonnay and Sauvignon Blanc are coming to be the focus of production. Prices $8–$12. There also is a proprietary white under the Sanel Winery label. Price $7. Earlier Villa Baccala and Fawn's Glen labels are to disappear. Production approaches 15,000 cases. The plan is to grow to the capacity of the owner's 40-acre vineyard.

Baldinelli Vineyard   Amador   T   **
Proprietor Ed Baldinelli makes White Zinfandel (just off-dry, just off-white), Zinfandel (subtle and polished though not without weight), Cabernet Sauvignon, and a bit of Sauvignon Blanc, all from his 70 acres of vines e. of Plymouth in the Shenandoah Valley. The first crush was '79. Production is about 11,000 cases per year. Prices $4–$7.

Bale Mill Cellars
Second label owned by Charles F. Shaw Winery & Vineyards; used for moderately priced varietal wines.

Ballard Canyon   Santa Barbara   T   **
Gene Hallock's family winery and rolling 45-acre vineyard nestle in the Santa Ynez Valley between Solvang and Los Olivos. The first crush was in '78. Production has edged past 10,000 cases. Prices $5.75–$13. Predilection is for sweet whites and pinks (Johannisberg Riesling at 2% and 4% r. s., Sauvignon Blanc at 1% r. s., Blanc de Cabernet Sauvignon at 1.5% r. s., Rosalie's Blushing Brunch Cabernet Blanc at 3.5% r. s.). Also Chardonnay and Cabernet Sauvignon. Rieslings have drawn most of the favorable notices.

Ballatore
A label of E. & J. Gallo for a flavorful sparkling Muscat.

Balling
Measure of sugar in grapes, which corrects small errors in *Brix* scale.

Balverne Vineyards   Sonoma   T   nyr
Winery and 250 hilly acres of vines hide away s. of Healdsburg in Chalk Hill area. The wines have been steady to excellent since the debut vintage, '80. Production nears the planned maximum of 45,000 cases. Prices $6–$12. The roster includes Chardonnay (rich fruit flavors nicely buttressed by French oak; first tries aging well), Gewürztraminer (one of the drier, spicier models). Also: Healdsburger (off-dry, Riesling-based proprietary white), Sauvignon Blanc (splendid first effort in '81), Scheurebe (much the drier of two producers of this Ger-

man hybrid), Cabernet Sauvignon (woodier, headier than the whites), Zinfandel.

Bandiera
One of several labels produced by California Wine Co.

Barbera
The Piemontese grape and its wine (see p. 21).

Barberone
A generic wine-type based on the character of off-dry San Joaquin Barbera, and usually containing some "Barbera."

Barengo Winery
A label currently used by Lost Hills Winery for specialty items and/or regional markets. Lost Hills operates in cellars founded by Dino Barengo in 1946.

Bargetto's Santa Cruz Winery Santa Cruz T, S */**
Family-owned cellar in town of Soquel focuses increasingly on varietal whites from Santa Barbara County grapes, esp. Chardonnay, Gewürztraminer, and regular and *Botrytis*-affected Johannisberg Riesling. Also: Cabernet Sauvignon and Zinfandel. Santa Cruz Cellars is a second label. Total production of 35,000 cases includes substantial proportion of well-received fruit wines. Sales are mostly in California. Prices $4–$12.50.

barrel-fermented
Fermenting whites in barrels as opposed to tanks is a source of early complexity. Widely practiced for Chardonnay, it is used somewhat less for Sauvignon Blanc, rarely for Chenin Blanc and French Colombard. The technique sometimes is noted on labels.

Bay Cellars Alameda T nyr
Richard Rotblatt makes a bit more than 1,200 cases per year of Carneros Pinot Noir, Napa Valley Clarion (blend of Bordeaux varieties), and Santa Maria Valley Chardonnay. The first vintage for the Emeryville winery was '82. Prices $9–$12.

Beau Val Wines Amador T *
A quartet of partners produces 600 to 1,200 cases annually in a tiny cellar in the Shenandoah Valley. They have made Zinfandel and Zinfandel Blanc regularly, and sometimes have offered Sauvignon Blanc and Barbera. Price $6.25, mostly for local sale.

Beaulieu Vineyard Napa T, D ***
From the 1930s through the 1960s, it was the royal house of Napa, mainly because of strong, stylish Georges de Latour Private Reserve Cabernet Sauvignons. Since the early 1970s, the Rutherford winery has run more with the pack, not be-

cause it has declined but because it is running in an ever faster field. Founded by de Latour in 1900, it has been owned by Heublein, Inc., since 1972. Annual production in 325,000 case range, nearly all from Napa grapes. Prices $5–$22.

• Cabernet Sauvignon, Georges de Latour Private Reserve. Designed by the legendary André Tchelistcheff, who gave wines from ripe grapes an extra year in American oak to temper intense flavors imparted by the then owner's family vineyard. Resulting early complexity did not keep them from aging well in bottle (though recent vintages have matured swiftly). '69 '70 '72 '75

• Cabernet Sauvignon, Rutherford (known as "Napa Valley" until 1979). Lighter wine from broader spectrum of vineyards than de Latour, but still distinctive, age-worthy. Released younger, at lesser price. '77 '80

• Cabernet Sauvignon, Beautour. Unlike above two, blended with Merlot. Soft, approachable young.

Also: Sauvignon Blanc (tart, refreshing, melon-like varietal flavors; fine since '81, but too often overlooked), Chardonnay (tart, delicate to neutral), Pinot Noir (erratic, as most are, but good value in cool seasons). Claret, Burgundy, and Chablis are dry, vinous, consistent good values.

Bel Arbres

Label owned by Fetzer family but maintained independently of their Fetzer Vineyard label. Currently it is used mostly for several varietal blush wines.

Bell Canyon

Label owned by Burgess Cellars of Napa is used for episodic releases of sound, standard varietals from their own cellars and bulk purchases.

Bella Napoli San Joaquin T *

One of the last old-time country jug wineries in the San Joaquin Valley. Hat family makes some 5,000 cases of white and red table wines from its vineyard near Manteca. Sales are local.

Bellerose Vineyard Sonoma T nyr

Proprietor Charles Richard is trying to fashion a Medoc-style wine from his 35-acre Dry Creek Valley vineyard by blending substantial proportions of "Cabernet Franc," "Merlot," and "Petit Verdot" with "Cabernet Sauvignon." At least partial success greeted the first two vintages, '79 and '80. The wine is called Cuvée Bellerose since 75% varietal requirement came into effect.

Belli & Sauret Vineyards San Luis Obispo T nyr

A grower-owned label going back to a '78 Zinfandel, Belli &

Sauret is building a small cellar to be ready for the '85 crush, though some of its annual 7,000 cases will continue to be made in leased space. Since '82, the wine-types are Chardonnay, Sauvignon Blanc, White Zinfandel, and Zinfandel, all from the owner's three vineyards in the Paso Robles area. Prices $5–$9.

Belvedere Wine Co. Sonoma T nyr
This producing winery w. of Healdsburg in the Russian River Valley hides modestly behind labels trumpeting the identities of independent growers who supply the grapes for its finest wines: Bacigalupi Russian River Chardonnay and Pinot Noir, Robert Young Alexander Valley Cabernet Sauvignon, York Creek Napa Valley Cabernet Sauvignon, and Winery Lake Carneros Chardonnay and Pinot Noir. The inaugural vintage was '80; production is about 18,000 cases. Prices $10–$12. The firm also acts as a negotiant, buying regular lots of ready-to-bottle Cabernet Sauvignon, Chardonnay, and White Zinfandel, plus episodic lots of other varietals for its Belvedere "Wine Discovery" bottlings. Prices $3–$5.

Beringer Vineyard Napa T **/***
An old-time label, it has patiently edged up in critical esteem after declining through the 1950s and 1960s. The renewed vigor owes to Nestlé, Inc., ownership since 1969. Production is about 400,000 cases, mostly from 2,000 acres of owned or leased vineyards in the Napa Valley and Sonoma's Knights Valley. The winery offers several single-vineyard lots able to compete with best. Prices $4.50–$19. The firm also sells about 1 million cases per year of $4–$7 varietals and generics under its second, jug label, Los Hermanos.

• Cabernet Sauvignon, Private Reserve. Usually from Lemmon-Chabot Ranch e. of St. Helena (spicy, fleshy), sometimes from State Lane Vineyard e. of Oakville (herbaceous, leaner). Regular bottlings from Knights Valley steadily attractive, approachable early. '78 '79 '80

• Chardonnay, Estate. The "regular" bottling is often the most attractive at dinner for focusing closely on fruit flavors, but the Private Reserve editions do well in comparative tastings for being rich, well marked by oak. '80 '81

• Johannisberg Riesling, Knights Valley. Late-harvest bottlings are more delicate than most (± 4% r. s.). Pure delights in '73, '76; spectacularly perfumed in '82. Also: Chenin Blanc, Fumé Blanc (separate Napa, Knights Valley bottlings both steady, straightforward), Gewürztraminer (spot-on varietal character), Pinot Noir (Small Lot '76 points in a hopeful direction).

Bernardo Winery San Diego T, D *
Old-line country jug winery near Escondido sells general selection of standard wines, mostly at the cellar door.

Black monukka
A Muscat-related grape and, rarely, a dessert wine from it.

Black Muscat
Dark-skinned Muscat grape variety and, occasionally, a dessert wine from it.

Blanc de Blanc
Literally white (wine) from white (grapes). It is a commonly used descriptive term on labels of sparkling wines, and occasionally is used as name of generic white table wine.

Blanc de Cabernet Sauvignon, Blanc de Pinot Noir
Same as Blanc de Noir, but varietal.

Blanc de Noir
Literally white (wine) from black (grapes), achieved by draining or pressing juice away from skins immediately on crushing so that little or no color is extracted. Frequent descriptive term for both sparkling wines and generic table wines of varying hue from white to partridge eye to outright rosé.

Blanc Vineyards Mendocino T nyr
The winery first crushed in '82. It makes Sauvignon Blanc and Cabernet Sauvignon from the owning Blanc family's 140 acres of vines. The label is Robert Blanc. Current production is 1,500 cases. Prices $7.50–$8.50.

Blush
A synonym—more accurate in most cases—for *blanc de noir*.

Boeger Winery El Dorado T */**
The family winery and 35-acre vineyard are near Placerville, where vines have grown since Gold Rush days. Greg Boeger makes 5,000 cases yearly from his own vines plus leased 25 acres in the area. Prices $4–$9. Principal wines are Chenin Blanc, Sauvignon Blanc, Cabernet Sauvignon, and Zinfandel, plus generics called Hangtown Red and Hangtown White after an early mode of local justice. All are sound, sturdy, straightforward.

Bogle Vineyards Yolo T nyr
One of two pioneers in a burgeoning vineyard and winery district behind Sacramento River levees at Clarksburg. The family winery's production is currently level at 18,000 cases. The label is best known for the proprietary Sarah's Rosé. Also: Chenin Blanc, Petite Sirah. The first vintage was '78. Prices $4.50–$5.

bond
Shorthand for bonded winery or bonded wine cellar. A bond is a federal permit to make and store wine commercially.

Bonet, Jacques
A label owned by Italian Swiss Colony, used for inexpensive bulk-process sparkling wines.

Bonny Doon Vineyard Santa Cruz Mountains T nyr
Randall Grahm is only one of many who sees Pinot Noir as a sort of holy grail, but is much lonelier in his fascination with Rhônish grapes and wines. Above the town of Bonny Doon, his winery sits amid 20 acres planted to such as "Marsanne," "Rousanne," and "Viognier" as well as "Pinot Noir." While his own vines mature, the early wines (beginning with '81s) come from grapes purchased in Sonoma and Oregon. Prices $12–$20 for Claret (from traditional Bordeaux grapes), Pinot Noir, Chardonnay, and Syrah. Annual production is about 5,000 cases.

Borelli Winery, Ciriaco San Joaquin T *
A small cellar s. e. of Lodi, owned by Ciriaco's descendants. The first vintage was '79. Production of 5,000 cases includes Zinfandel plus generic red, white, and rosé, all modestly priced for local sale.

Borra's Cellar San Joaquin T *
A family-owned winery and 30-acre vineyard on the s. w. side of Lodi made its first wines in '79. Annual volume hovers around 3,000 cases of Barbera, White Barbera, and Zinfandel. Sales are mostly local; price $5. The wines are steady, straightforward.

Botrytis cinerea (alias Noble Mold)
Often shortened to *Botrytis,* a curious mold that complicates but does not spoil the flavor of grapes while concentrating their qualities through dehydration. It is responsible for ultra-sweet (to 35% r. s.) dessert wines, usually Gewürztraminer, Johannisberg Riesling, or Sauvignon Blanc-Sémillon, but occasionally Chardonnay. Such wines are identified on labels as Late-Harvest, Individual Bunch Selected, or Individual Berry Selected, etc. They are counterparts to Sauternes of France, or Auslesen to Trockenbeerenauslesen of Germany, products of the same beneficent mold.

Bouchaine Vineyard
The principal label of Chateau Bouchaine.

Bounty
Label belonging to California Growers Winery.

Brander Vineyard, The Santa Barbara T ***
Owner-winemaker C. Frederic Brander specializes in Sauvignon Blanc grown on the winery property at Los Olivos in Santa Ynez Valley. Annual production is about 6,500 cases (including several attractive Blanc de Noirs under secondary, St. Carl label). First vintage was '81. Prices $8.50 for Brander, $4.75–$6.50 for St. Carl.
• Sauvignon Blanc. Superbly designed, age-worthy wine with none of the regional cooked asparagus flavors until time brings hints of them. Fattened with Sémillon, complicated by partial barrel fermentation. Versatile with food. '81 '82 '83

Braren-Pauli Winery Mendocino T nyr
Partners Larry Braren and Bill Pauli produce about 4,000 cases per year of Chardonnay, Sauvignon Blanc, and Zinfandel from their vineyards in Potter and Redwood valleys, plus a bit of Cabernet Sauvignon from leased vines in Alexander Valley. First vintage was '80. Prices $6–$9; all sales in California. The early wines have been sound, and straightforward.

Breckenridge Cellars
Brand of Giumarra Vineyards.

Brix
Measure of sugar in grapes and thus potential alcohol in wines. An error in the scale was corrected in the more widely used Balling scale, but Brix remains the commoner term of the two.

Bruce Winery, David Santa Cruz Mountains T **
High in hills w. of Los Gatos, the cellars of the iconoclastic Dr. David Bruce have earned their reputation for wines of extraordinary power and individuality, some from his own 25 acres at the winery, others from grapes purchased nearby and as far away as Amador County. The last couple of vintages have been tamer, more traditional. Annual production is edging toward 25,000 cases; prices $4–$18. Best known for:
• Chardonnay. Usually dark gold, frequently high in alcohol, sometimes with a bit of residual sugar, always pungent of the grape variety. The '81 leaned in gentler directions; the '82 seemed more like the old days.
Also: Cabernet Sauvignon, Pinot Noir (embarking on a new course through whole berry fermentation), Zinfandel, and generic Old Dog Red and Old Dog White.

Brut
Descriptive label term for sparkling wines. Indicates dry (typically .5% to 1% r. s. for *méthode champenoise* wines, often more for transfer process and Charmat bottlings).

Buehler Vineyards Napa T **
Small winery and 60-acre vineyard of John Buehler family nestle in steep hills e. of St. Helena, above Lake Hennessy. The debut '78s were heavy, heady; the '80s and later have been better balanced and more polished. The roster includes Cabernet Sauvignon, Zinfandel (stylish '81), Pinot Blanc (aromatic, firm), and White Zinfandel from the home property, plus Chardonnay from grapes purchased in the Russian River Valley. Annual production nears 12,000 cases on the way to a maximum 20,000. Prices $5–$10.

Buena Vista Sonoma T **/***
The original cellars of Agoston Haraszthy s. of Sonoma town are now just a showplace; winemaking goes on in a modern facility amid the winery's 1,700-acre vineyard straddling the Napa-Sonoma county line in Carneros. A resurgence begun in 1970 under the ownership of Young's Market of Los Angeles gained pace in 1979 with new German owners, A. Racke. Winemaker Jill Davis has shown a sure touch across the board since her arrival in 1981. Production is about 90,000 cases yearly, and growing with the vineyard. Prices $5.50–$9, and to $18 for Special Selections.

- Gewürztraminer. Reliably spicy, drier than many.
- Chardonnay. Refined but definite smack of fruit; oak stays in background. Watch esp. for Special Selection bottlings. '80 '81
- Cabernet Sauvignon. Dark, firm, slow to evolve if '79, '80 are true expressions.

Also: Sauvignon Blanc (spot-on Sonoma-grassy character), Spiceling (fresh, off-dry proprietary based in "Gewürztraminer," "Riesling"), Pinot Noir (still finding a way, but '81 Special Selection is highly promising).

Bulk
Trade term for any wine not yet packaged for sale to the consumer. Often misused to indicate inexpensive wines better identified as "jug wine."

Bulk process
See: Charmat process.

Burger
The white grape variety and, very rarely, its wine.

Burgess Cellars Napa T **/***
One-time pilot Tom Burgess bought the original Souverain winery and 22 acres of vineyard in hills e. of St. Helena in 1972. He is now making 30,000 cases per year from holdings around the Napa Valley expanded to 70 acres, plus purchased

grapes. The best reputation is for sturdy, even heavyweight reds. Prices $5.95–$15.95.

• Cabernet Sauvignon. Big, thick, sometimes heady, but always definably Cabernet. '79 '81

• Zinfandel. Same general vein as Cabernet, but shows delicacy, subtlety at times, esp. '81.

Also: Chardonnay (partially barrel-fermented, and as gutsy in its way as the reds). A second label, Bell Canyon, covers lesser and less expensive ($4–$6.75) lots of the same varietals.

Burgundy
Generic label term for red wine. No content by variety is required or implied.

Bynum Winery, Davis Sonoma T **
Nestled into an old hop barn on a curve of the Russian River some miles downstream from Healdsburg, Bynum's 20,000-case winery gets most of its grapes from partners with nearby vineyards. Prices $5.50–$12.50. The wines were rustic, uncertainly styled in early years. Recently they have begun to show complexity, polish. Roster includes Chardonnay (most impressive of the lot), Sauvignon Blanc (straightforward, consistent good value), Cabernet Sauvignon, Pinot Noir, Zinfandel.

Cabernet Franc
A black grape variety and, increasingly, its wine.

Cabernet Sauvignon
Finest of California's black grapes and its wine (see p. 21).

Cabernet Sauvignon Blanc
See Blanc de Noir

Caché Cellars Solano T **
Pilot Charles Lowe is taking a flier at making Monterey Chardonnay and Pinot Noir, Napa Valley Cabernet Sauvignon, and California Sauvignon Blanc at his cellar just w. of U. C.-Davis. The first vintage was '78. Lowe's early efforts have been fairly well received. Prices $7.50–$12. He makes about 5,000 cases annually.

Cadenasso Winery Solano T, D *
Veteran winemaker Frank Cadenasso sells unpretentious wine from his nearby 65-acre vineyard only at the cellar door in Fairfield. Grignolino is the specialty. Prices $1.50–$3.75 (the high price for a flavored specialty called Passionata).

Cadlolo Stanislaus T, D *
Through several recent ownerships, a small winery in the town of Escalon has continued to sell sound valley wines to a local clientele. The mainstays are French Colombard and red table wine.

Cain Cellars Napa T nyr
Winemaking began with the '81s for the Jerry Cain family. The plan is for 30,000 cases from an eventual 200-acre (currently 70) family vineyard on Spring Mountain w. of St. Helena. Present production is 18,000 cases of Chardonnay (bought-in grapes), Sauvignon Blanc, Cabernet Sauvignon, and Merlot. Prices $7.50–$11. The first whites (esp. the '82 Sauvignon Blanc) were attractive; the first reds were due in '85.

Cakebread Cellars Napa T **
Proprietor Jack Cakebread likes wines in his own mold—burly and assertive. He and his winemaker son, Bruce, have gotten just such results since the first vintage, '76, though recent efforts have been tamed considerably. Their short list includes Sauvignon Blanc (pungently varietal, often austere, mostly from their own 22 acres around the winery at Oakville), Chardonnay (same vein as Sauvignon Blanc, from purchased grapes), and Cabernet Sauvignon (dark, tannic, often heady, increasingly from 20 acres adjoining the winery, and bought in 1982). Production currently is in the 35,000 case range. Prices $9.50–$14, with small lots of "Rutherford Reserve" Cabernet exceeding the latter figure.

Calafia Cellars Napa T */**
Randall Johnson makes Sauvignon Blanc (noticeably flavored by wood), Cabernet Sauvignon (dark, ripe), Merlot, and Zinfandel from grapes purchased in the Napa Valley. He works in leased space pending construction of his own winery. The first vintage was '79. Annual production is about 2,500 cases, and growing slowly. Prices $7.75–$13.50. There is a second label, Redwood Canyon Cellars, for wines that present themselves year to year as targets of opportunity.

Calera Wine Co. San Benito T **/***
The quest for a perfect California Pinot Noir landed proprietor Josh Jensen high in the w. hills of San Benito County with 14 acres of that variety in limaceous soils, and a cellar built over the dramatic bones of an old limekiln. Since the founding, in 1975, the second focus has shifted from Zinfandel (still in the roster, still dark, plummy, and heady) to Chardonnay (ripe and toasty). Both are from bought grapes. Production is 12,000 cases. Prices $4 (for the generic red) to $25.
• Pinot Noir. The home vineyard divides into three blocks called Selleck, Reed, and Jensen.

California Growers Fresno T, S *
Begun as a coöp during the 1930s, the firm has changed owners twice in recent years without changing the wines much.

Production centers on French Colombard, Chenin Blanc, and generics from San Joaquin Valley grapes. There is also a Charmat sparkling wine. The flagship label is Le Blanc. Others are Growers and Bounty. Production is about 300,000 cases. Prices $2–$4.

California Soleil Napa T nyr
The grower-owned label of Ray Mayeri goes on Johannisberg Riesling from his vineyard at Yountville in the Napa Valley. There are three styles—early harvest, regular, and late harvest—all made at a Napa winery that buys "Pinot Noir" from him. The effort is for low alcohols (10%) and a range of sweetness. The first vintage was '82. Production approaches 3,000 cases. Prices $5.95, and to $9.95 for half bottles of late harvest at 18% r. s.

California Villages
A brand belonging to Gibson Wine Co.

California Wine Co. Sonoma T **
The company's cellars in Cloverdale produce 85,000 cases of wines for at least four, sometimes five labels. The proprietors have sound geographic reasons for their pluralist approach.
Arroyo Sonoma is a regional label for wines from Sonoma grapes, primarily from 200 acres of affiliated vineyards at Schellville in the Sonoma Valley and in Dry Creek Valley. The roster includes Cabernet Sauvignon (soft, balanced, bouqueted early), Chardonnay, Fumé Blanc, Zinfandel, and a pair of generics accurately called Dry Red and Dry White. Prices $7–$12.
Bandiera is a catchall label for lower-priced ($2.99–$6) varietals and generics that give consistent value for money. In particular: Zinfandel and the generics. Also Cabernet Sauvignon and Chardonnay.
John B. Merritt is, in effect, the label for reserve and special wines. Named after California Wine Co.'s winemaker, the label goes on particular lots of Cabernet Sauvignon, Chardonnay, Sauvignon Blanc (all understated for fruit flavors, and noticeably wood-aged), and both regular and late-harvest Johannisberg Rieslings. Prices $6.50–$15.
Potter Valley, temporarily suspended in 1984, is a line of wines from an affiliated 140-acre vineyard in Mendocino County's Potter Valley sub-district. When it is around, the wine to watch is Sauvignon Blanc.
Sage Creek is the Napa label, which draws on a 200-acre vineyard in the Chiles Valley sub-district. The wines are Cabernet Sauvignon, Chardonnay, and Fumé Blanc—styled much as the John B. Merritts are. Prices $7–$11.

Callaway Vineyards and Winery Temecula T **
The first and by far largest explorer of a southern California district first planted to vines in the 1960s, Callaway dates from 1974. Founder Ely Callaway sold to Hiram Walker & Sons, Inc., in 1981. Current production exceeds 135,000 cases on the way to a planned 150,000, every drop white wine: Chardonnay (soft, pleasant, free of oak, so straightforwardly varietal), Fumé Blanc (dry, marked by a curious perfume that appears to be regional), Sauvignon Blanc (same as Fumé but with perceptible .8% r. s.). Also: White Riesling, Chenin Blanc, Sweet Nancy (botrytized Chenin Blanc named after Nancy Callaway, and made only in the occasional year when the weather is right). Prices $4.75–$8.75, to $15 per half bottle for Sweet Nancy. Experiments in process in 1984 may lead to other styles and/or varietals on the list.

Cambiaso Sonoma T */**
Since the repeal of Prohibition, a reliable source of jug generics; since the mid-1970s also a source of varietal wines at bargain prices. Now owned by a Thai distilling company, the Healdsburg winery approaches 100,000 cases annual production, mostly from purchased Sonoma grapes but including others from as far away as the Sierra Foothills. Generics offer the best values ($3); Chenin Blanc and Zinfandel seem the best-regarded of the varietals (to $7.99) by winemaker Bob Fredson, member of a long-time winemaking family in the region. Also in the list: Sauvignon Blanc, White Zinfandel, Cabernet Sauvignon, Petite Sirah.

Caparone Vineyards San Luis Obispo T **
To date, owner Dave Caparone has specialized in sturdy, intensely varietal Cabernet Sauvignon and Merlot from Central Coast (mostly Santa Maria Valley) grapes, but he also has in mind to champion Nebbiolo and Brunello in California. To that end he has planted his small vineyard to those varieties in hopes Paso Robles will succeed where many other regions have failed. The first vintage should be '85. Also, Caparone has begun making Pinot Noir from the Santa Maria area. The winery, n. w. of Paso Robles town, dates from 1979. Production is about 3,500 cases. Price $10.

Carbonic maceration
Technique developed in Beaujolais district of France in which clusters are fermented whole to make red wine for early consumption, as opposed to regular technique of crushing and destemming the berries before fermenting. If bottled straightaway, resulting wines are intensely aromatic (the perfume can be and usually is close to banana oil), with noticeable spritz

from trapped CO_2. Most wines called "Nouveau" (or variations thereof) are made this way, though the vogue for them has faded. Some proprietors blend small proportions of carbonic maceration wine into conventionally fermented lots of Pinot Noir for complexity, extra liveliness.

Carey Cellars, J. Santa Barbara T **
Three doctors J.—father and sons—own 45 acres of rolling vineyard and a winery in the Santa Ynez Valley n.e. of Solvang. Their first crush was '78. Annual production is at 5,200 cases, with 7,000 the planned peak. Prices $4.50–$12. The label is best regarded for Cabernet Sauvignon-Blanc and Sauvignon Blanc (distinct regional overtones of canned asparagus). Also on the list: Chardonnay, Cabernet Sauvignon, and Merlot.

Carignane
A black grape variety and, from a few, its wines (see p. 22).

Carlo Rossi
A label belonging to E. & J. Gallo, used for their lowest-priced generics, sold mainly in jugs.

Carmel Bay Winery Monterey T */**
Housed at Monterey County Airport, the tiny part-time winery belongs to stockbroker Fred Crummey and schoolteacher Bob Eyerman. Production, begun in 1977, is about 1,500 cases per year. Prices $5–$10. The wines include a hefty proportion of Zinfandel plus Cabernet Sauvignon, Pinot Noir, Chenin Blanc, and Sauvignon Blanc, all from purchased Monterey County grapes.

Carmel Valley
An AVA formed by the watershed of the Carmel River in coastal Monterey County. See maps.

Carmenet Sonoma T nyr
The newest offspring of Chalone Vineyards occupies 40 acres atop Sonoma Mountain, high above the Sonoma Valley floor and Sonoma town. The first crush, '82, yielded Sauvignon Blanc (from Edna Valley, which will continue to be the source) and an estate-grown Cabernet Sauvignon-Cabernet Franc-Merlot blend, to be known simply as Sonoma Valley Red. Production is 15,000 cases per year. Prices $9–$12. The Gavilan Vineyards Napa Valley French Colombard, formerly made at Chalone, is now made at this property. Price $4.

Carmine
A black grape hybridized at U. C.-Davis (from "Merlot," "Cabernet Sauvignon," and "Carignane"), and its wine.

Carnelian
A black grape hybridized at U. C.-Davis (from "Cabernet Sauvignon," "Merlot," and "Grenache"), and its wine (see p. 22).

Carneros
An AVA covering the southern tip of two other AVAs, Napa Valley and Sonoma Valley. See maps.

Carneros Creek Napa T **/***
Winemaker Francis Mahoney and partners set out in 1972 to make outstanding Chardonnay and Pinot Noir from grapes grown at or near their cellar in Carneros. They also are exploring Cabernet Sauvignon and Sauvignon Blanc from other parts of Napa—and have dropped Zinfandel from the roster after 10 years of varied experiments. Annual production is approaching the planned maximum of 25,000 cases; price range is $4.50–$16.
• Pinot Noir. Velvety texture provides the backdrop for complex aromas of fruit, oak, and time. Distinctively Californian, but pleasing to Burgundy fanciers nonetheless. '77 '79
Also: Cabernet Sauvignon (frequently identified by vineyard source; characters of the wines have varied accordingly, from silky-soft to big, rough-hewn, tannic), Chardonnay (extra-ripe, well marked by oak, has tended to be at best early), and two styles of Sauvignon Blanc (the one called Sauvignon Blanc is a shade less dry than the one called Fumé Blanc).

Cartlidge & Brown
Merchant-owned label used for Napa varietals made at Stratford Winery, which has a partially overlapping ownership. Early Chardonnays ('81, esp.) were impressive.

Casa de Fruta San Benito T nyr
A 14-acre vineyard supplies grapes for four varietal wines sold only at the door of the owner's adjacent roadside tourist attraction e. of Hollister.

Casa Nuestra Napa T nyr
N. of St. Helena, the cellar specializes in Chenin Blanc from the owning Kirkham family's vineyard. Their other wines are Cabernet Sauvignon and a proprietary red, Tinto, based in Gamay. An attractive, off-dry '83 Chenin Blanc showed marked improvement over earlier vintages. First crush was '80. Annual production is 1,000 cases. Prices $5–$7.50.

Cassayre-Forni Napa T **/***
Winery s. of Rutherford belongs to winery designer Paul Cassayre and winemaker Mike Forni, whose first vintage on their

own property was '77, though the label goes back to '76 with wines made in leased space. Annual production goal is 10,000 cases. Prices $6–$12. List includes well-received Napa Chardonnay, two Napa Chenin Blancs (one dry, one at 1.5 r. s.), hearty Sonoma (Dry Creek) Zinfandel, and a balanced but distinctly sturdy Napa Cabernet Sauvignon, all from purchased grapes.

Castoro Cellars San Luis Obispo T nyr
Niels Udsen made his first wines, '79s, in leased space, and continues that arrangement. Chardonnay, Fumé Blanc, White Zinfandel, Cabernet Sauvignon, and Zinfandel all come from purchased Paso Robles area grapes. Volume is 3,000 cases and growing slowly, so far in local markets. Prices $3.50–$5.75.

Caswell Vineyards Sonoma T nyr
After several years of photographing wine professionally, Dwight Caswell moved around to the other side of the camera in 1983. His small vineyard and winery near Sebastopol in the Russian River Valley is meant to go to 10,000 cases in time. In 1984, his second season, production was 1,000 cases of Cabernet Sauvignon, Chardonnay, and Rosé of Zinfandel. Prices $4–$10.

Caymus Vineyard Napa T ***/****
Most of the label's fame rests on its Cabernet Sauvignon, some on a Pinot Noir Blanc called Oeil de Perdrix, but owner Charles Wagner's wines get good marks across the board. The winery is e. of Rutherford on 70 acres of vineyard that straddle the Napa River. Annual production ranges around 35,000 cases, including a second label, Liberty School (for Cabernet Sauvignon and Chardonnay bought in bulk and finished at Caymus). Prices $5–$14, and to $30 for the reserve Cabernet Sauvignon. The founding date is 1970.

• Cabernet Sauvignon. Rich in varietal flavors, but with an enticing overtone of berries or even flowers as counterpoint to the essential herbaceousness. Consistently subtle, complex, balanced, they age better than most. '74 '77 '78 '79 '80

• Oeil de Perdrix (Pinot Noir Blanc). Truer to partridge eye ideal than most. Preserves excellent varietal character while tasting more white than rosé.

Also: Chardonnay (sound, steady), Sauvignon Blanc (intermittently produced from purchased grapes and somewhat variable in character), Pinot Noir (attractive in the ripe Napa style), Zinfandel.

Central Coast
Informally, a term linking all coastal counties from Santa

Clara s. to Santa Barbara as a wine-producing district. More formally, it refers only to San Luis Obispo and Santa Barbara counties, the wineries and grape growers of which have formed the Central Coast Wine Growers Association. A proposed AVA would encompass all counties in the informal definition, but would exclude parts of some of them.

Centurion
Black grape variety hybridized at U. C.-Davis. Plantings remain minuscule.

Chalk Hill
AVA in Sonoma County, extending along w.-facing hills between Windsor and Healdsburg. See maps.

Chalk Hill Winery
A second label for Donna Maria Vineyards.

Chalone
A one-winery AVA for Chalone Vineyards.

Chalone Vineyards Monterey T ****
At 2,000 feet in the Santa Lucia Mountains e. of the Salinas Valley town of Soledad, a splendidly isolated winery and 145-acre vineyard with Burgundian ideals and a track record of almost annual success under the direction of Richard Graff. Annual production is 15,000 cases, reaching for 18,000. Price range $6–$18, to $25 for reserve bottlings available only to a mailing list.
• Chardonnay. Deep gold. Intense, austere flavors from grapes are overlain by grace notes of damp earth and buttery oak. Can age but early complexity allows early enjoyment. '77 '79 '81
• Pinot Blanc. Same style as Chardonnay, but the variety renders the wine somehow less austere.
• Pinot Noir. The greatest success of the lot. For many Europeans, California's closest challenger to a fine red Burgundy. Enormously subtle and complex, beautifully balanced. '75 '77 '78 '80
Also: Chenin Blanc (poor man's Chardonnay).

Chamisal San Luis Obispo T **
Norman Goss and family's 57-acre vineyard and 3,000-case winery in Edna Valley are devoted almost entirely to an estate Chardonnay (dark, toasty, woody), but the Gosses make an occasional Cabernet Sauvignon just to keep a hand in. The label dates to '77 for Cabernet, to '79 for Chardonnay. Price $12.

Champagne
Accepted designation for California sparkling wines made by *méthode champenoise,* transfer process, or Charmat process.

The term is generic, with no requirement as to grape varieties used. The word usually is modified by Natural, Brut, Extra Dry, or Sec to describe sweetness. Sometimes it is modified by Blanc de Blancs or Blanc de Noirs to reveal the color of grapes used. Sparkling wines other than white can be called Pink Champagne, Champagne Rosé, or Champagne Rouge.

Chandon
The label of Domaine Chandon.

Chanticleer Vineyards
A merchant-owned label founded in 1982, it offers 3,000 cases per year of Sonoma County Chardonnay, Sauvignon Blanc, Zinfandel, and proprietary red and white. Prices $4.50–$8.50

Chappellet Vineyard Napa T ***
Donn Chappellet's spectacularly scenic vineyard produces wines of stately charms. The vines face n. from lofty Pritchard Hill, e. of Rutherford. The family's 110 acres, supplemented by three adjoining leased blocks, yield an annual 30,000 cases of distinctive Cabernet Sauvignon, Chardonnay, and Chenin Blanc, plus a bit of White Riesling. All four have been well received since the winery's founding in 1969; current winemaker Cathy Corison may have the finest touch of all. Prices $7.50–$12.50, and to $18 for Signature bottling of Cabernet Sauvignon.
• Chardonnay. Subtle fruit flavors and light touch of oak marry slowly in wines of body and texture. Best vintages have lasted 10 years. '80 '81
• Chenin Blanc. A model of what the grape can do made dry and given a bit of oak aging. Vintages vary little.
• Cabernet Sauvignon. Dark-hued and rich in varietal flavors. Typical vintages of the '70s started out austere. More recent vintages have been gentler from the start, but seem just as long-lived. '75 '77 '79 '80

Charbono
A black grape variety and, from very few, its wine (see p. 22).

Chardonnay
White grape variety and its much-praised wine (see p. 16).

Charis Vineyards Sonoma T nyr
Dry Creek Valley grower Jack Florence is making 1,700 cases a year of Cabernet Sauvignon and Sauvignon Blanc in leased space, using only his own grapes. The first vintage was '81. Prices $6.75–$7.

Charles Krug
See: Krug, Charles.

Charles Lefranc
See: Lefranc, Charles.

Charles F. Shaw Vineyard and Winery
See: Shaw Vineyard and Winery, Charles F.

Charmat process
Method of producing sparkling wine by conducting the secondary fermentation in a large tank, then filtering and bottling the wine under pressure. Identified on labels as either Charmat or Bulk Process, the wines are almost inevitably modest in character and price.

Château Boswell Napa T nyr
From a cartoon of a stone castle n. of St. Helena come conventionally styled, rather attractive Napa Cabernet Sauvignons, if the debut '79 accurately forecasts things to come. Grapes are purchased. Case production is about 2,000 annually. Price $16.

Chateau Bouchaine Napa T nyr
Jerry Luper (ex-Freemark Abbey, ex-Ch. Montelena) is in charge of a Carneros winery devoted primarily to Chardonnay and Pinot Noir made from grapes bought in its home district. The label is Bouchaine Vineyard. The first vintage, '80, yielded wines more distinctly flavored by new oak than by grapes. Total production of 20,000 cases per year also includes a Chardonnay from farther n. in the Napa Valley, and a tiny bit of Napa Valley Sauvignon Blanc. Prices $10–$15.

Chateau Chevalier Napa T nyr
Venerable winery and vineyard, w. of St. Helena on first steep slopes of Spring Mountain, changed hands in 1984; the property is now owned by the proprietor of Far Niente, who plans to increase production from 5,000 to 25,000 cases, keeping Cabernet Sauvignon, Chardonnay, and Pinot Noir as principal wine-types. Under former owner Greg Bissonette, wines were known for raw power. New style remains to be established. Prices unsettled in 1984, but figure to be lower than those of the sister winery.

Chateau Chèvre Napa T **
One-time pilot Gerald Hazen turned a one-time goat barn into a 4,000-case winery in 1979. Production is limited to Merlot (darker and more tannic than most) from an 8-acre vineyard surrounding the winery at Yountville, and Sauvignon Blanc from another, 11-acre Hazen property n. of Napa City. Prices $8–$12.

Chateau de la Vallée
Brand of Sierra Wine Co. for generics packaged in cartons.

Chateau de Leu Solano T nyr
A family-owned winery and 80-acre vineyard a few miles n. of the Sacramento River near Fairfield, it offers straightforward, estate-grown Chardonnay, Sauvignon Blanc, Chenin Blanc, and De Leu Blanc (a proprietary white of "Colombard" and "Chenin Blanc"). Annual production is about 10,000 cases, with room to grow to 25,000. Prices $2.75–$7.50. The first crush was '81.

Chateau du Lac
Reserve wines label for Kendall-Jackson.

Château Julien Monterey T nyr
The firm crushed its first wines in '83, but the label goes back to '81 with purchased lots. The emphasis is on Chardonnays, one identified as Monterey County, several others from identified vineyards: Cobblestone, Paraiso Springs, and Rancho Tierra Rejada. The rest of the table wine roster is Fumé Blanc (off-dry, no oak), Sauvignon Blanc (dry, oak-aged), Cabernet Sauvignon, and Merlot, plus red and white generics. Nearly all of the grapes are purchased from growers in Monterey and San Luis Obispo counties. There also is a pair of Sherry-types. Production has edged past 20,000 cases. Prices $5.25–$15, and to $25 for a Reserve Chardonnay.

Chateau Montelena Napa T ***
A partnership of four revived a famous pre-Prohibition label in 1969. The name is now more prestigious than ever, principally because of its Chardonnays, first made by Miljenko Grgich, then by Jerry Luper. The winemaker now is Bo Barrett, son of the principal partner. Winery n.e. of Calistoga has 90 acres of vines adjoining, mostly "Cabernet Sauvignon." Grape purchases in Napa and Sonoma contribute the rest of 25,000 cases of annual production. Prices $7–$16.
• Chardonnay. Exquisitely delicate under Grgich (1972–73), more assertively varietal and oaky under Luper (1974–80). Barret apparently takes the latter approach.
• Cabernet Sauvignon. Silky under Grgich, it has evolved steadily to its present dark, forcefully tannic profile.
Also: Johannisberg Riesling (off-dry), Zinfandel (stylistic mirror to Cabernet), both in small quantities.

Chateau Moreau
Brand of Gibson Vineyards.

Chateau St. Jean Sonoma T, S ***/****
From an impressive first vintage ('74) onward, this Sonoma Valley winery at Kenwood has stayed at the forefront in California Chardonnays and late-harvest Johannisberg Rieslings. Winemaker Richard Arrowood specialized from the

beginning in making several vineyard-designated bottlings of each type each year, and has added Fumé Blanc and Gewürztraminer to the lists with enough success that the cellars now turn out more than 120,000 cases per year, almost all white. Prices $4.75–$18, and to $22.50 per half bottle of Special Select late-harvest wines. In 1984, the three founding partners sold Ch. St. Jean to Suntory, the Japanese distillers. The property included 77 acres of vines, the winery, and a just-getting-started sparkling wine cellar located in a separate facility in the Russian River Valley village of Graton. The announced goal is to hold the status quo at Kenwood while building the sparkling wine cellar to a minimum of 25,000 cases.

• Chardonnay. The distinctive anchors in recent vintages have been Robert Young Vineyard (Alexander Valley) and Belle Terra Vineyard (also Alexander Valley). They and their peers in an ever-changing list that reaches as many as eight separate vineyard-identified lots per year have grown a bit more delicate of flavor and texture during the 1980s than they were in the 1970s, but keep a characteristic little fillip of bitterness in the finish. '79 '81

• Fumé Blanc. The leaders are the Estate and Petite Etoile bottlings. Like the Chardonnays, they are distinctly varietal, but a bit lighter of heart.

• Late-harvest Johannisberg Riesling. Lusciously sweet and ripe, they smell of Riesling but have more of the texture of a fine Sauternes. The most consistent source is Robert Young Vineyards.

Also: Gewürztraminer, Vin Blanc (Gewürztraminer-dominated, dry). From the sparkling wine cellar, Brut and Brut-Blanc de Blanc.

Chenin Blanc

White grape variety and its wine (see p. 17).

Chianti

Generic wine-type mainly represented by inexpensive, off-dry reds from the San Joaquin Valley, but sometimes by drier coastal wines several shades truer to the Italian original.

Chiles Valley

In hills e. of St. Helena, a small vine-growing valley forming part of the Napa River watershed, so usually considered part of the main Napa Valley. Not an AVA.

Chispa Cellars Calaveras T nyr

Cellar in Sierra Foothills town of Murphys opened in 1977. The annual 400 cases of rustic Zinfandel come from purchased local grapes. Price $6, for mostly local sales.

Christian Brothers Winery Napa/Fresno T, S, D [**]
Owned by the Catholic teaching order, the properties include 1,200 acres of vines and two substantial cellars in the Napa Valley for table and sparkling wines, plus 1,200 acres and two big cellars in the San Joaquin Valley for dessert wines and brandies. The Brothers also buy substantial tonnage to round out an annual volume in the 1.25-million-case range for wines, and 1.35 million for brandies. Long a bastion of sound, inexpensive non-vintage varietals, the winery has slowly shifted over to good to distinctive vintage-dated wines. The flagships are Napa Fumé (straightforward varietal), Chardonnay (nicely tinged with oak), and Cabernet Sauvignon (good varietal flavors embodied in an approachable wine). The generics are notably good values. Too often overlooked is a vintage Port plenty rich enough for winter nights by the fire. Prices $3–$12, and to $15 for a fine late-harvest Johannisberg Riesling.

Cienega Valley
An AVA running s. from Hollister along the w. side of San Benito County. See maps.

Cilurzo Vineyard and Winery Temecula T *
Vincenzo Cilurzo's main lighting job is the Merv Griffin television show. His moonlighting job is making wine. The family's 40-acre vineyard was the first commercial one in its region in 1968. From its grapes, Cilurzo produces Chardonnay, Chenin Blanc, Sauvignon Blanc, Cabernet Sauvignon, and Petite Sirah, plus off-beat proprietary blends such as Chenite (Chenin Blanc + Petite Sirah) and Vincheno. The style is as unpretentious as the specialty items suggest. Volume is 8,000 cases. Prices $4–$6.95, and to $12.50 for late-harvest whites.

Ciriaco Borelli Winery
See: Borelli Winery, Ciriaco.

Claiborne & Churchill San Luis Obispo T nyr
The notion is to make Alsatian-style Gewürztraminer, Riesling, and Edelzwicker from grapes purchased in Edna Valley. Winemaker-owner Clay Thompson, working in leased space, made 550 cases of much-praised '83s, his starting vintage. In '84 he went to 1,100 cases; the near-term goal is 5,000. Thompson also plans to build his own winery by 1986. Prices $4.50–$8.50

Claret
A generic term, long out of vogue, is coming back on the labels of dry reds, some of them from Bordelais grape varieties.

Clarksburg
A deep-soiled AVA in Sacramento and Yolo counties, it threads behind levees along the Sacramento River delta w. of Sacramento almost as far as Fairfield. Its Chenin Blancs have distinctive, appealing melon-like overtones.

Claudi, Vincent
A merchant-owned label with close ties to a winery in the Alexander Valley produces 2,500 cases of varietal Sonoma wines sold only in southern California. Prices are moderate.

Clear Lake
An AVA encircling Clear Lake in Lake County. See maps.

Cline Cellars   Contra Costa   T   nyr
The winery opened in 1983 in the town of Oakley, in cellars previously known as Firpo. Proprietor Fred Cline, who learned winemaking at his Italian grandfather's knee, plans to go from 2,000 to 10,000 cases of Sémillon, Zinfandel, and Muscat, among other varietals. Prices $5–$8. Much of the fruit is to come from vineyards in the immediate neighborhood.

Clos du Bois   Sonoma   T   **/***
A well-established Healdsburg winery with 1,000 acres of vineyards divided among several sites in Dry Creek and Alexander Valleys, Clos du Bois offers seven varietals, with several Cabernet Sauvignons and Chardonnays designated by vineyard. The first vintage was '74. Production currently exceeds 100,000 cases (in a larger winery that also produces for another label with overlapping ownership, River Oaks). Prices $5.50–$18, and $15 for half bottles of late-harvest Johannisberg Riesling.
• Cabernet Sauvignon. A Dry Creek bottling labelled as Woodleaf defines both regional and varietal character while tasting noticeably of oak. Briarcrest does much the same job for Alexander Valley. '74   '78   '79
• Chardonnay. A Dry Creek edition called Flintwood has a tart austerity that recommends it with fish. Calcaire is the softer, riper counterpart from Alexander Valley. '79   '81
Also: Gewürztraminer (off-dry at 1.3% r. s., good varietal), Johannisberg Riesling (affably routine), Sauvignon Blanc (promising '83).

Clos du Val Wine Co.   Napa   T   ***/****
The property of a French-American family was an overnight success with its first vintage, '73. Bordeaux-born and -trained winemaker Bernard Portet has gone from strength to strength with Cabernet Sauvignon and Merlot, and has thought origi-

nal thoughts about Zinfandel. This, the original roster, has been augmented in the 1980s by Sauvignon Blanc, Sémillon, Chardonnay, and Pinot Noir. Most of the grapes come from winery-owned vineyards around the cellars at Stag's Leap, and in Carneros. "Zinfandel" is bought from Howell Mountain. A second label, Granval, puts more emphasis on varietal character than does the main one. Annual production approaches 40,000 cases. Prices $4.50–$14, and to $30 for Reserve Cabernets.

• Cabernet Sauvignon. Supple and subtle from youth onward, it has shown a steady ability to age gracefully. '75 '78 '79 '80

• Merlot. A softer, gentler echo of the Cabernet.

• Zinfandel. Antithesis of the Cabernet. Richly flavored, distinctly tannic, and usually headier. Hard to know whether to drink early for freshest fruit flavors or wait for elements to come together. '77 '79

Also: Sauvignon Blanc (new with '80s, straightforward in flavor, delicately rigged), Sémillon, Chardonnay (same vein as Sauvignon), Pinot Noir (gentle, altogether Californian).

Cloudstone Vineyard Santa Clara T nyr
The part-time winery of Peter and Judith Wolken produces about 500 cases per year of Monterey Chardonnay-Ventana Vineyard, Lake County Cabernet Sauvignon, and California Zinfandel. The first crush at the cellar in hills behind Stanford University was '81. Prices $9–$14.

Cobb Mountain Lake T nyr
Owner-winemaker Jim Downing founded his cellar in '81 to make local Sauvignon Blanc, Cabernet Sauvignon, and Zinfandel, plus a generic white. Chenin Blanc from his own vines near Middletown will join in '85. Production is headed toward 1,000 cases. Prices $3.50–$10, locally to date.

Cocktail Sherry
Generic name for a relatively dry sherry-type. It is synonymous with Dry Sherry. The wines may or may not have a smack of *flor*.

Cold Duck
Sparkling wine-type typically containing some Concord, though there is no legal requirement. A sweet sipper, it has faded steadily from favor after a brief heyday during the 1960s.

Cole Ranch
A single-property AVA s. w. of Ukiah in Mendocino County. The 150-acre area has 61 acres in Chardonnay, White Riesling, and Cabernet Sauvignon. Fetzer Vineyards Cole Ranch

Cabernet Sauvignon has been much praised in recent vintages.

Coloma Wine Cellars San Joaquin T, D *
Small firm sells a broad range of everyday wines only through its own outlets at Lodi and in the Sierra Foothills. Prices $3.25–$4.50.

Colony
The primary brand of Italian Swiss Colony.

Concannon Vineyard Alameda T **/***
One of the Livermore Valley's finest names before Prohibition continues as a well-regarded label. Indeed, new owners (Distillers Co., Ltd., since 1982) have revived its fortunes considerably with the continued help of the founding family and new winemaker Sergio Traverso. The cellars and 180 acres of vines flank Livermore to the e. Annual production of about 100,000 cases comes from the home vineyard plus grapes purchased in Monterey, San Luis Obispo, and elsewhere. Prices $3.75–$9.
• Sauvignon Blanc. The Estate bottling is opulent in texture but restrained in the vigorous flavors of the grape. A second, California bottling is rather the reverse. '81 '83
• Petite Sirah. The warmth of Livermore tempers it into a fat, velvety wine without compromising its ability to age well. '79 '80
Also: Chardonnay (gentle, appealing), Zinfandel Rosé (dry, rich in fruit), Cabernet Sauvignon (the only Livermore appellation wine of this variety). The generics give good value.

Congress Springs Vineyard Santa Clara T **/***
In steep hills w. of Saratoga, partner-winemaker Dan Gehrs thinks the best way to preserve the Santa Cruz Mountains as a district is to make wines from nowhere else. Thus he makes an annual 6,000 cases, mostly of white wine . . . all from 10 acres at the winery and another 50 scattered around wooded hills s. of the San Francisco peninsula. His first crush was '76. Prices $5–$15.
• Chardonnay. Barrel-fermented, but more fruity, less toasty than most of its peers. Attractive when young. May age fairly well. '81
• Sémillon. Some variation in character, but best are firm, complex. '81
Also: Chenin Blanc (zesty, fruity), Pinot Blanc, Cabernet Sauvignon (tannic, big), Pinot Noir, Zinfandel.

Conn Creek Napa T **
The winery of Bill and Kathy Collins and partners is e. of Rutherford but its two vineyards are e. of Yountville and n. of St. Helena. The oldest wine under the label is a Cabernet

Sauvignon '73. Current production is a shade more than 20,000 cases. Dark, intensely flavored, markedly oaky Cabernet Sauvignon is the flagship (first-rate in '74 and '79). Also in the list: Chardonnay (main bottling is buttery rich, oaky; a second, less expensive one subtitled Chateau Maja is lighter and fruitier), and Zinfandel (dark, full of varietal flavor, usually a bit heady but deftly balanced in that style). Prices $7.50–$13.75.

Conrad Viano Winery
See Viano Winery, Conrad.

Conrotto Winery, A. Santa Clara T *
In the old Hecker Pass District w. of Gilroy, Jim Burr has taken over the one-time country jug winery of his father-in-law, Anselmo Conrotto, and turned it toward varietals without changing the style much. The list includes Chardonnay and Cabernet Sauvignon as well as Chablis, Grenache, and Zinfandel. Prices $2.75–$6.50; all sales are in central California.

Conti Royale
Brand of East-Side Winery for 10-year-old brandy.

Cook-Ellis Santa Cruz T nyr
The husband-wife team of Rebecca Cook and Jim Ellis graduated from home winemaking in time to make '81s. They now make an annual 1,000 cases of Chardonnay, Fumé Blanc, and Pinot Noir—all from purchased Monterey grapes—at a ridgetop (2,100-ft. elevation) winery beyond a village called Corralitos. Their goal is 10,000 cases. A small part will come from their own 8 acres of vines. Prices $6.95–$8.95, only in California at present.

Cook Winery, R & J Yolo T *
In the burgeoning Clarksburg region, behind levees on the n. bank of the Sacramento River, the family-owned 400-acre vineyard and 50,000-case winery of Roger and Joanne Cook first crushed in '79. Specialty is Chenin Blanc in several styles: wood-aged Extra Dry, steel-aged Very Dry, and steel-aged Semi-Dry. Other wine-types under their label include: Cabernet Sauvignon, Petite Sirah (steady, attractively vinous), Merlot Blanc, Petite Sirah Rosé, plus generics. Prices $3.39–$7.

Corbett Canyon San Luis Obispo T, S nyr
Substantial winery in Edna Valley, owned by Glenmore Distillers, is building toward annual production of 75,000 cases of varietals and "Coastal classic" generics, primarily from Central Coast counties grapes. The label began with '83s, but winemaker Cary Gott (ex-Montevina) arrived in '82 before Glenmore changed the name from Lawrence Winery. The list

includes Chardonnay, Sauvignon Blanc, Cabernet Sauvignon, and a Zinfandel from Amador County, all modest in character but well made. Prices $4.50–$8. The company also owns Shadow Creek, a label for *méthode champenoise* sparklers (reliable values) made elsewhere from Sonoma County grapes.

Cordtz Brothers Sonoma T **
A family-owned winery near Cloverdale makes about 13,000 cases a year of Sauvignon Blanc (conventional, agreeable), Chardonnay, a dry Gewürztraminer, Cabernet Sauvignon and Zinfandel (both reds tend to be plummy, extra-ripe), plus a red table wine. All are principally from Alexander Valley grapes. The first crush was '79. Prices $4–$8.

Cosentino Wine Co. Stanislaus T, S nyr
At a base in Modesto and on other premises, young proprietor Mitch Cosentino makes (and sometimes buys) a broad spectrum of wines from Sacramento County, the Sierra Foothills, and Napa for his two labels. Special lots of Chardonnay (light, approachable immediately), Sauvignon Blanc (subtle, balanced), and Cabernet Sauvignon are sold as Cosentino; prices $6–$12. The great proportion of 15,000 cases (en route to a planned 50,000) goes into the world as Crystal Valley. The types include Chardonnay, Sauvignon Blanc, Cabernet Sauvignon (clean, lively with fruit flavors), generics, and several Charmat sparkling wines; prices $4.75–$7. Cosentino founded the winery in 1980.

Costello Napa T nyr
New in 1982, the winery and a 38-acre vineyard are just n. of Napa city. The announced roster is dominated by Chardonnay, but includes bits of Sauvignon Blanc and Gewürztraminer. Most of the latter is dry, but John Costello makes late-harvest lots when the weather is right. Production is already at the planned peak of 9,000 cases. Prices $6.95–$10.75.

Coturri & Sons, H. Sonoma T *
Family-owned winery near Glen Ellen in Sonoma Valley makes self-described "natural" (no preservatives, no fining) Chardonnay, Gewürztraminer, Johannisberg Riesling, Sémillon, Cabernet Sauvignon, Pinot Noir, and Zinfandel, all from local grapes. Since first crush, '79, wines have been idiosyncratic. Chardonnays are typically dark-hued, sometimes cloudy. Cabernet Sauvignon has been dark, pruney to raisiny. Prices $6.50–$11.25. Production presently is 2,000 cases; the proprietors were searching in 1984 for a site to build a 15,000-case cellar.

Cranbrook Cellars
Label of Monticello Cellars.

Cream Sherry
Generic name for sweetest (about 8% r. s.) sherry-types.

Crémant
Label term to identify sparkling wines with lesser carbon dioxide content than required for Champagne. Presently used only by Schramsberg.

Crescini Santa Cru T nyr
The part-time winery of Richard and Paule Crescini yields about 850 cases per year of Monterey Chenin Blanc, Napa Cabernet Sauvignon, and Napa Merlot, all sold locally, mostly from the winery in Soquel. The inaugural vintage was '80. Prices $5.50–$7.50.

Cresta Bella
Brand of Gibson Wine Co. for inexpensive generic wines.

Cresta Blanca Mendocino T, S, D **
Winery name dates to pre-Prohibition times in Livermore Valley, but currently operates at n. side of Ukiah. Its current owner, Guild Wineries and Distilleries, was actively seeking a buyer in 1984. Grapes for its table and sparkling wines come from Guild members, mainly in Mendocino. Dessert wines come from a Guild winery in the San Joaquin Valley. Volume is stretching toward 100,000 cases. Prices $3.30–$6, and to $11.50 for sparkler, for roster encompassing most familiar types. Whites are straightforward; reds tend to smack sharply of American oak. One curiosity is an intensely varietal Champagne of Chardonnay.

Creston Manor San Luis Obispo T nyr
In 1982, a small partnership (which includes Christina Crawford, Joan's daughter and writer of *Mommy Dearest*) launched a 95-acre vineyard and 7,500-case winery in the remote s. e. quarter of the Paso Robles viticultural district. A subtly appealing if quick-maturing Sauvignon Blanc won immediate praise. Other wines on the list: Chardonnay, Cabernet Sauvignon, and two Pinot Noirs (one conventional, one carbonic maceration). All come from the home and other San Luis Obispo vineyards. Prices $9–$11. The long-range goal is 40,000 cases.

Cribari & Sons, B.
Label owned by Guild Wineries and Distilleries, used for broad range of inexpensive wines.

Cronin Vineyards Santa Clara T nyr
Duane Cronin takes time from the computer business to make an annual 500 cases of Chardonnay (of the toasty-woody school), Cabernet Sauvignon, Merlot, and Pinot Noir from a

number of vineyards near the winery, and in Napa, Sonoma, and Monterey counties. Volume may grow to 2,000 cases, but the winery will remain a part-time venture. Prices $8.50–$15; sales are highly localized. Cronin's first vintage was '80.

Crystal Valley
The principal label for wines of the Cosentino Wine Co.

Cucamonga
Time-honored district in San Bernardino County just e. of Los Angeles County line is rapidly disappearing beneath the onslaughts of suburban housing developments and industrial parks. See maps.

Culbertson Winery, John San Diego S nyr
Small specialist in *méthode champenoise* sparkling wines draws from vineyards amid the avocado orchards dominating terrain around town of Fallbrook, and from Temecula. Technically adept first vintage was '80. It and subsequent '81 Brut and Natural (the latter divided into regular and late-disgorged lots) have commanded critical attention for crisper, cleaner character than expected from the growing region. Prices $14.50–$19.50. Volume of 8,000 cases in 1984 is planned to increase to a maximum 12,000.

Cuvaison, Inc. Napa T [**]
Cellar near Calistoga has undergone several changes of ownership since its founding in 1970. Current proprietor (since 1979) is a Zürich banker who has invested heavily in vineyards at opposite, Carneros end of valley. Key wine is Chardonnay (pleasingly straightforward varietal flavors in well-balanced wine), followed by Cabernet Sauvignon. Announced style beginning with '81 is for early drinkability. Vintages through '79 were austere, designed to age. Current production is about 25,000 cases. Prices $11–$12. A second label, Calistoga Cellars, is used for slightly lesser and less expensive Chardonnay ($6.99) and Pinot Noir ($5.99).

cuvée
As in France, where the word originates, a label term signalling a specific blend or lot. Most commonly used with sparkling wines, but sometimes with table wines (e.g., Spring Mountain Cabernet Sauvignon Les Trois Cuvées, etc.).

Cygnet Cellars San Benito T *
Since its first crush, '78, a small cellar in the w. hills of the Paicines River Valley has specialized in late-harvest reds—both dry and sweet—principally Zinfandels and Carignanes. Alcohols have ranged to 19.5%. There is also a Chardonnay. Prices $5–$13. Annual volume about 2,000 cases.

d'Agostini Winery Amador T *
Old-line winery and 125-acre vineyard e. of Plymouth in Shenandoah Valley changed hands in 1984, and is now changing spots. Style was pure country under the d'Agostini family. With Armagan Ozdiker (the name is Turkish) at the reins, the emphasis still is on Zinfandel and Muscat Canelli, but White Zinfandel and Sauvignon Blanc have joined the list, and the cellars are being modernized. Production is about 50,000 cases. Prices $2.99–$5.99, and scheduled to go up a bit as distribution expands.

Daniel Society, John Napa T nyr
The name of a Bordeaux-Napa partnership pays tribute to the long-time owner of Inglenook Vineyards. Christian Moueix is the Bordelais. Marcia Smith and Robin Lail—the daughters of John Daniel—are the Napans, and the vineyard owners. They began with '83 to make a traditional Cabernet Sauvignon-Cabernet Franc-Merlot blend to be called "Dominus." In favorable vintages there is also to be a 100% Cabernet Sauvignon called Daniel Estate. First release is due in 1986.

Daumé Winery, The Ventura T nyr
Founded in the town of Camarillo in 1982 by Los Angeleno John Daumé, the 2,000-case winery produces Chardonnay, Pinot Noir, and *vin gris* from grapes purchased in the Central Coast, mostly the Santa Maria Valley. Prices $4.99–$7.99.

David Bruce Winery
See: Bruce Winery, David.

Davis Bynum Winery
See: Bynum Winery, Davis.

Deer Park Winery Napa T **
Family-owned cellar and 5-acre vineyard in hills e. of St. Helena, first crushed in '79. Proprietor-winemaker Dave Clark makes about 6,000 cases per year of Chardonnay, Sauvignon Blanc, Petite Sirah, and Zinfandel—all well made, straightforwardly varietal, all from purchased Napa grapes. Prices $6.50–$9.50.

Dehlinger Winery Sonoma T **/***
Tom Dehlinger owns the winery and a 14-acre vineyard in Russian River Valley just e. of Forestville. First crush was '76. Production has grown from 3,000 to 8,500 cases of increasingly stylish wines. Roster includes Chardonnay (excellent varietal, well polished), Cabernet Sauvignon (splendid in '79), Zinfandel, and Pinot Noir ('79 and '80 both fine). All the reds are a notch or two on the dark and tannic side of center, and age-worthy. New with the '84s, a Blanc de Noir styled after still Champagne. Prices $7.50–$10.

Delicato Vineyards San Joaquin T, S *
Family-owned winery near the town of Manteca produces several million gallons of reliably sound San Joaquin Valley wines. The owning Indelicatos sell a good deal in bulk, but about 300,000 cases go to market under their Delicato label. The style is for instant drinking. Both Petite Sirah and Zinfandel, for example, are affably off-dry, with a minimum of tannins. All but 7 of 22 wines are to be had in jugs; several come in bag-in-a-box packages. Prices $1.79–$5.25. The winery dates from 1935, but its growth began only during the 1970s.

DeLoach Vineyards Sonoma T [***]
Cecil DeLoach first bonded in 1975, and settled into current stride in time to make striking array of '79s. Wines since then have been far more consistent than the vintages that yielded them. The winery and 150 acres of vineyards are just e. of Forestville in the Russian River Valley. Production, mostly estate, has edged past 25,000 cases; prices $5.75–$12.50.
• Chardonnay. Splendid evocation of varietal flavors is tempered but not obscured by oak from partial barrel fermentation and aging. Early vintages suggest age-worthiness, but patience is hard to cultivate. '80, '81, '82, '83
• Pinot Noir. The most individualistic in style of these wines is pungently fruity, well marked by oak. '79, '82
• Zinfandel. Dark, rich in fruit, balanced at mortal levels of alcohol, it is perfect wine for tomato sauces and other spicy fare. '79, '80
Also: Gewürztraminer (intense varietal, just off-dry), Fumé Blanc, White Zinfandel (crisp, fresh "blush" wine).

Demi-sec
Descriptive term for sparkling wines of considerable sweetness (usually 2% r. s. and up). Has largely given way to "extra dry."

dessert wine
In practical use, any wine too sweet to be taken with regular meals, i.e., anything from late-harvest Gewürztraminer to Port-types. In legal definition (for tax-collecting purposes), any sweet or dry wine of 17% alcohol or more.

Deutz San Luis Obispo S nyr
Deutz, pure and simple, will not be the label, but the French firm's name should figure somewhere in the identity of the *méthode champenoise* winery they launched in 1983, near the Pacific shore at Arroyo Grande. Deutz is buying grapes in the nearby Santa Maria Valley while its own 150 acres come into bearing. Volume is planned to grow quickly to 60,000 cases. The first wines are to go to market in 1986.

Devlin Wine Cellars Santa Cruz T */**
Another small cellar reaching out from the Santa Cruz Mountains hideaway for grapes—in this case as far n. as northern Sonoma County, as far s. as Edna Valley. Proprietor Chuck Devlin first crushed in '78; current production is about 2,500 cases of Chardonnay, Cabernet Sauvignon, and Merlot—heavyweights all. Prices $4.99–$8, only from the winery at Soquel.

Diablo Vista Winery Solano T **
Robert Polson and family bought a small existing winery in 1982, having sold grapes to it for some years. Growers in Dry Creek Valley, they plan to shift the name over to Lake Sonoma during 1985–86 (but will keep Diablo Vista as a second label). A longer-range plan is to move the winery from Benicia to Dry Creek. Meanwhile, production is 1,500 cases and growing slowly. The wines include Cabernet Sauvignon (good varietal, distinct oak from aging), Merlot, Zinfandel (ripe, vinous), and Chenin Blanc, all from the owners' 32 acres. Prices $6.90–$10.50.

Diamond Creek Vineyards Napa T **
Al Brounstein's winery and 20-acre vineyard in hills s. w. of Calistoga produce only Cabernet Sauvignon—blended with Cabernet Franc, Malbec, and Merlot in the Bordeaux tradition. Three lots totalling 2,500 cases are named after sections of the vineyard, Gravelly Meadow, Red Rock Terrace, and Volcano Hill. All are dark, tannic, meant to improve through the decades. Because of this, the proof is not yet in though the first vintage was '75. Price $20.

Diamond Oaks Vineyards Sonoma T nyr
Winery of Dinesh Maniar settled at Cloverdale in 1983 after earlier stints in San Francisco and Napa. The roster of wines: Cabernet Sauvignon, Chardonnay (oaky), and Sauvignon Blanc, from 155 winery-owned acres in Sonoma (Alexander Valley at Cloverdale and Chalk Hill area near Windsor) and Napa Valley (near Calistoga and e. of Napa city in Wild Horse Valley). Prices $7.50–$10.50. Separate lots of the same varietals sell as Diamond Oaks-Thomas Knight selection; prices $4.99–$5.49. Total production is 15,000 cases, on the way to a planned capacity of 45,000.

Dolan Vineyards Mendocino T nyr
A 3,000-case winery in the Redwood Valley n. of Ukiah belongs to Fetzer Vineyard's talented winemaker, Paul Dolan, who moonlights to produce Chardonnay (powerfully bouqueted after aging in French oak) and Cabernet Sauvignon

from selected local grapes. Prices $11–$12. The first wines were '80s.

Domaine Chandon Napa S [***]
At Yountville, the American offshoot of Moët-Hennessy met with instant success after its founding in 1973. Under the expert direction of Moët *chef de caves* Edmond Maudière, production shot to nearly 300,000 cases in time for the 10th Anniversary Cuvée. The projected maximum is around 400,000 cases. The firm has 800 acres in vines at Yountville, Carneros, and in the Mayacamas Mountains to the w. Prices $13.50, and to $38 for a reserve bottled only in magnums.
• Napa Brut. A blend dominated by Chardonnay and Pinot Blanc but with an enriching proportion of Pinot Noir, it has remained subtle and deft season after season.
• Napa Blanc de Noirs. Fuller than the Brut but equally dry, it harkens back to the partridge eye styles of France in the 1950s and earlier. Pinot Noir is the great majority, its flavors almost bold enough to identify as varietal.
Also: Panache, a "Pinot Noir"–based apéritif styled after *ratafias* of Champagne.

Domaine Laurier Sonoma T ***
Named after native laurels in Sonoma-Green Valley n. of Forestville, the 30-acre vineyard and 11,000-case winery of Jacob and Barbara Shilo made attractive '78s in its first outing. The label's reputation has grown each year since. Prices $9–$13.
• Chardonnay. Toasty overtones are restrained. So are varietal flavors in a stylish, consistent wine. '81 '82
• Cabernet Sauvignon. Goal seems to be balance rather than power, but varietal flavors intense all the same. '79, '80
• Sauvignon Blanc. Stylistic twin of the Chardonnay is not grassy, as Sonomans from these cool reaches can be, but rather a compilation of delicate flavors. '81 '82 '83
Also: Pinot Noir (the most variable to date).

Domaine Marville Napa T nyr
Mike Marville retired early as a consulting engineer to buy 30 acres of vines near Oakville. He made his first Johannisberg Riesling (off-dry, fine varietal flavors) and Cabernet Sauvignon from them in '82, and will add a Chardonnay from '85. The announced style is lighter across-the-board, in keeping with the trends of the times. Production approaches 5,000 cases, and will increase by 1,200 as the "Chardonnay" matures. Prices $6–$7.

Domaine Michel Sonoma T nyr
The only wines from this vineyard in Dry Creek Valley are to be Chardonnay and Cabernet Sauvignon. The first vintage

was '82; the first Chardonnay is due for release in 1985. The winery is under the direction of Mike Rowan (ex-Jordan).

Domaine Mumm Napa S nyr
Domaine Mumm may or may not be the label of the joint venture of G. H. Mumm & Co, in France and Seagram Wine Co. in the U. S. That decision will come when Guy Devaux (ex-Gold Seal in New York) has his small lots of '83s ready for disgorging. Fine points of the long-term style remained to be set late in 1984, though it is a sure bet most or all of the grapes will come from Napa, and the general approach to style from Mumm. The first wines are due on the market in '85 or early '86. A 40,000-case cellar was abuilding in 1984 on the property of Sterling Vineyards, the Seagram-owned half-sister of this company.

Donatoni Winery Los Angeles T **
Airline pilot Hank Donatoni operates his 1,200-case winery right at the end of a runway of his home base, LAX. The wines are Cabernet Sauvignon and Chardonnay, both from a Paso Robles vineyard called Nepenthe. The first crush was '79. Prices $8.50–$11. Sales are local.

Donna Maria Vineyards Sonoma T nyr
First crush for owner Frederick P. Furth's winery was '80, though his 175-acre vineyard in Chalk Hill district e. of Windsor goes back to 1974. The early wines—all from the estate—have been sound. The roster leans toward Chardonnay (good varietal character heartily kissed by oak), Cabernet Sauvignon (on the dark, tannic side but not to excess, also oak-kissed), Sauvignon Blanc, and Pinot Noir. Prices $6–$10. A second label, Chalk Hill Winery, goes on Chardonnay, Sauvignon Blanc, and other varietals from grapes purchased in the immediate region. Prices $6–$7. Total production nears 25,000 cases on the way to a planned limit of 45,000 cases.

Doré Signature Selection, J. Patrick
A substantial (225,000 cases a year) merchant label which draws widely for a full roster of varietal and generic table wines. Most of the varietals are from coastal vineyards as far n. as Mendocino, as far s. as San Luis Obispo. Prices for varietals $3.99–$4.95, for generics $2.50. The wines have tended to be reliably attractive near-termers.

dosage
Liqueur added to sparkling wines at bottling to set the final sweetness, perhaps add particular flavors. It can be composed of sparkling or still wine, Madeira, brandy, and/or sugar in whatever combination a proprietor feels will help produce a "house style."

dry
For winemakers, the absence of fermentable grape sugar in a wine, thus a descriptive term for a wine not sweet. For marketing purposes, "dry" on a label indicates only that the wine is not too sweet to go with meals, hence a subjective note. Sometimes modified to "bone-dry" (no residual sugar) or "off-dry" (perceptible sweetness but not enough to limit the wine's use to dessert).

Dry Creek Valley
An AVA in Sonoma County, running w. and n. from Healdsburg. See maps.

Dry Creek Vineyard Sonoma T **/***
Proprietor David Stare grows (50 acres) and buys most of his grapes in immediate Dry Creek Valley area, but also reaches into neighboring Alexander Valley and Russian River Valley. Since opening in 1972, the winery's reputation for whites has been particularly steady. Case production about 50,000. Prices $6–$10, to $14 for reserve bottlings.
• Sauvignon Blanc. Perfect evocation of the Sonoma grassy character in youth, it ages until a galaxy of aromas suggests a whole Italian delicatessen. '81, '82, '83
• Chardonnay. Focus is on fruit flavors of a ripe, slightly heady wine that ages well (the '76 was fine in 1984). '78 '80 '81
• Chenin Blanc. Ringingly clear of its variety, and dry.
• Cabernet Sauvignon. Tends to be heady, a bit blunt, but some vintages ('74, '77) have turned charming with age. '79
Also: Gewürztraminer (including late-harvest, most years), Merlot, Petite Sirah (overlooked by too many), Zinfandel.

Dry Sherry
One of several variant names for relatively dry (to 2.5% r. s.) sherry-types intended as appetizers. Essentially synonymous with Cocktail Sherry.

Duboeuf & Son, Georges Sonoma T nyr
One of France's major producers of Beaujolais has been trying his hand at a similar type in California since 1980. Originally called "Gamay Beaujolais" but now known as "Gamay Duboeuf," it is a carbonic maceration wine from Sonoma and Mendocino grapes, fermented and aged in steel, but not released early enough to be called "Nouveau." The results have met considerable success with people looking for a fresh, zesty quaff. From '84, it will have as a running mate a Sonoma Chardonnay styled after St. Véran. Production is 8,000 cases. Prices $4.50–$8.

Duckhorn Vineyards Napa T **/***
At the winery's founding, in 1976, emphasis was on Merlot. The game still is wines from Bordeaux varieties, but Cabernet Sauvignon and Sauvignon Blanc have joined in as equal partners. All the grapes come from Napa Valley vines; an increasing proportion is winery-grown. Production is 10,000 cases. Prices $9–$15.
• Merlot. Darker and with a bit more tannic spine than most of its Napa peers. '78 '80
Also: Sauvignon Blanc (first effort straightforward, balanced) and Cabernet Sauvignon (dark, tannic, sometimes a bit heady).

Dunn Vineyards Napa T nyr
Another busman's holiday winery, this one was founded in 1978 by Randall Dunn, the winemaker at Caymus Vineyard. Production is 1,000 cases of Cabernet Sauvignon priced at $13. The wines are intense in flavor and tannic, characteristic of their origin in the lean upland soils of Howell Mountain e. of St. Helena, but not exaggerated. The early vintages appear balanced to age well.

Durney Vineyards Monterey T **
For years after debut '77 vintage, the winery was a lonely outpost on high hills above Carmel Valley. There are neighbors now, but the 142 acres of winery-owned vineyards remain the largest and most distinctive source in the region of Cabernet Sauvignon (dark, tannic, austere) and Chenin Blanc (dry, with good varietal fruit). Also: Johannisberg Riesling, Gamay Beaujolais. New-in-1983 winemaker Dan Lee (ex-Jekel Vineyards) may change the styles somewhat. Production is at 15,000 cases a year. Prices $6.50–$12.50.

Duxoup Wine Works Sonoma T nyr
Possibly, Deborah and Andy Cutter named their winery Duxoup because *A Night at the Opera* is hard to fit on a label. Possibly, they did it because they favor various dishes from duck as accompaniments to their balanced, distinctly varietal Syrah (subtler than most), Napa Gamay (all wine, no tutti-frutti), and Zinfandel. In any case, their grapes come from Dry Creek Valley, the first vintage was '81, production approaches the planned maximum of 2,000 cases, and prices are $6–$10.

Eaglepoint Vineyard
Label owned by Scharffenberger Vineyards and used by them for Chardonnay and Blanc de Noir not selected for sparkling wine cuvées of the primary label.

Early Burgundy
Little-planted black grape variety and its seldom-made wine.

East-Side Winery San Joaquin T, D *
Long-established growers' cooperative on e. side of Lodi was a pioneer producer and marketer of varietal table wines from San Joaquin Valley grapes, especially Ruby Cabernet and Emerald Riesling. Both of these varietals are gone, but Chenin Blanc, French Colombard, White Zinfandel, Zinfandel, and Grand Sirah are mainstays of lists dominated by the new-in-1984 Oak Ridge Vineyards label. Prices $2.90–$4.75. The old principal label, Royal Host, now covers generic table wines and dessert wines. Two specialties are Mission 1773 Angelica Antigua (dark, sweet, beginning to be complex) and a 10-year-old brandy called Conti Royale. Annual production approaches 1 million cases.

Eberle Winery San Luis Obispo T **
Winemaker-proprietor Gary Eberle moved a short way w. of his former cellar (Estrella River) in the Paso Robles area to make Cabernet Sauvignon and Chardonnay on his own. The cellars date from 1983; the first vintage (made in leased space) was '79. Production nears 10,000 cases. Price $10. With the '84s, a Cabernet Blanc joins the roster.

Edmeades Vineyards Mendocino T **/***
Family-owned winery and 35-acre vineyard w. of Philo in Anderson Valley nudges 24,000 cases of annual production, mostly from its own 32 acres, but partly from locally purchased grapes. Prices $4.95–$12.
• Chardonnay. Excellent fruit and some style. '79 '80 '81
• Zinfandel (especially vineyard-identified DuPratt, Pacini bottlings). Deep riches of varietal flavor seldom found in wines of their restraint and balance. '75 '78 '79
Also: White Riesling, Gewürztraminer, and proprietaries called Rain Wine, Whale Wine, and Opal.

Edna Valley
One of the state's smaller AVAs rolls s. from the town of San Luis Obispo. See maps.

Edna Valley Vineyards San Luis Obispo T ***
The winery, built in time to make the '80s, is a joint venture of Chalone Vineyards (the winemaking side) and Paragon Vineyards (the grower). The first wines were '77s made at Chalone. Paragon's vines flank the cellar at the upper end of Edna Valley. Production is about 30,000 cases. Prices $5.50–$12.50.
• Chardonnay. Made to mirror Chalone's own via the same

regimen of barrel fermentation and long aging in a damp cellar, it is thus one of the forcefully toasty school and much prized as such.
Also: Pinot Noir, *vin gris* from "Pinot Noir."

Ehlers Lane Winery Napa T nyr
Founded in 1983 in an old stone cellar n. of St. Helena, the winery makes Sauvignon Blanc, Chardonnay, and Cabernet Sauvignon. The first vintage yielded 13,000 cases; the plans are for a maximum of 20,000, all from purchased Napa Valley grapes. Prices $9–$14.

El Dorado
A small AVA anchored on the El Dorado County town of Placerville in the Sierra Foothills.

Eldorado Vineyards El Dorado T nyr
Recently revived by the original owners after a three-year hiatus, it is a small winery e. of Placerville which makes about 750 cases per year of Zinfandel and others. The earlier wines were rustic.

Elliston Vineyards Alameda T nyr
The Ramon Awtrey family founded its 500-case cellar in the town of Sunol to revive a similarly tiny pre-Prohibition winery. The first vintage was '80. The principal wines are Chardonnay and Cabernet Sauvignon from local vines that, with the winery, fall barely outside the Livermore Valley. Prices $6.95–$7.95, mostly at the cellar door.

Emerald Riesling
A white grape developed at the University of California, Davis, and its wines. See page 17.

Emile's
Label belonging to the Guglielmo Winery and used by it principally for generic jug wines.

Enz Vineyards San Benito T *
In the Lime Kiln Valley (a limestone corner within the Cienega area), a family-owned winery produces about 12,000 cases per year of sound, somewhat heavy wines. The label dates from 1973; a 40-acre vineyard goes back much further. The roster includes French Colombard, Fumé Blanc, Zinfandel, Pinot St. George, and a flavored apéritif called Limestone. Prices $5.30–$7.70.

Estate Bottled
In spite of recent tightening of regulations, still a fuzzy term on labels. Some proprietors use it to indicate wines made by them from grapes surrounding the winery. Other use it to identify wines made from any and all grapes owned or bought

within the AVA in which the winery is located—this latter the only genuine restriction on the term's use.

Estrella River San Luis Obispo T, S [**]
The largest cellar in the Paso Robles AVA draws selected lots from its 860 acres of vines to make 100,000 cases of varietal table wines, and, beginning with '83, *méthode champenoise* sparklers. First crush was '77. Wines have settled in as sound, straightforward. Of greatest interest: Cabernet Sauvignon (affable early), Chardonnay (subtly flavored), Muscat Canelli (well made off-dry sipper). Syrah, from Australian budwood, is singular by pedigree but only modest in character. A more distinctive wine is a late-harvest Muscat Canelli. Prices $4.50–$9, to $15 for reserve bottlings. The winery offers lower-priced ($3–$4.50) non-vintage bottlings labelled just "Estrella."

Evensen Winery Napa T [**]
The only wine is Gewürztraminer, about 800 cases of it a year, from the owner's 8 acres of vines between Rutherford and Oakville. Bone-dry, redolent of its grape, with a proper bitter fillip at the finish, it has won an audience of fervent admirers. First crush was '79. Price $6.50.

Extra Dry
As in France, a label term designating perceptibly sweet sparkling wines (in practice from 1.5% to 3% r. s.). It is used interchangeably with "Sec." There is no requirement as to grape varieties, but the expensive ones lean on Chenin Blanc for flavor, the inexpensive Charmat bottlings on Muscat.

Fairmont Napa T [**]
A veteran winemaker with experience in sizable firms in both Australia and California, George Kolarovich launched his own label with a 1,600-case lot of '78 Napa Valley Cabernet Sauvignon made in leased space. He since has added Chardonnay and Sauvignon Blanc to the roster under the same regime. All the wines are polished and polite. Prices $6–$8.

Falcon Crest
Second label of Spring Mountain.

Far Niente Napa T ***
In the original, now much gussied-up stone cellars at Oakville, a partnership of three has restored to life one of Napa's great pre-Prohibition labels. First crush was '79. The roster is limited to Chardonnay and Cabernet Sauvignon (debut '82, due to appear in 1985, seemed supple, polished on the way from barrel to bottle). The wines are in much subtler taste than the restoration of the building. Prices $18–$20. Production is at

16,000 cases annually, on the way to a planned peak of 26,000, when all will be estate-grown.

• Chardonnay. Estate and Napa Valley bottlings both toasty from barrel fermentation, well scented with oak, and still discernibly varietal. Nicely balanced. '81

Farview Farm San Luis Obispo T nyr

The label belongs to a grower with 51 acres just w. of U. S. 101 at Templeton in the Paso Robles area. The annual 7,000 cases of Chardonnay, White Zinfandel, Zinfandel, and Merlot (sound, straightforward) from his grapes will for the foreseeable future be made by the owner's winemaker in leased space at a local winery. Prices $5–$7. '79 was the first vintage.

Felton-Empire Santa Cruz T */***

The property in the village of Felton once was famous for Cabernet Sauvignon when it was Hallcrest. Now the winery is best known for Gewürztraminers and Johannisberg Rieslings, all off-dry, many of them *Botrytis*-affected and outright sweet. The quality is, by the rules of nature, uneven, but the best are splendid and very fairly priced. The reds, on the other hand, are seldom successes. Prices $6.50–$16, and to $12 for half bottles of some late-harvest whites. Annual production nears 13,000 cases, a bit from the home property, but mostly from grapes purchased in Mendocino, Sonoma, and Santa Barbara counties.

• Johannisberg Riesling. Rich, ripe varietal flavors. '82
• Gewürztraminer. Rich, ripe varietal flavors. '82

Also Chardonnay, Pinot Noir (extremely erratic but sometimes of interest), Cabernet Sauvignon.

Fenestra Winery Alameda T **

Lanny Replogle, an academic when he is not making wine, has operated at various locations in the Livermore Valley since 1976 (originally as Ventana Winery). From purchased grapes, Replogle makes Monterey Chardonnay (thoroughly marked by oak), San Luis Obispo or Livermore Valley Sauvignon Blanc (also oaky). Monterey Cabernet Sauvignon (ultra-herbaceous), Napa Merlot, and Livermore Zinfandel. Annual volume is about 2,700 cases; prices $4.50–$11.

Fenton Acres

Original name of small winery now known as Rochioli.

Ferrara Winery San Diego T, D *

In the town of Escondido, an old family winery is broadening its long-time role as a local supplier of jug wines with the addition of varietal table wines.

Ferrer, Gloria Sonoma S nyr

The Spanish *cava* makers, Freixenet, have launched a California *méthode champenoise* winery at the w. edge of the Carneros. In 1984 they assembled a cuvée from bought wine to launch the label with a non-vintage Brut-Cuvée Emeralda. Simultaneously they started construction of a cellar scaled to make 80,000 cases a year, began planting 80 acres of vines in front of it, and made their first wines (Pinot Noir-Chardonnay blend from several Sonoma districts, styled as Brut) in leased space. The debut non-vintage Brut is priced at $11. The first of their own wines is scheduled to appear in 1986.

Fetzer Vineyard Mendocino T, S **

It is not exactly a rags-to-riches story, but almost. The late lumberman Bernard Fetzer planted 200 acres in Redwood Valley and launched a small winery there in 1968. Ten of his 11 children now oversee a 600,000-case business with three cellars spread s. along the Russian River as far as Hopland. One cellar is devoted to *méthode champenoise* sparklers, to appear beginning in 1986. Most of the grapes are purchased from growers in Mendocino and Lake counties; some come from Sonoma and elsewhere. Prices $3.25–$10.

• Cabernet Sauvignon. Full of flavor and nicely polished. Home vineyard and Cole Ranch bottlings show signs of being able to age with the best.

• Zinfandel. Ricetti Vineyard is dark and tannic; Lolonis Vineyard is pale and gentle; Scharffenberger Vineyard falls between them.

Also: Chardonnay-Sundial (fresh, light, free of oak), Fumé Blanc (excellent straightforward varietal flavors), Johannisberg Riesling-Lake (lovely smack of apricot buoyed by 1.8% r. s.). Of particular value are generics Premium Red and Premium White. The Fetzers also own the Bel Arbres label, used principally at present for blush wines.

Ficklin Vineyard Madera D ***

From classic Portuguese grape varieties (Tinta Madeira, Tinta Cao, Touriga, and Souzao) come an annual 10,000 cases of "Tinta Port." The grapes are planted in the Ficklin family vineyards in San Joaquin Valley s. of town of Madera. The third generation is now in charge of a cellar that began with a stellar '48, which continues in fine fettle. Using developed skills and reserve stocks, the Ficklins coax out one of California's few truly distinctive dessert wines, one which has some of the qualities of vintage-character Port, and some of Ruby Port. Price $7.

Fiddletown

Small Sierra Foothills AVA east of Shenandoah Valley in Amador County.

Field Stone Winery Sonoma T */**
The late mechanical genius Wallace Johnson (developer of the first workable mechanical harvester) bonded his Alexander Valley winery in 1977 in part to test equipment of his design. It has wobbled a bit since his death in 1979, but appears back on track with the crush of '84. Best known for a fresh, fragrant blush wine called "Spring Cabernet," it also offers Gewürztraminer (serviceable), Cabernet Sauvignon (inky-dark and extra woody in '78, '79), Petite Sirah. Annual volume is 12,000 cases; prices $5–$10, to $16 for special Cabernet Sauvignon-Hoot Owl Creek.

Field Winery, James Arthur
Since 1976, James Arthur Field, the man, has responded nobly to the need for genuinely dry everyday wines by buying rather good ones in bulk, blending them to a high standard, and selling the results in 1.5-liter jugs under his name at $3.99. There are only two table wines—Burgundy and Chablis. In 1984 he added a dry Charmat sparkler (priced at $3.39 a bottle) to his roster for the same reason. Alas for all others, he markets his annual 40,000 cases only in California.

Filippi Vintage Co., J. Cucamonga T, S, D *
Like others in its region, it sells a long list only through its own outlets scattered throughout southern California. Bread-and-butter Chablis, mellow Sauterne, Burgundy, and Zinfandel come mainly from 400 acres of family-owned vineyard at and near the winery s. of the industrial town of Fontana. Volume averages 130,000 cases a year. Prices $1.85–$3.95.

Filsinger Vineyards & Winery Temecula T */**
Family-owned cellar produces about 6,500 cases per year, mostly from the Filsinger's own 60 acres. First crush was '80. Roster includes Chardonnay (soft, agreeable), Sauvignon Blanc (very ripe), Emerald Riesling, and Zinfandel. Prices $3.75–$7.50, and to $11.50 for a late-harvest Johannisberg Riesling.

Firestone Vineyard Santa Barbara T **
Jointly owned by the Leonard Firestone family and Suntory (the Japanese distilling firm), the 300-acre vineyard and ultra-modern winery have been major factors in the Santa Ynez Valley since Firestone's first crush, '75. The whites have been approachable early, the reds often a bit overdone for alcohol and oak flavors. The firm has announced a goal of restyling its reds to more mortal dimensions. Of particular note: Chardonnay (affable, straightforwardly varietal), Johannisberg Riesling (pleasing fruit, sipper-sweet), Gewürztraminer (matched pacer to Riesling). Also: Sauvignon Blanc, Cabernet

Sauvignon, Merlot, Pinot Noir. Annual production of 75,000 cases is priced $4–$15.

Fisher Vineyards Sonoma T **/***

Fred J. Fisher elected to be a specialist with his first crush, '79. His 7,000-case winery makes only Cabernet Sauvignon and Chardonnay from 19 acres of vineyard at the winery site in hills e. of Santa Rosa; a second, 50-acre vineyard is in the Napa Valley e. of Calistoga. Prices $8.50–$14.

• Chardonnay. Slightly toasty, distinctly woody, but balanced by fine fruit. (A second, less expensive bottling called Everyday Chardonnay is simpler, fruitier.) '81

• Cabernet Sauvignon. Restrained; usually subtle, sometimes a bit oaky. '79

Fitzpatrick Winery El Dorado T nyr

A family-owned 4,500-case winery draws on 19 acres of its own plus nearby vineyards in El Dorado and Amador counties to produce Sauvignon Blanc–Clockspring Vineyard, Eire Bann (a proprietary Sauvignon Blanc–Chenin Blanc blend), Chardonnay, Chenin Blanc, and a pair of vineyard-identified Zinfandels. The early wines have been sound if a bit roughhewn. The first crush was '80. Prices $5–$9.

flor

Curiously flavorful yeast can be grown naturally as floating film on dry Sherry-types in partially filled barrels, or can be cultured and mixed (as "submerged flor culture") into tanks. Both techniques are used in California, and sometimes are announced on labels.

Flora

White grape developed at U. C.-Davis, and its wine.

Flora Springs Wine Co. Napa T **/***

After a small start with the fine vintage of '78, the winery got up to projected 15,000-case speed quickly between 1980 and 1984. Owned by John Komes and family, it draws on family-owned grapes from three separate properties (one at the winery s. of St. Helena, one a mile e., the third e. of Oakville) to make a short roster of increasingly well-received wines. Prices $8–$15.

• Sauvignon Blanc. Appealingly fruity, dry, refreshingly tart. '82 '83

• Chardonnay-Estate. Well marked by oak, but distinctly varietal. Well balanced. (A barrel-fermented lot is mostly toasty.)

• Cabernet Sauvignon. Leans noticeably toward the dark, tannic style.

Fogarty Winery, Thomas Santa Cruz Mountains T nyr

Fogarty, like most in his area, casts widely for grapes. His roster of Chardonnay and Pinot Noir, plus a bit of Cabernet Sauvignon, draws on vineyards at home, and in Monterey and Napa counties. The first crush was '81. Annual volume is 6,500 cases. Prices $12–$15.

Folie à Deux Napa T nyr
In a small cellar just n. of St. Helena, Dr. Larry and Evie Dizmang made their first wine in 1981. The debut Chardonnay was airy-light, subtle, and neatly balanced. Also on the list: dry Chenin Blanc, Cabernet Sauvignon, and a proprietary cheerfully named Folie Blanc. Current production is about 2,000 cases, to come increasingly from the owners' 15 acres of young vineyard. Prices $4.50–$12.

Folle blanche
A white grape and, only from Louis M. Martini, its wine.

Foppiano Wine Co., Louis J. Sonoma T [**]
An old-line family firm in the Russian River Valley at the w. side of Healdsburg, it began marketing varietals under its own label in 1970 after a long career in the jug trade. The always reliable wines are growing ever more stylish. Some come entirely from 200 family-owned acres of vines at the winery; most have a proportion of purchased Sonoma grapes. Of particular note: Petite Sirah (dark, tannic, rich in varietal flavors, slow to age), Zinfandel (gentle, skillfully balanced), Fumé Blanc (distinct regional grassy character). Also: Chardonnay, Chenin Blanc (from Clarksburg), and Cabernet Sauvignon. The good-value second line of jug generics is called Riverside Farms, made mostly from Sonoma grapes. Total production is more than 125,000 cases per year; prices for the Louis J. Foppiano label $5.50–$10, for Riverside Farms $2.50–$3.50.

Forman Winery Napa T nyr
Ric Forman (ex-Sterling, now Charles F. Shaw) is one of many winemakers who moonlights in a winery of his own. In his case, the debut vintage is '83, the volume 3,000 cases. The roster starts with a Cabernet Sauvignon-Cabernet Franc-Merlot-Petit Verdot blend from his own vines (due for release in 1986), and stops with a Chardonnay from purchased grapes (released in autumn 1985). Forman has a thoroughly developed, Bordeaux-influenced style familiar to all who knew his wines at Sterling. Prices $12–$13.

Fortino Winery Santa Clara T */**
Not much stainless steel, no centrifuge, no pretensions, just straightforward wine well made in the best Italian rustic tradition. Ernest Fortino's annual production at an ever-growing cellar e. of Gilroy is edging up past 20,000 cases, most of it sold in the San Francisco region. Prices $4–$8.50. In a roster

with 22 entries: Charbono (one of few, from riper grapes than all the rest), Petite Syrah (thick, with broad hints of warm growing conditions), and a rare Mission Blanc. Also: Cabernet Sauvignon, Ruby Cabernet, White Zinfandel.

Fountaingrove
Before Prohibition a famous winery, it is now a brand of Martini & Prati, used mostly for a Cabernet Sauvignon.

Franciscan Vineyards Napa T **
The wines of this 80,000-case cellar n. of Rutherford have been only slightly more consistent than its ownership, but there are promises of a new steadiness on both counts. The Peter Eckes Co. of Germany became the fourth owner in seven years in 1979, and is still the proprietor. Most of the wines come—as they have since the early going—from 436 acres of owned vineyards, split 50:50 between Napa Valley and Alexander Valley. Prices $2.50–$10.50, to $13.50 for reserve wines, and to $25 for a late-harvest Johannisberg Riesling. The well-received types: Johannisberg Riesling (off-dry, straightforward), Cask 321 Burgundy (well marked by its time in American oak), Cabernet Sauvignon (also well marked by American oak, whether the Napa Valley, Alexander Valley, or Reserve bottling). The curiosity piece is a carbonic maceration Charbono called Harvest Nouveau. Also: Chardonnay (Alexander Valley, Napa Valley, and Reserve Bottlings), Fumé Blanc.

Franken Riesling
An occasional synonym for the white grape "Sylvaner" and its wine.

Franzia Brothers San Joaquin Valley T, S, D *
An old-line firm, now corporately owned by The Wine Group, it makes about 5 million cases per year at its sprawling winery in the San Joaquin County town of Ripon, nearly all of it from valley grapes, most of it generic and in the traditional off-dry style of everyday wines from this region. Franzia sells under its own name and many other labels (all identifiable by the telltale Ripon address). Prices $2.50–$3. As benchmarks, consider: Zinfandel, Chenin Blanc, Chablis. As an oddity: almond-flavored Charmat sparkler.

Fred's Friends
Whimsical label belonging to Domaine Chandon is used for a tart, austere Chardonnay drawn from candidates for Chandon cuvées.

Freemark Abbey Napa T [****]
No other winery comes to mind for placing high on lists of connoisseurs so consistently with each of its major types. Cel-

lar just n. of St. Helena produces about 28,000 cases per year, mainly from vineyards of three of its owning partners. Prices $6.75–$14, and to $32 for Edelwein.

• Chardonnay. Year in, year out, it balances to perfection while hiding the flavors of oak in its varietal fruit, and vice versa. Fine young, better with 2 to 5 years in bottle. '78, '80, '81

• Cabernet Sauvignon. Much overlooked because it runs in the shade of the companion Cabernet Bosché, but steadily one of Napa's most polished and long-lived Cabernets (the '70 is still gaining). '73 '75 '79 '80

• Cabernet Bosché. From a single grower at Rutherford, it is the flagship red. Styled in same vein as regular.

• Edelwein, Edelwein Gold. *Botrytis*-affected Johannisberg Rieslings offered only when the vintage cooperates. Splendid first offering from '73 followed by '76, '78, '82.

Also: Johannisberg Riesling (off-dry, affable).

French Colombard

The white grape and its wine (see p. 18).

French oak

A shorthand term used by tasters to remark flavors produced by fermenting and/or aging any wine in barrels or tanks coopered from oak grown in French forests. (As opposed to: Yugoslav oak and American oak, which impart subtly different characteristic flavors.) Sometimes "French" is refined to Alliers, Troncais, Limousin, or another specific forest, from which the wood allegedly has come.

Fretter Wine Cellars Alameda T **

Part-time winery located in Oakland/Berkeley hills offers 1,000 cases of Napa Cabernet Sauvignon, Merlot, Pinot Noir, Gamay, and Chardonnay under the names of the vineyards from which they come. A fair proportion of sales are direct from the winery on the heels of an ofttimes outrageously funny, always instantly effective annual release letter by the proprietor, Travis Fretter, but the wines do get into local stores. Prices $3.50–$12. The first vintage was '77.

Frey Vineyards, Ltd. Mendocino T nyr

In Redwood Valley, Dr. and Mrs. Paul Frey and their 12 children organically farm 40 acres of vineyard and organically make 5,000 cases of wine divided among 10 varietal types ranging from French Colombard to Cabernet Sauvignon. Since the first vintage, '80, the wines have had a rough-hewn, home-made quality about them, but are consistent and sound as near-term drinkers. Prices $3.99–$9.

Frick Winery Santa Cruz T **
Judith and William Frick are two more seekers after the perfect Pinot Noir. They also make Chardonnay, Petite Sirah, and Zinfandel. The latter is from San Jose; the others come from vines in Monterey and Santa Barbara counties. Debut vintage was '77. A volume of 3,500 cases presses hard against the walls of a cellar in downtown Santa Cruz. Prices $6–$11.

Fritz Cellars Sonoma T **
In a dramatic, dug-into-the-earth hillside winery in Dry Creek Valley, the winery makes Chardonnay (ripe, deftly marked by French oak) and Fumé Blanc (same vein as Chardonnay) from owner Arthur Fritz's nearby 90-acre vineyard. Cabernet Sauvignon (dark and a bit heady) and Zinfandel come from purchased Dry Creek area grapes. First crush was '79. Current production is 20,000 cases. Prices $6–$9.

Frog's Leap Wine Cellars Napa T nyr
A winemaker and a physician are partners in a winery named (honest) after a frog farm that once flourished on the creek that runs through the property n. of St. Helena. Wry wit aside, the early wines offer quality and style at sensible prices. They are Sauvignon Blanc (complex, firm, able to age) and Zinfandel (perfect varietal character and excellent balance in the debut '79). With the '82s, Chardonnay and Cabernet Sauvignon join the roster. Volume is 7,000 cases, on the way to a planned maximum of 9,000. Prices $8–$11.

Fumé Blanc
Alternative name for the white grape "Sauvignon Blanc" and its wine (see p. 19).

Gainey Vineyard Santa Barbara T nyr
A showplace winery in the Santa Ynez Valley, Gainey's oldest wine is a bought-in '82 Chardonnay; the first crush on its own premises was '84. As 54 acres of Chardonnay, Sauvignon Blanc, Johannisberg Riesling, and a bit of Cabernet Sauvignon mature, it is to become a 10,000-case estate operation. Meanwhile, the same varieties are being purchased from Santa Barbara County vineyards. The plan is to sell from the winery and at selected restaurants only. First prices $8–$10.

Gallo Winery, E. & J. ubiquitous T, S, D **
Brothers Ernest and Julio command the American market, command the respect of the industry, and, increasingly, command the interest of critics. The scale cannot be grasped: 300 million gallons of cooperage feed annual sales in the 40- to 50-million-case range. The firm owns or controls fermenting facilities in Napa, Sonoma, and throughout the San Joaquin

Valley to feed its huge aging and bottling cellars at Modesto. The scope is an effect caused by three facts: the wines are infallibly consistent, agreeable to drink, and sell at easy prices. Under the main label, Gallo is well regarded for Chablis Blanc (barely off-dry bread-and-butter white), Hearty Burgundy (red matched pacer to Chablis Blanc), Cabernet Sauvignon (good varietal deftly balanced—a special '78 is aging better than most from its vintage), Sauvignon Blanc (straightforward), Livingston Cellars Cream Sherry (at its price, remarkably complex and harmonious sweet Sherry-type). The firm also produces wines under these labels: André, Ballatore (wonderfully fruity sparkling Muscat), Boone's Farm (fruit wines), Carlo Rossi (the jug label), and more. Prices $2–$9. Its brandy, E & J, is the nation's best-seller.

Gamay (also Napa Gamay)
The black grape variety and its wine (see p. 22).

Gamay Beaujolais
The black grape variety and its wine (see p. 22).

G & D (Gambarelli & Davitto)
A label belonging to Italian Swiss Colony.

Gavilan
A second label of Chalone Vineyards and/or Carmenet for a Napa Valley French Colombard.

Gemello Winery   Santa Clara   T   **
Tucked away behind a bowling alley on an interminable commercial street in suburban Mountain View, Gemello dates from 1934. It clings to a durable reputation for good-value, sturdy reds fashioned first by John, then Mario, Gemello, and now a Gemello niece, Sandra Obester. Annual production is a shade more than 1,500 cases of Alexander Valley Cabernet Sauvignon and Petite Sirah, and Amador Zinfandel and White Zinfandel. Prices $4.95–$12, mostly at the cellar door.

generic
The categoric term for wines of no required grape variety. Most such wines are named after a color (Red Table Wine, Vino Rosso, Vin Rosé) or a place where a supposedly similar type originated (Burgundy, Chianti, Sherry). Wines named after places are also called, sometimes, semi-generic.

Gentili Wines, J. H.   San Mateo   T   nyr
In the San Francisco suburb of Redwood City, Jim Anderson's winery produces about 1,000 cases a year of Napa Valley Chardonnay and Cabernet Sauvignon, and Amador Zinfandel and White Zinfandel. The plan for the new-in-1981 winery is

to grow a bit. Prices $5.50–$13; sales are local. The name, incidentally, is the maiden name of the proprietor's mother.

Gerwer Winery El Dorado T nyr
In the Sierra Foothills s. of Placerville, Vernon Gerwer's cellar is producing about 3,000 cases of Chenin Blanc, Sauvignon Blanc, White Zinfandel, Ruby Cabernet, Zinfandel, and a proprietary red, all from local grapes. Gerwer plans to expand to 7,000 cases. The founding date was 1981. Prices $3–$7.

Gewürztraminer
Pink-skinned grape variety and the white wine from it.

Geyser Peak Sonoma T, S */**
Revitalized in 1972 by Jos. Schlitz Brewing Co., then sold in 1983 to local vineyardist Henry Trione, the 1.5-million-case-per-year winery at the n. end of Alexander Valley offers select varietal table wines under its new Trione label, a broad range of varietals, generics, and *méthode champenoise* sparklers under the Geyser Peak name (prices $3.25–$6.75, and to $10 for sparklers). The firm also offers some distinctly lesser generics in jugs and bags-in-boxes under the name of Summit (prices $3 per 1.5-liter jug). Some 1,100 acres of owned grapes provide much of the fruit for the top two lines. Whites have outshone reds in the past. Most admired types have included Fumé Blanc (straightforward), Johannisberg Riesling, Zinfandel.

Gibson Vineyards Fresno T, D *
A well-established producer of standard generic table and dessert wines offered under several labels in bottles, jugs, and boxes. French Colombard and Zinfandel are the only varietals. Gibson is the first label, Silverstone Cellars the principal one (for wine-in-a-box). Others include California Villages, Cresta Bella, and Woodbrook. The winery draws nearly all of its grapes from the Fresno area. Annual production is about 1.5 million cases. Prices $2–$3 for the table wines.

Girard Winery Napa T nyr
A family-owned winery e. of Oakville, it draws most of its grapes from a 50-acre estate vineyard at the winery, but also buys from independent Napa growers. Girard will become an estate winery when a second vineyard in steep hills w. of Yountville matures. Current volume is 12,000 cases on the way to 15,000. Since its first vintage, '81, the tendency has been toward distinctly oaky Chardonnay, and dark, tannic, oaky Cabernet Sauvignon. The dry Chenin Blanc and Fumé Blanc have been fresher. Prices $6.40–$14.

Giumarra Vineyards Kern T, D *
Along with larger agricultural interests, members of the Giumarra family own 6,000 acres of wine grapes and a 1 million–case winery e. of Bakersfield. Most of a broad array of attractively fruity generics and varietals come from Giumarra and other San Joaquin Valley vineyards in Kern and Tulare counties, but some varietals are firmed up with some Central Coast grapes. Even the latter drink best in the first bloom of youth. Prices $2.65–$3.75. A second label, Breckenridge Cellars, is reserved for jug table and dessert wines priced at the equivalent of $1.

Glen Ellen Winery Sonoma T ***
From its first vintage under the ownership of Bruno Benziger and family, the Sonoma Valley winery has produced balanced, distinctive wines that give pleasure in the drinking. The Benzigers own 40 acres at the winery at Glen Ellen and another 15 nearby in the Carneros area, supplementing their grapes with purchases in Sonoma County. Production is 40,000 cases. Prices $3.99–$10.

• Chardonnay-Les Pierres. Crisp, invitingly fruity. '81
• Sauvignon Blanc-Estate. A lesson in varietal character and yet restrained and complex. A Sonoma Valley bottling is not far off the pace. A third bottling called Fumé Blanc smacks a bit more of oak after longer aging in wood. '81 '83
• Cabernet Sauvignon. Restraint all around going back to a fine '79.

Also: Proprietor's Reserve Chardonnay, Proprietor's Reserve Cabernet Sauvignon (both good values at lesser prices than the main bottlings).

Gold Peak
Brand of Lamont Winery used for low-priced jug generics.

Golden Chasselas
Synonym for the grape variety "Palomino."

Gran Val
Second label of Clos du Val Wine Co. used for more straightforwardly varietal wines than those under the main label.

Grand Cru Sonoma T **/***
In the Sonoma Valley town of Glen Ellen, the cellar was launched in 1972 and purchased by Walt and Bettina Dreyer in 1981. It has expanded steadily to a current level of 25,000 cases using grapes bought locally, elsewhere in Sonoma County, and from Clarksburg. Prices $4.50–$9, and to $14 for a reserve Cabernet.

• Gewürztraminer. Consistently pleasing, varietally distinctive sipper at +2% r. s. (plus occasional super sweetie).

• Chenin Blanc. Drier than most, with agreeable regional overtones of Clarksburg grapes.
Also: Fumé Blanc (good fruity/melony varietal), Cabernet Sauvignon (dark, plummy-ripe in both regular and Collector bottlings). White Zinfandel added with vintage of '84 as running mate to lesser-priced Cabernet Sauvignon and Sauvignon Blanc, all subtitled Vin Maison, all good value.

Grand Noir
Little-planted black grape (116 acres in state) used only for blending.

Granite Springs El Dorado T nyr
Les and Lynne Russell make 7,000 cases a year from their own 23-acre vineyard s. of Placerville, and from grapes purchased nearby. The label dates from '80; the winery's first crush in its own premises was '81. Types are Chenin Blanc, Sauvignon Blanc, White Zinfandel, Cabernet Sauvignon, Petite Sirah, Zinfandel, and a pair of generics. The wines thus far have been sound if a bit rough-hewn. Prices $4.25–$8.

Gray Riesling
White grape and its wine (see p. 18).

Green & Red Vineyard Napa T */**
On a hillside looking down into Pope Valley, Jay Heminway has 16 acres of "Zinfandel" and "Chardonnay," a 2,000-case winery, and room to grow just a bit. His first vintage was '77, when he made only Zinfandel. The current roster has Chardonnay and White Zinfandel as added starters. The wines to date have been sound if a bit common.

Green Hungarian
White grape and its wine (see p. 19).

Greenstone Winery Amador T, S, D nyr
Two couples own a 7,000-case winery in San Joaquin Valley at the w. edge of Amador County, not far e. of Lodi. The first wines came from '81. The partners also own 23 acres of vines. The style of the table wines began as deliberately affable, mostly off-dry, for casual consumption, but appears to be migrating toward drier and woodier. The roster includes French Colombard (dry, estate-bottled, and well regarded), Zinfandel Rosé, White Zinfandel, and Zinfandel, all from Amador grapes. Prices $3.50–$5.75.

Greenwood Ridge Mendocino T nyr
Proprietor Allan Green makes 2,000 cases of Cabernet Sauvignon and Johannisberg Riesling (regular and late-harvest) from his rolling 8-acre vineyard high above the shoreside town of Elk. Since the first vintage, '80, the regular Riesling has

been off-dry, and intensely flavorful. The debut Cabernet was just coming to market in late 1984. Prices $6.75–$9.75, and to $20 the half bottle for the late-harvest Riesling.

Grenache
Black grape variety and its red or (usually) rosé wine (see p. 22).

Grgich-Hills Napa T ***/****
Miljenko Grgich, in partnership with vineyardist Austin Hills, makes for his own winery much the same kinds of delicate, subtle wines that first won him fame at Chateau Montelena. The winery n. of Rutherford produces about 20,000 cases per year, after much smaller beginnings in 1977. Most of the grapes come from Hills's 140 acres e. of Rutherford and n. of Napa city. Prices $7.50–$17.
• Chardonnay. Distinctive for liveliness, freshness in the mouth. Though nicely kissed by oak, varietal flavors dominate even after several years in bottle. '80 '81
• Johannisberg Riesling. Regular bottling (1.2% r. s.) sips well but is crisp enough for food, and profits from a year in bottle; a late-harvest bottling at 6% r. s. is purely for dessert.
• Zinfandel. From Sonoma grapes. Enticing, fresh, berry-like flavors dominate it. '79 '80
Also: Sauvignon Blanc (pungently varietal), Cabernet Sauvignon (first vintage, '80, released only in 1984).

Grignolino
Black grape and its wine (see p. 22).

Groth Vineyards & Winery Napa T nyr
Dennis and Judith Groth have ambitious plans for an estate winery based in a 121-acre vineyard site e. of Oakville and supplemented by a second vineyard of 40 acres near Yountville. From '84 came 20,000 cases of Cabernet Sauvignon, Chardonnay, and Sauvignon Blanc. The first crush, '82, yielded less than half that; the plan calls for a peak 35,000. Winemaker Nils Venge (ex-Villa Mt. Eden) produced a first round of sturdy wines well marked by new oak. Prices $8.50–$13.

Grover Gulch Winery Santa Cruz T */**
Long-time home winemakers Dennis Bassano and Reinhold Banek launched their 1,000-case winery at Soquel in 1979 to make sturdy, ripe, old-fashioned red varietals from aged, unirrigated vineyards in the Hecker Pass area of southern Santa Clara County. Prices $6.60–$9.50, mostly at the cellar.

Growers
Label of California Growers.

Guasti
Label belonging to M. LaMont.

Guenoc Valley
One-winery AVA in southern Lake County, near the Napa County line.

Guenoc Winery Lake T nyr
A major effort of the family Magoon in Guenoc Valley, the winery makes 70,000 cases annually from a 270-acre vineyard on a huge old ranch that once belonged to Lily Langtry. Since the first vintage, '80, the wines have been sound, steady, straightforwardly varietal. They include Cabernet Sauvignon (straightforward), Chardonnay (pleasing mélange of toasty and fruit flavors), Chenin Blanc (pleasing varietal), Petite Sirah, Sauvignon Blanc (flowery rather than grassy), and Zinfandel (well-proportioned red).

Guglielmo Winery, Emilio Santa Clara T *
One of southern Santa Clara Valley's old-time, no-frills jug wineries has, in recent years, added varietals to its line. Generic jugs labelled just as "Emile's" remain weighty in the old, country style, and good buys as such. The "Emilio Guglielmo" varietals (Sémillon, Fumé Blanc, Grignolino Rosé, Gamay Beaujolais, Petite Sirah, Zinfandel among them) follow the pattern set by the jugs. The family's 125 acres of vines are supplemented by bought Santa Clara and San Luis Obispo grapes to bring production to an annual 70,000 cases, available mostly in California. Prices $4.50–$7.

Guild Wineries & Distilleries San Joaquin T, S, D *
The largest grower cooperative winery in California has 1,000 members channelling grapes through several wineries in the San Joaquin Valley, and sending 3 million cases of wines and brandies out into the world under eight to a dozen labels. The major ones for table and dessert wines in standard bottles are B. Cribari and Roma. Roma Vino d'Uva, Tavola, Vintners Choice, and Winemasters identify generics in jugs. The main sparkling wine label is Cook's. J. Pierrot is carbonated wine. In all cases the flavors tend toward the heavy, off-dry ones that come with thoroughly ripe grapes. Prices $3–$5 for Cribari and Roma, $2–$3 for the others. Guild's brandies go by the names Guild, St. Marks, and Old Ceremony. Price $10. The firm also has a line of coolers called Quinn's.

Gundlach-Bundschu Vineyard Co. Sonoma T ***
Bundschus have farmed grapes in the Sonoma Valley continuously since 1858, but Jim Bundschu's reactivation of the pre-Prohibition winery dates only from 1973. Production is 40,000 cases, nearly all from the 110-acre home property

called Rhinefarm, plus another family-owned 190-acre vineyard on the opposite, n. w. corner of Sonoma town. The exceptions are two vineyard-identified specialties. Prices $2.99–$12.

• Cabernet Sauvignon. Dark, tannic, a bit heady, complex in its varietal character. Companion Batto Ranch follows same outlines, but has distinctive flavors of its own. From '81 onward, Special Reserve from home vineyard is to join the list. '78 '79 80

• Chardonnay. Excellent varietal not much masked by wood, whether estate or companion Sangiacomo Vineyard. '81 '82

• Gewürztraminer. Only when the year is cool enough to endow it with pungent aromas of its grape variety will winemaker Lance Cutler let it out of the house.

• Merlot. In much the same style as the vineyard's Cabernet Sauvignons. '79

Also: Kleinberger (gentle, pear-like flavors, from an off-beat German variety), Zinfandel (much in vein of Cabernets).

Hacienda del Rio Sonoma T nyr

In the Russian River Valley n. of Windsor, the winery—not to be confused with Hacienda Wine Cellars—got started with tiny lots of '81 Pinot Noir and Zinfandel (highly attractive) from locally purchased grapes. By '84 partners Bert Williams and Ed Selyem were up to 700 cases, on the way to 2,000. Prices $7.50–$10, only in local markets.

Hacienda Wine Cellars Sonoma T ***

In Sonoma Valley on e. edge of Sonoma town, Crawford Cooley's 20,000-case winery produces consistently appealing wines, mostly from affiliated vineyards (40 acres at the winery, 70 near Cloverdale in northern Sonoma County), partly from purchased grapes. Prices $5.50–$12, and to $15 for a reserve Chardonnay. Under winemaker Steve MacRostie's able direction, best regarded for:

• Cabernet Sauvignon. Dark-hued, tannic, but never to excess. '77 '79 '80 '81

• Gewürztraminer. Refined, just off-dry. Ages well. '79, '81

• Chardonnay. Austere. Ages slowly but well.

Also: Chenin Blanc (typical Clarksburg flavors, just off-dry), Sauvignon Blanc (debut '83 highly promising), Pinot Noir (tends to be heady, but '82 is charming change of pace).

Hafner Vineyard Sonoma T nyr

A new-in-1982 winery on the Hafner family's well-established 100-acre vineyard e. of Healdsburg in the Alexander Valley, it produces only Cabernet Sauvignon and Chardonnay. Annual production is about 8,000 cases. Price $11 for the Chardonnay; the debut Cabernet is scheduled for release in 1986. Except for select restaurants, sales are from the winery only.

Hagafen T nyr
Kosher without the Concord! A small partnership started with a Kosher Johannisberg Riesling '80 (distinctly sweet and unusually flowery) that has since branched out to include Chardonnay-Winery Lake (very toasty), Pinot Noir Blanc, and Cabernet Sauvignon, all from Napa Valley grapes. Volume is about 5,000 cases. Prices $5.75–$13.50.

Handley Cellars Mendocino T nyr
From '82 and '83, Milla Handley produced only Chardonnay, one lot from Anderson Valley grapes (tart, cleansing, deftly complicated by French wood), the other from the family's Handley Vineyard in Sonoma County. Price $12.50. With '84 she added a small lot of *méthode champenoise* Brut (a blend of "Pinot Noir" and "Chardonnay") which will not be released before 1986. Total production approaches 1,300 cases.

Hanns Kornell Champagne Cellars
See: Kornell Champagne Cellars, Hanns.

Hanzell Sonoma T ***
On a slope n. w. of Sonoma town, James D. Zellerbach in 1957 set California Chardonnay and Pinot Noir on new courses with judicious use of new European barrels as a source of added complexity. Now, under the ownership of Barbara deBrye and the winemaking direction of Bob Sessions, Hanzell still ranks near the top for both varieties, though small production (2,500 cases per year) sells to initiates too fast for the label to keep itself in the limelight. Prices $16–$19.
• Chardonnay. Recent vintages have seemed riper, weightier, and more strongly marked by wood than earlier ones. They also appear to age more quickly. '81
• Pinot Noir. Complex, balanced, but more easily thought of as a chewy counterpart to a Rhône than a Burgundy. '77 '78
Also: Cabernet Sauvignon (debut '81, scheduled for release in 1985).

Harbor Winery Sacramento T, D **
Winemaker-proprietor Charles Myers earns most of his daily bread as a professor of English at a local university, but finds time to make an annual 1,500 cases of Napa Chardonnay, Napa Sémillon (dark, ripe, figgy), and Amador Mission del Sol (an age-worthy dessert wine of intriguing character). Sales are mostly to local familiars; prices $6.50–$9.

Hart Vineyards Temecula T nyr
Production has jumped up from 1,000 to 7,000 cases since Joe Hart founded his winery in 1980. The roster includes Cabernet Sauvignon, Merlot, Chardonnay, Sauvignon Blanc, and Cabernet Blanc. All but the Merlot come from local vines; it will, too, when Hart's 11-acre vineyard matures. Prices $4.50–$9.

Hawk Crest
The second label for Stag's Leap Wine Cellars.

Haywood Winery Sonoma T nyr
Peter Haywood's 84 acres of vines and 8,000-case winery occupy some of the steep slope looming above the Sonoma town plaza in Sonoma Valley. The first crush was '80. The label won quick respect for a memorable Chardonnay '81 (rich, complex fruit flavors only lightly tinted with oak) and a fine Johannisberg Riesling. Other wines on the list: Spaghetti Red, Cabernet Sauvignon, Zinfandel, and Estate White. Prices $4.25–$11.

Hecker Pass
A long-time district of country wineries that extends westward from the Santa Clara County town of Gilroy, it is losing vineyard acreage to an expanding local population, but gaining in number of wineries. Simultaneously, emphasis has shifted from generic jugs to varietal bottles. Not an AVA.

Hecker Pass Winery Santa Clara T, D **
Of several family wineries strung along the Hecker Pass Highway w. of Gilroy in southern Santa Clara County, Mario Fortino's has an edge over most for subtlety and style in its reds. Prices $5–$7. From Fortino's own 14-acre vineyard come some 5,000 cases per year. Of note: Carignane, Petite Sirah, Ruby Cabernet, and Zinfandel. Also: several varietal rosés, Cream Sherry, Port.

Heitz Cellars Napa T ***/****
Joe Heitz helped launch revolutions in style and price in California with the legendary Chardonnay '62-Lot C-22, then with his Cabernet Sauvignon '66-Martha's Vineyard, and all its successors. He still keeps the pot aboil with superb wines made to his individualistic sense of style. The Heitzes own 115 acres of vineyard at and near their hidden-in-the-hills winery e. of St. Helena. Bought grapes are usually for vineyard-designated wines. Production nears the planned maximum of 40,000 cases per year. Prices $4–$14, to $30 for Martha's Vineyard, and to $45 for library Cabernets.
• Cabernet Sauvignon-Martha's Vineyard. Everybody's long-time benchmark for pure Napa Cabernet. Pervasive aromas of

mint and spice box render the wine readily identifiable to its followers. After an extra, third year in wood (a basic Heitz tenet) the wine has early charm in spite of its intense varietal character and sturdy backbone of tannin. The oldest vintage is not too old yet. '69 '70 '73 '74 '75 '77

• Cabernet Sauvignon-Bella Oaks Vineyard. Similar in style to Martha's, Bella Oaks distinguishes itself for having a little less spice box, a little more herbaceousness, and a little more tannin. '76 '77

• Cabernet Sauvignon. The "regular" often includes some wine from the above two vineyards; sometimes it runs even up with them for quality; usually it is a considerable bargain. '78 '79

Also: Chardonnay (just coming back to form after replanting of prized vineyard), Grignolino Rosé (the house specialty, remarkably aromatic and bone-dry), Pinot Noir, Zinfandel, Chablis (an oak-aged poor man's Chardonnay), Burgundy (counterpart red to the Chablis).

Herbert Vineyards El Dorado T nyr

The label belongs to Frank and Beverly Herbert, independent growers with 14 acres s. of Placerville. They have an annual 1,000 cases of sound, steady Sauvignon Blanc, White Zinfandel, and Zinfandel made by John MacCready at the latter's nearby Sierra Vista winery. The first vintage was '80. Prices $4.50–$6.

Hidden Cellars Mendocino T nyr

A partnership winery, it is indeed hidden in the hills e. of Ukiah. The first crush, 1981, yielded a fine *Botrytis*-affected Johannisberg Riesling. Other wines in the roster: Johannisberg Riesling (a sipper at 2% to 3% r. s.), Gewürztraminer (bone-dry), Sauvignon Blanc (appealing varietal flavors mix it up with distinct oak), and two Zinfandels, one of mortal dimensions, the other late-harvest. All come from Mendocino County grapes. The plan is to grow from the current 9,000 cases of production to 15,000 by 1986. Prices $7.25–$8, and to $10 per half bottle for a late-harvest Zinfandel.

Hill Winery, William Napa T **

An Oklahoma money wiz turned Napa grape grower and winery owner, Hill has several hundred acres of vineyard scattered through the Mayacamas Mountains and down to the edges of the Silverado Country Club. Production began with a '78 Cabernet Sauvignon, and is currently at 25,000 cases on the way to a planned 40,000. The only wines are Cabernet and Chardonnay, but there are at least two of each—a less expensive Silver Label advertised as a near-termer, a more expensive Gold Label held out as an ager. There is also a reserve Chardonnay aborning in 1984. Gold Label Chardonnays through '81 were overweight, over-woody; '82 pulled back a bit. Gold Label Cabernet Sauvignons were of the inky dark, ever tannic sort from '78 through '80, but the '81 was much more deft and complex. Prices $10.50–$16.50, and to $25 for reserve Chardonnay.

HMR San Luis Obispo T [**]
Founded in 1965 by Dr. Stanley Hoffman, the winery was bought in 1982 by a group of investors from Los Angeles. They are changing the winemaking styles. The company produces 30,000 cases a year of Chardonnay, Chenin Blanc, Sauvignon Blanc, Pinot Noir Blanc, Cabernet Sauvignon, and Pinot Noir from 82 acres of owned vineyard in w. hills of Paso Robles area, plus bought grapes from other vineyards in the region. Both vineyard and winery have room to grow. Prices $5.29–$8, and to $15 for a reserve Cabernet. A second label, Santa Lucia Cellars, is for generics priced $3–$4.

Honig Cellars, Louis Napa T nyr
After two vintages as HNW, the label changed to Honig for '83. Early production focused on Sauvignon Blanc from a winery-owned 54-acre vineyard near Yountville. Chardonnay and Cabernet Sauvignon from '84 will expand the list. Current production nears 10,000 cases, on the way to a planned maximum of 30,000, all from the winery's own grapes. The first three vintages of Sauvignon Blanc were somewhat inconsistent. Price $8.

Hop Kiln Winery at Griffin Vineyards Sonoma T, S [**]
The winery—it is indeed in a one-time hop kiln—gets a good deal of favorable attention for dark, rough-hewn Petite Sirahs and bone-dry, pungently spicy Gewürztraminers. Other varietals: Chardonnay, Cabernet Sauvignon, Pinot Noir, and Zinfandel. The winery also has two proprietary wines. One is a white called A Thousand Flowers. The other specialty, a stylistic twin of the Petite Sirah, is called Marty's Big Red after owner Dr. Martin Griffin. Most of the annual 8,000 cases come from his adjoining 65-acre vineyard w. of Healdsburg in the Russian River Valley. Prices $5–$10, and to $15 for late-harvest Johannisberg Riesling and Zinfandel.

Houtz Vineyards Santa Barbara T nyr
The first crush, '84, yielded 1,000 cases of Chardonnay, Sauvignon Blanc, and Cabernet Sauvignon. The first release is scheduled for 1985. The grapes come from David and Margy Houtz's 16 acres of vines near Los Olivos. Their planned peak production is 4,000 cases.

Howell Mountain
A small, upland AVA ranged along the 1,400-ft. level of the Mayacamas Mountains e. of St. Helena, in the Napa Valley. It is devoted mostly to "Cabernet Sauvignon" and "Zinfandel."

Hultgren & Samperton Sonoma T */**
A new-in-1979 winery, in the Russian River Valley w. of Healdsburg, makes about 10,000 cases per year divided equally between Chardonnay and Cabernet Sauvignon. Both come from grapes purchased in Sonoma County, mostly in Dry Creek Valley. The label was launched with some bought-in '79s; the first crush was '80; a recent change in winemakers may signal a shift in style. Sales are primarily along the Atlantic seaboard.

Hunter Vineyard, Robert Sonoma S nyr
A joint venture of vineyardist Robert Hunter and the Duckhorns of Duckhorn Cellars in the Napa Valley, the *méthode champenoise* sparkling wine house makes what it calls "Brut de Noirs"—a name coined to suggest that the wine is not as weighty as many sparkling Blanc de Noirs. It is vintage-dated, of "Pinot Noir" and "Chardonnay." All but a small fraction come from Hunter's 45-acre vineyard in Sonoma Valley, n. w. of the town of Sonoma. The second vintage, '81, was very tart, with hints of underripe fruit flavors. Annual volume in 1984 was 8,000 cases, with plans to expand. Price $14.

Husch Vineyards Mendocino T [**]
Hugo Oswald and family bought a winery and 35 acres of Anderson Valley vineyard in 1979 from founders Tony and Gretchen Husch. The Oswalds make about 10,000 cases per year from this vineyard and another, 160-acre property at Talmage, just s. e. of Ukiah. The latter gives its name, La Ribera, to some lots. Many of the wines have been attractive, especially the Chardonnay (rich in fruit flavors, seemingly balanced to age), Cabernet Sauvignon (distinct but subtle varietal character), and Gewürztraminer (lively, distinctly varietal). Also: Chenin Blanc, Sauvignon Blanc (regular one is dry; variety sometimes also offered as a late-harvest wine), Pinot Noir. Prices $5–$9.75

Inglenook Navalle
A label belonging to Heublein, Inc., now run separately from Inglenook Vineyards. The winemaking goes on at Madera; company headquarters is in Connecticut. The line includes San Joaquin Valley varietals (notably Chenin Blanc, French Colombard, Zinfandel) and generics. Annual volume is about 7 million cases. Prices $3–$4.

Inglenook Vineyards Napa T **/***

This old-time Napa label has lurched uncertainly through the years since a family ownership sold it to corporate interests in 1964, but in 1984 it begins again to look something like it did in the old days. Heublein, Inc., the current owner, has made it into a purely Napa winery again (see: Inglenook Navalle), is plunging a large budget into upgrading the winemaking facilities, and has found a talented winemaker in John Richburg. Production is 150,000 cases of varietals, another 100,000 of two generics. Prices $4–$9, and to $18 for reserve Cabernet.

• Cabernet Sauvignon. Made at three price levels (Cabinet, Estate, and Reserve), all from Napa Valley grapes. All three have been attractive, but the Reserve—still from some of the vineyards that once made the label one of the premiers—can give more pleasure than many newcomers more in the news. '75 '77 '78 '79 '80

Also: Chardonnay (same three gradations as Cabernet, the finest beginning to show striking form). Charbono, Merlot, Pinot Noir, and Sauvignon Blanc (Estate is good, Reserve is even closer to the first rank) may be found in Estate and Reserve bottlings. Estate only: Chenin Blanc, Gewürztraminer, Johannisberg Riesling, Petite Sirah, and Zinfandel, along with Napa Chablis and Burgundy.

Iron Horse Ranch & Vineyards Sonoma T, S **/***

A winery near Forestville in Sonoma-Green Valley produces Chardonnay, Pinot Noir, and *méthode champenoise* sparkling wines from 100 handsome surrounding acres of Barry and Audrey Sterling, plus Cabernet Sauvignon and Sauvignon Blanc from partner-winemaker Forrest Tancer's 14 acres in Alexander Valley. Overall production of 25,000 cases splits about evenly between still and sparkling wines. Prices $6–$13.50 for still wines, $16–$18 for the sparklers.

• Pinot Noir. Tancer courts the grape's flavors first, but backs them neatly with a touch of European oak. '79 '81

• Blanc de Noirs. Sparkler is plush in texture but subtle in flavor. '81

• Brut. Dominant sparkler by volume shows finesse and polish. '81

Also: Cabernet Sauvignon, Sauvignon Blanc (both ripe, pleasing in flavor, a bit weighty compared to many), Chardonnay (austere, well kissed by oak, apparently best through first three years in bottle), Blanc de Blancs (tart, cleanly made sparkler).

Italian Swiss Colony Sonoma/San Joaquin Valley T, S, D *

Allied Grape Growers sold ISC to Heublein, Inc., in the mid-

'60s. Two decades later, the same grower coöp is the major stockholder in a company it formed to buy the wineries and labels back. The showcase cellar at Asti, in northern Sonoma County, also makes the pride wines of the house: vintage-dated varietals with Sonoma appellations and the Colony label. Three other cellars in the San Joaquin Valley produce some or all of the wines for other labels: Colony generics and proprietaries, Lejon, Petri, and Gambarelli & Davitto generics, and Lejon and Jacques Bonet Charmat sparkling wines. Total production is about 6 million cases. Prices $3.99–$4.99 for the Sonoma varietals, $1.89–$2.99 for the other table wines, $2.99–$4.99 for the sparklers. Among the early releases, a non-vintage Colony Classic Zinfandel had lovely varietal flavors (and a softening dollop of sweetness), while vintage-dated Gewürztraminer and Pinot Noir Rosé were a shade heavy, perhaps overripe.

Jacaré
A proprietary label of Heublein, Inc., used for a standard-quality, somewhat sweet white wine.

Jacques Bonet
A label of Italian Swiss Colony.

Jaeger-Inglewood Vineyard Napa T nyr
The William Jaeger family—major growers and partners in Freemark Abbey and Rutherford Hill—have established their own aging cellar and label to make 4,000 cases of Merlot from one of their smallest vineyards, a parcel located just s. of St. Helena. The debut '79 was released with the '80 and '81 in 1984. Prices $11–$13.

Jefferson Cellars
A label of Monticello Cellars for generic wines of some excellence.

Jekel Vineyard Monterey T **/***
In the Arroyo Seco district w. of Greenfield, the 330-acre vineyard and +50,000-case winery of William and August Jekel yielded a technically flawless and absolutely delicious Johannisberg Riesling from the first crush, '78. That wine has remained the flagship of the house. Prices $6.50–$10.50, and to $16 for reserve Cabernet Sauvignon and Chardonnay.
• Johannisberg Riesling. Distinctive combination of regional and varietal flavors come very close to a perfectly ripe, crisp, right-off-the-tree apple. '81, '83
Also: Cabernet Sauvignon (strong on oak), Chardonnay (some appealing fruit flavors but heartily kissed by oak; short-lived to date), Pinot Blanc, Gamay Beaujolais.

JFJ Bronco Winery Stanislaus T, S *
A substantial winery e. of Modesto produces sound, steady generics, most packaged in jugs, for the equivalent bottle price of $2–$2.50, and Charmat sparklers for slightly more. Owned by members of the Franzia family that founded Franzia Brothers, its volume is about 2 million cases per year, almost all from San Joaquin Valley grapes. The labels are JFJ Bronco and CC.

Jimark Winery Sonoma T nyr
Winemaker James Wolner and grower Mark Michtom are partners in a 12,000-case cellar s. of Healdsburg that is devoted mainly to making Chardonnay and Cabernet Sauvignon from Michtom's vineyard in Alexander Valley, and selling it under the Michtom Vineyard label. The first full vintage was '81. Prices $6–$7.50. The winery also buys wines in bulk and blends them for release under the Limerick Lane label.

Johannisberg Riesling
A more popular alternative name for the grape "White Riesling" and its wine.

Johnson-Turnbull Vineyards Napa T **/***
Attorney Reverdy Johnson and architect William Turnbull collaborate to make about 2,000 cases of Cabernet Sauvignon per year from their 20-acre vineyard between Oakville and Rutherford. Since the first vintage, '79, very well-made wines have been dark, with the minty, spicy overtones that the mid-section of the Napa Valley produces with seeming ease. Price $12.50.

Johnson's of Alexander Valley Sonoma T **
The winery and 45-acre vineyard of the brothers Will, Jay, and Tom Johnson sit in the middle of Alexander Valley e. of Healdsburg. From it come an annual 8,000 to 10,000 cases of sound, straight-ahead Cabernet Sauvignon, Chenin Blanc, Johannisberg Riesling, Pinot Noir Blanc, Pinot Noir (subtle and stylish in cool vintages such as '77 and '79), White Zinfandel, Zinfandel, and late-harvest Zinfandel. Prices $4.50–$12.50.

Jordan Vineyard and Winery Sonoma T ***
The spectacular evocation of a Bordeaux château built by oil millionaire Thomas Jordan occupies a hilltop in Alexander Valley n. e. of Healdsburg, while 250 acres of "Cabernet Sauvignon" and "Merlot" plus 50 of "Chardonnay" fill the lowlands before it. The first vintage was '76. Annual production is 70,000 cases; prices $16–$17.

• Cabernet Sauvignon. Skillful winemaking adds layers of flavor to a pungent varietal character that seems to come from this wine's vineyard. Thus far best at about 4 years, though

the '80 seems more complex than its predecessors, so perhaps able to improve over a longer life.
Also: Chardonnay (well made, well marked by oak).

Joseph Phelps Vineyards
See: Phelps Vineyards, Joseph

Joseph Swan Vineyards
See: Swan Vineyards, Joseph

jug wines
A casual description of everyday wines packaged in containers of 1.5 liters and up.

Kalin Cellars Marin T nyr
Microbiologist Terry Leighton started out to explore the variations in *Botrytis*-affected wines, and search for the perfect Pinot Noir. He has since spread his interest to include Cabernet Sauvignon and Chardonnay (as many as 3 vineyard-designated lots per year). Another specialty is Sémillon. The results from his winery-in-a-warehouse in San Rafael have been as erratic as the goals promise, but agreeable as well as fascinating. Production is, at his maximum, 6,000 cases per year. Prices $9–$20.

Karly Wines Amador T **
From the debut '79s onward, owner-winemaker Lawrence (Buck) Cobb has put more polish and finesse on his Shenandoah Valley Fumé Blancs and Zinfandels than most of his peers, yet does not rob the wines of their innate strengths. His own 18 acres are supplemented by local purchases. The other regular wine in the annual 5,000-case production is a Chardonnay from Santa Maria Valley grapes. An irregular one is Petite Sirah from his own vines, available only at the winery. Cobb's long-range goal is 7,500 cases per year. Prices $6–$12.

Keenan Winery, Robert Napa T **
Robert H. Keenan's family-owned 46-acre vineyard and 9,000-case winery high up on Spring Mountain produce only Cabernet Sauvignon (blended with a bit of Merlot from elsewhere in the valley) and Chardonnay (there are two bottlings, an Estate and a Napa Valley). An '82 Merlot from purchased grapes is the baby that will make three on its release in 1985. Keenan's first vintage was '77. Both ongoing wine-types have had the intense flavors associated with hillside grapes, even when blended. They also have had marked contributions from oak aging, and have been persistently heady.

Kendall-Jackson Vineyard Lake T nyr
One of the brighter stars in Lake County's renascence as a

winegrowing district, Kendall-Jackson hit the ground running with five well-made, appealing '81 wines. Subsequent vintages have done as well as the first. Production is at 65,000 cases, partly from 65 acres of winery-owned vines in the Clear Lake district at Lakeport, mostly from grapes purchased as close as next door and as far away as Santa Barbara. Chardonnay accounts for two-thirds of the total. Prices $5.50–$18. In addition to Chardonnay (excellent fruit flavors dominate), the roster includes Johannisberg Riesling (fine, ripe, a sipper at 9% alcohol and 3% r. s.), Sauvignon Blanc (enticing floral aromas), Cabernet Sauvignon (the estate '81 was approachable early but seems to have the balance to age for some years), and Zinfandel (winemaker Jed Steele brought along three favored sources of old-vines Mendocino Zinfandel when he joined Kendall-Jackson in 1984). A second label, Château du Lac, has been reserved for special lots of estate Chardonnay and Sauvignon Blanc (subtle in texture and flavor).

Kennedy Winery, Kathryn   Santa Clara   T   **
The proprietor set out in 1979 to be the ultimate specialist, producing only 400 to 800 cases of Cabernet Sauvignon from her patch of vines near downtown Saratoga. After a brief digression, that is again the program. Prices $5.50–$12. Nearly all sales are in California.

Kenwood Winery   Sonoma   T   **/***
The owning Lee family bought an old jug winery near the Sonoma Valley town of Kenwood in 1970. Over the next decade they methodically turned it into a 100,000-case producer of well-regarded varietal wines, nearly all of them from purchased Sonoma County grapes, a considerable proportion from the home valley. Prices $4.50–$14, and to $25 for the Artist's Series Cabernet Sauvignons.
• Sauvignon Blanc. Deft, dry, with pronounced varietal character.
• Chardonnay-Beltane Ranch. Fat, rich, usually a bit heady. For the bold. '81
• Cabernet Sauvignon-Jack London Vineyard. Leans toward the dark, tannic, and heady, but does not tip too far to discourage gentle palates. The Artist's Series goes a small step farther along the same route. '79
Also: Gewürztraminer (affable, off-dry), Johannisberg Riesling (same as Gewürz), Chenin Blanc (still the same vein), Pinot Noir-Jack London Vineyard (back to the ripe, heady school of thought).

Kenworthy Vineyards   Amador   T   *
A family-owned, 1,800-case cellar located e. of Plymouth in the Shenandoah Valley district, it specializes in hearty, some-

times rustic Zinfandel and Cabernet Sauvignon, both from local grapes, and a Chardonnay from El Dorado County fruit. The first vintage was '79. Production is about 1,500 cases. Prices $7–$9, mostly in central California.

Kirigin Cellars   Santa Clara   T   *
Nikola Kirigin Chargin trained at Zagreb, matured in large San Joaquin Valley wineries, and retired to the Hecker Pass district in south Santa Clara County to make wines that suggest his palate still favors Yugoslavia. Opol Rosé is the particular case in point. Others on the list: Burgundy, Pinot Noir, Zinfandel. An annual 10,000 cases come mainly from his adjoining 45 acres of vines. Most of the wine sells in the immediate neighborhood. Prices $4–$7.50.

Kistler Vineyards   Sonoma   T   **/***
On top of a top-of-the-world ridge separating the Sonoma Valley from Napa, Steve Kistler, with help from Mark Bixler, began with the vintage of '79 to make varietal wines according to their idea of ancient, handcrafted standards. The grapes have been purchased at several label-identified vineyards. When their own 40 acres mature, half of the production will be estate, the other half from Dutton Ranch (Sonoma-Green Valley). Thus far the results have been uneven, though fascinating. The sure factor through the first three vintages was strong flavors of oak all around. Annual production is around 7,500 cases. Prices $12–$14.
• Chardonnay. Heavy, toasty wines of early vintages have given way to subtler ones, esp. in '81.
Also: Cabernet Sauvignon (ample wood, even more tannin in '81), Pinot Noir.

Kleinberger
A white grape and—only from Gundlach-Bundschu Wine Co. —its wine.

Knights Valley
AVA in southeastern Sonoma County, just across the line from Calistoga in the Napa Valley. See maps.

Knights Valley Estates
Vineyards in Knights Valley belonging to Beringer Vineyards, and identified as the source of Cabernet Sauvignons and superior *Botrytis*-affected Johannisberg Rieslings.

Konocti Cellars   Lake   T   [**]
The winery was founded in 1979 by a cooperative of 26 growers in and near Lakeport, in the Clear Lake district. Since 1983 it has been half-owned by the founders, and half by the guiding family of Parducci Wine Cellars. Production is approaching 30,000 cases, all from member vineyards. The potential is

for 100,000. The types are Johannisberg Riesling (good varietal, just off-dry), Fumé Blanc (lean, firm, flavorful of its grape), Cabernet Sauvignon (balanced, straightforward), and Cabernet Blanc (bone-dry, without a hint of blush). Prices $5–$5.50.

Korbel & Bros., F. Sonoma S **/***
California's pioneer great name in *méthode champenoise* sparkling wines still competes around the top with its best efforts. The home vineyards near Guerneville, toward the western limit of the Russian River Valley, provide only a small part of the grapes needed for an estimated annual production of 735,000 cases. Bought grapes have come from as far s. as Santa Maria Valley. Prices $11.18–$17.46.
• Natural. A non-dosage wine from a blend of varieties, it is tart and bone-dry.
• Blanc de Noirs. Purely of "Pinot Noir," the first vintage of it was '79. As with most, flickering hints of varietal character play against well-developed yeasty notes.
Also: Blanc de Blancs (100% Chardonnay), Brut, Extra Dry, Sec, Rosé, Rouge.

Kornell Champagne Cellars, Hanns Napa S **/***
In cellars n. of St. Helena, owner–Champagne master Hanns Kornell hears a different drummer than others in California. Having kept a fondness for the Sekts of his native Germany since founding his firm in 1952, he leans on "Riesling" where others dote on "Chardonnay," "Pinot Blanc," or "Pinot Noir." Production for his label is about 80,000 cases per year, all from purchased still wines. Prices $10.75–$18.
• Sehr Trocken. Translates from German as "very dry," a technical and a sensory truth. Four to seven years on tirage give it both yeasty flavors and the taste of well-aged Riesling.
Also: Blanc de Blancs (all Chenin Blanc; affably fruity), Brut, Extra Dry. Rosé, Rouge.

Krug Winery, Charles Napa T, D **
One of the Big Four that nursed Napa's reputation for vintage-dated varietals from post-Prohibition into the wine boom of the 1960s, it has now settled into the pack of Napa wineries. Owned by C. Mondavi & Sons and directed by Peter Mondavi, the winery n. of St. Helena offers steadily good, sometimes exceptional varietals. Most of them come from 1,200 acres of Napa vineyard, scattered from St. Helena s. to the Carneros. Total production of 1.5 million cases includes a hefty proportion of San Joaquin jug wines labeled C. K.-Mondavi. The winery is best known for Chenin Blanc (the name was invented here; the style is sweetly sippable) and Cabernet Sauvignon (approachable early but balanced neatly enough to

age rather well, sometimes extraordinarily well). Also: Chardonnay (quick to mature), Gewürztraminer, Blanc Fumé, Johannisberg Riesling (too much overlooked among the off-drys). Prices $3.50–$10, and to $25 for older vintages of reserve Cabernet. C. K.-Mondavi $2.63–$2.74.

Kruse Winery, Thomas   Santa Clara   T, S   */**
The writer of the world's best back labels helped turn the Hecker Pass district away from jug generics and toward varietals after his arrival in 1971. Kruse makes about 4,000 cases per year, winning most of his compliments for sturdy, honest country reds (Cabernet Sauvignon, Pinot Noir, Zinfandel). He also makes Gilroy White, French Colombard, Sauvignon Blanc, and a tiny bit of an inimitable *méthode champenoise* sparkling wine. All of the wines are from local grapes. Prices $2.25–$5, and to $10 for the sparkler.

La Cienega
An AVA reaching s. and w. from Hollister in San Benito County. See maps.

La Crema Vinera   Sonoma   T   */***
Since its first vintage, '79, the winery has been erratic, with its best being impressively stylish and its worst rather less than enjoyable because of winemaking flaws. Located in Petaluma, it buys all of its grapes, most from Sonoma, some from Napa, some from Monterey. Chardonnay and Pinot Noir are the mainstays. Cabernet Sauvignon and Merlot have appeared under another label, Petaluma Cellars. All four types carry vineyard designations. Annual production is about 7,000 cases. Prices $5–$14.50, and to $18 for reserve Chardonnays and Pinot Noirs.
• Chardonnay. To date the flagships, especially from Winery Lake (Napa-Carneros), Dutton Ranch (Sonoma-Green Valley), and Ventana (Arroyo Seco).
Also: Pinot Noir (thus far, sure to be strongly marked by wood), *vin gris*.

La Jota Vineyard Co.   Napa   T   nyr
The 30-acre vineyard and 4,500-case cellar of William and Joan Smith hides in high, forested hills to the e. of St. Helena. They began making Cabernet Sauvignon and Zinfandel with the vintage of '82, and plan to release their first wines in 1986.

La Marque
A small-volume merchant label used for good-quality varietal wines from varying sources.

La Mont Winery, M.   Kern   T, D   *
A substantial San Joaquin Valley winery named after the Bakersfield suburb in which it sits, it produces a long list of every-

day valley varietals and generics from local and other grapes. Of several labels, M. Lamont is the flagship, used only for varietals, mainly Cabernet Sauvignon, Chardonnay, Chenin Blanc, and French Colombard. Capistro is for white varietals only. Ambassador, Gold Peak, Guasti, Mission Valley, and Mountain Gold are the labels for generics. DiGiorgio Fresh Pak is for bag-in-a-box generics. Prices range from $2. Lamont sells about 1 million cases a year under these labels. A Canadian brewing and winemaking company, John LaBatt, Ltd., is the owner.

La Montana
A brand of Martin Ray Vineyards used for blended (as opposed to vintage-dated) varietals. Not to be confused with Las Montanas.

La Vieille Montagne Napa T nyr
John and Shawn Guilliams make 1,000 cases of Cabernet Sauvignon from their 7 acres of vines just s. of St. Helena plus bought grapes from a vineyard on Mt. Veeder. They also make a bit of Johannisberg Riesling. The first Cabernet vintage, '81, yielded 300 cases scheduled for release in 1985 or 1986. The debut Johannisberg, '84, is to be released during 1985.

Laird Vineyards Napa T nyr
Veteran Napa grower Ken Laird began with the vintage of '80 to make Cabernet Sauvignon and Chardonnay from his own grapes, which are spread among several properties as far s. as Carneros and as far n. as St. Helena, but are concentrated around Yountville. Early volume is about 5,000 cases, produced in leased space. Price $11.50.

Lakespring Winery Napa T **
At Yountville, the 16,000-case winery is a reliable source of sound, steady, fairly priced varietals from grapes purchased mostly in Napa, except for a proportion of "Sauvignon Blanc" from San Luis Obispo County. Prices $6–$11. The roster includes Cabernet Sauvignon, Merlot (one of the house's most impressive types), Chardonnay, and Sauvignon Blanc (both whites have pleasing fruit along with a touch of wood; both tend to be a bit heady).

Lamb Winery, Ronald Santa Clara T *
Lamb's cellar n. w. of Gilroy divides an annual production of less than 1,000 cases between Monterey Chardonnay, San Luis Obispo Chardonnay, and Monterey Chenin Blanc . . . a recent reversal of form. In the early vintages nearly all the wines were red, sturdy rather than polished. The whites are due for release in early 1985. Prices $6–$12.

Lambert Bridge Sonoma T **
From 80 acres of grapes in three separate blocks in Dry Creek Valley, Gerard Lambert's winery produces an annual 28,000 cases of Cabernet Sauvignon (austere, tannic, strongly varietal) and Chardonnay (leaner, less ripe than most, but pungently flavored of both fruit and wood for all of that), plus a bit of Merlot. The first crush was '75. Prices $10.50–$13.

Landmark Vineyards Sonoma T **
The early wines by partner-winemaker William Mabry were erratic, as he trained on the job, but he has worked hard at his craft, with the result that recent vintages are growing ever steadier and ever finer. From 80 acres of family vineyards in Alexander Valley and Sonoma Valley, the production is 22,000 cases. Landmark offers four bottlings of Chardonnay (reserve, Alexander Valley, Sonoma Valley, and Sonoma County; fine fruit, understated oak, esp. in Alexander Valley '82), Cabernet Sauvignon, and Petit Blanc, a proprietary blend of Chardonnay, Chenin Blanc, and Sauvignon Blanc. Prices $4.50–$10, and to $14 for reserves.

Las Montanas Sonoma T nyr
Cabernet Sauvignon, Gamay Beaujolais, and Zinfandel from bought Sonoma and Napa grapes make up the roster of Aleta Apgar Olds's 700-case winery in Sonoma Valley. All are identified as "Natural," by which is meant made without additives. Her fledgling vineyard is organically farmed, as are those of her suppliers. The label began with '80s. Prices had not been established late in 1984.

Las Tablas San Luis Obispo T *
In the Paso Robles district near Templeton, the family-owned winery produces small lots of thick, old-fashioned Zinfandel and white table wine, mostly for a local trade.

late-harvest
A label term, it has no precise definition or legal standing. On whites (Johannisberg Riesling, Gewürztraminer, Sauvignon Blanc, Sémillon), it usually signifies a sweet, *Botrytis*-affected wine, but may only signify sweetness. On reds (esp. Zinfandel), it sometimes suggests sweetness, but more surely denotes alcohol in excess of 14%.

Laurel Glen Sonoma T nyr
From his well-established 30-acre vineyard on slopes above the Sonoma Valley town of Glen Ellen, violist-turned-winemaker Patrick Campbell coaxed a promisingly subtle, stylish Cabernet Sauvignon in his first vintage, '81. That year yielded 1,400 cases; Campbell reached a peak 4,500 cases with his '83. Price $12.50.

Lazy Creek Vineyards Mendocino T nyr
Retired San Francisco waiter Hans Kobler and his wife craft 1,500 cases of Chardonnay, Gewürztraminer, and Pinot Noir from their small vineyard w. of Philo, in the Anderson Valley. The wines have given steady good value since the inaugural vintage, '79. Prices $6.50–$7.75.

LeBlanc, L.
The principal brand of California Growers covers modestly priced San Joaquin Valley Chenin Blanc, French Colombard, and generics.

LeDomaine
A brand of Almadén Vineyards used for inexpensive transfer-process sparkling wines.

Lefranc, Charles
A brand of Almadén Vineyards, it covers an abbreviated line of select varietals (Cabernet Sauvignon, late-harvest Johannisberg Riesling, high-alcohol Zinfandel) and generics that are pricier than but not necessarily preferable to bottlings under the regular label. A move was afoot in 1984 to improve the quality.

Leeward Winery Ventura T **/***
Partners Chuck Brigham and Chuck Gardner make 8,500 cases per year at a winery near the Pacific shore in the city of Ventura, a good distance from the nearest vineyard, but in exactly the climate they want to barrel-ferment the Chardonnays that have made their name. The label began with '79s. Prices $5.25–$15.

• Chardonnay. The principal bottlings among as many as 4 are vineyard-identified, from Ventana Vineyard (Arroyo Seco) and MacGregor (Edna Valley). Both have the toasty flavors inherent in barrel fermentation, but maintain a welcome fruity edge as well.

Also: A proprietary Santa Maria Valley Pinot Noir Blanc called "Coral," and Amador Zinfandel.

Lejon
A label belonging to Italian Swiss Colony, used especially for Charmat sparkling wines.

Liberty School
A second label of Caymus Vineyard used for medium-priced varietals bought in bulk and blended for bottling.

Lime Kiln Valley
A tiny AVA within the larger Cienega Valley district in San Benito County.

Limerick Lane Cellars
A label belonging to Jimark Winery.

Live Oaks Winery   Santa Clara   T   *
Thick, old-fashioned Burgundy, Chenin Blanc (Extra Dry, Medium Dry, and Dolce), and Grenache Rosé (same range as Chenin Blanc) appear under Peter Scagliotti's long-time label. Scagliotti sells almost all of an annual 20,000 cases at the cellar door in the Hecker Pass district w. of Gilroy. Prices $4.26–$4.56.

Livermore Valley
An AVA e. of San Francisco Bay, in Alameda County. It is one of California's oldest and most distinguished wine districts, known especially for splendid Sauvignon Blancs.

Livermore Valley Cellars   Alameda   T   *
From the beginning vintage, '78, the wines—all white—from Chris Lagiss's 34-acre vineyard and 3,000-case cellar have been sound, and thoroughly homespun. The property is between Livermore and Pleasanton. The roster includes Chardonnay, Fumé Blanc, and Gray Riesling. Prices $4.95–$7.50.

Llords & Elwood Winery   Napa/Alameda   T, D   **
Jay Corley (the proprietor of Monticello) bought the firm and moved the table wine cellars to the Napa Valley in time to produce the '85s there. The dessert wine cellars are to remain at Fremont, in Alameda County, where they have been for years. Great Day D-r-ry and Dry Wit Sherries have been the standard-bearers for the label to this point; the table wines have been reliable but indistinct. Annual production is about 18,000 cases. Prices $5.35–$8.

Lohr, J.   Santa Clara   T   **
With a winery in downtown San José, 240 acres of vineyards w. of Greenfield in Monterey's Arroyo Seco district, 40 acres in the Napa Valley e. of St. Helena, and another 180 acres in Clarksburg, the firm produces an annual 300,000 cases from its own and purchased grapes. The label dates from 1975. Consistently attractive are Johannisberg Riesling (regular and late-harvest) and Pinot Blanc, as is a proprietary blend called "Jade." Chardonnay, Fumé Blanc, and Chenin Blanc round out the whites. Cabernet Sauvignon and Petite Sirah have not been quite the equals of their white mates. Prices $4.50–$9, and to $12 for a reserve Chardonnay.

Long Vineyards   Napa   T   ***
From 20 acres on Pritchard Hill e. of Rutherford, partners Bob and Zelma Long make an annual 1,500 cases of 4 varietals, half of them estate-grown, the other half from purchased

Napa grapes. The first crush was '77. Prices $9–$24.
• Johannisberg Riesling-Estate. Spectacular evocation of varietal character in both the drier (1% r. s.) and sweeter (3–4% r. s.) editions.
• Chardonnay-Estate. Early vintages aged quickly, but were delicious in youth. '81
Also: Cabernet Sauvignon (yet to declare itself), Sauvignon Blanc (first made in '84).

Longoria Wines, Richard Santa Barbara T nyr
Another busman's holiday cellar, this one belongs to Rich Longoria, the winemaker at Carey Cellars, J., nearby in the Santa Ynez Valley. He makes only two wines, Chardonnay and Pinot Noir, both from grapes purchased in Santa Barbara County. The first vintage was '82. Annual volume is about 900 cases. Price $11.

Los Hermanos
Second label owned by Beringer Vineyards is used for sound, agreeable medium-priced generics and varietals sold mostly in jugs.

Los Vineros Santa Barbara T nyr
The winery belongs to a partnership of 8 vineyardists, most of them with properties in the Santa Maria Valley. Since the label's first vintage, '80, the Chardonnay (fine regional fruit flavors, definite overtones from oak aging), Chenin Blanc, Gewürztraminer, Sauvignon Blanc (subtle, polished, the flagship), and Blanc of Cabernet have been steady, easy to enjoy early. Cabernet Sauvignon and Pinot Noir were first released in 1984. Annual production approaches 12,000 cases. Prices $4.75–$9.50.

Lost Hills Winery San Joaquin T, D **
In what used to be the Barengo Vineyards winery at the n. edge of Lodi, a corporate proprietorship is making a broad spectrum of varietals, generics, and a wine cooler, all from San Joaquin Valley grapes, quite a few of them local. Annual volume is about 500,000 cases (including small lots of table and dessert wines offered under the older Barengo label). The winemaking has been steady. Prices $2.19–$3.39.

Lower Lake Winery Lake T *
The Harry Stuermer family opened its winery in 1978, the first in Lake County since Prohibition. They are making 7,000 cases on the way to a planned maximum of 10,000, all from grapes purchased in the Clear Lake district. The style has been sound, if a bit rough-hewn. The types include Cabernet Sauvignon, Fumé Blanc, and a White Cabernet Sauvignon. Prices $5.75–$9.50, and to $12 for reserve Cabernets.

Lucas Winery, The San Joaquin T **
Dave and Tamara Lucas draw grapes from their 30 acres of old vines w. of Lodi to make small lots of White Zinfandel and Zinfandel (sturdy, even a bit weighty, but still with some polish). Most of the annual 1,500 cases sell at the cellar door, but a few get as far as San Francisco. Prices $5–$7.

Lyeth Vineyard & Winery Sonoma T nyr
Munro "Chip" Lyeth built an ambitious cellar amid 115 acres of vines s. of Cloverdale to make ambitious estate wines, a red from "Cabernet Sauvignon" and other Bordelais varieties, and a white from "Sauvignon Blanc," "Sémillon," and "Muscadelle." The first vintages, '81 for the red, '83 for the white, are to be released early in 1985. Volume is planned to reach the peak 30,000 cases swiftly. Prices $10–$15.

Lytton Springs Winery Sonoma T **
In a legendary spot for Sonoma Zinfandel just n. of Healdsburg in the Alexander Valley, the cellar concentrates on that varietal wine, a reserve bottling from its own ancient vines on a bench above the Russian River, a regular one from purchased grapes. It also produces a bit of White Zinfandel under a proprietary name, "Andrea." Even smaller lots of Chardonnay, Sauvignon Blanc, and Merlot—recent additions—are sold only at the winery at present. The first vintage was '76. Zinfandels from that and every year since have been dark, tannic, and a bit heady. There are about 10,000 cases per year. Prices $8–$12.

MEV
A label belonging to Mount Eden Vineyards.

McDowell Valley
A one-winery AVA e. of Hopland in Mendocino County.

McDowell Valley Vineyards Mendocino T **
From 360 acres in their own AVA, the Richard Keehn family grows and produces a long string of reliably appealing varietal wines. A particular pride of the house is a sturdy, distinctive, age-worthy Syrah. Zinfandel and Chenin Blanc, too, win consistent praise. Also on the list: Chardonnay, French Colombard (too much overlooked), Cabernet Sauvignon, and red and white table wine. Annual volume approaches 70,000 cases. Prices $4.50–$10.85, to $14 for the first of several newly introduced reserve bottlings (a '78 Cabernet Sauvignon), and to $18 for library wines only at the tasting room.

McHenry Vineyard Santa Cruz T nyr
A retirement venture, the winery will produce about 500 cases of Chardonnay and Pinot Noir when 4 acres of vines mature in wooded hills near the small resort town of Bonny Doon.

The two owning McHenry families made their first wines in '80. Prices $10–$14.50, all sold from the winery.

McLester Winery Los Angeles T nyr
Cecil McLester brings fruit from Paso Robles and Shenandoah Valley to his cellar at Los Angeles International Airport to make White Zinfandel, Zinfandel Rosé, Zinfandel Nouveau, and Zinfandel . . . along with Cabernet Sauvignon, Sauvignon Blanc, a Muscat-based dessert wine called Suite 13, and generics wryly called Runway White and Runway Red. The first crush was '80. Volume is 2,000 cases on the way to a planned 10,000. Prices $3–$9.

Madeira
A generic label term for a dry or just off-dry appetizer type. It is seldom used in California.

Madera
A proposed AVA in the San Joaquin Valley. See maps.

Madroña Vineyards El Dorado T *
An ambitious grower-winemaker in the Sierra Foothills above Placerville makes estate Cabernet Sauvignon, Chardonnay, and Johannisberg Riesling as well as the tried-and-true local staple, Zinfandel. The latter is offered by Richard Bush as both white and red. From the debut '80s onward, reds, esp., have been consistent if rough-hewn. Annual production from 35 acres approaches planned maximum, 10,000 cases. Prices $5–$8.50.

Malbec
A little-grown (in California) black grape and its wine.

malolactic fermentation
A bacterial fermentation converts malic acid into the less tart lactic acid. It may occur spontaneously or be induced during or after primary fermentation. It is sought as a complicating buttery or mildly cheesey flavor in many reds and a few whites. The occurrence sometimes is noted on back labels.

Malvasia Bianca
The Muscat-related white grape and its wine.

Manzanita Napa T nyr
Partners Steve Koster and Bob Holder launched their label with an '80 Chardonnay, and have since added a Cabernet Sauvignon, both from purchased Napa Valley grapes. Annual volume is 2,300 cases made in leased space. Price $14.

Marietta Cellars Sonoma T [**]
Since his first vintage, '79, owner-winemaker Chris Bilbro has produced a steady supply of agreeable Cabernet Sauvignons

(fat, distinctly varietal) and Zinfandels (same style) from purchased Sonoma County grapes. Subsequent additions are Old Vine Red and White Zinfandel. The cellars hide in hills w. of Healdsburg. Annual volume is 8,000 cases, the planned maximum. Prices $4–$9.

Marion, M.
An 85,000-case merchant label belonging to M. Dennis Marion. It covers Cabernet Sauvignon, Chardonnay, and White Zinfandel from varying sources. Prices $3.99–$4.95.

Mark West Vineyards Sonoma T, S **/***
N. of Forestville in lower Russian River Valley, vineyardist Bob and winemaker Joan Ellis emphasize Burgundian and Germanic varietals from their 62-acre vineyard, but make some wines from purchased grapes. Their first vintage was '76. Annual volume nears 25,000 cases. Prices $4–$10, and to $17 for sparkling wine.
• Chardonnay. Ever smoother and more stylish. Estate wine ages very slowly. '81
• Blanc de Noirs. In its first two outings, richly flavored, firmly structured sparkler. '81 (all "Pinot Noir"), '82 (80% "Pinot Noir," 20% "Chardonnay")
• Gewürztraminer. Just off-dry (.7–.9% r. s.), crisp, and pungently spicy. '79, '81, '83
Also: Johannisberg Riesling (sometimes as sweet *Botrytis*-affected type), Pinot Noir-Blanc, Pinot Noir, Zinfandel.

Markham Winery Napa T **
Proprietor Bruce Markham founded the winery in 1978 to take selected lots of Cabernet Sauvignon (definite smack of wood), Chardonnay (also noticeably flavored by oak), Chenin Blanc (refined varietal flavors, nicely balanced), and Johannisberg Riesling (off-dry, varietal) from his 300 acres of vineyard, in three blocks located n. of Calistoga, at Yountville, and n. of Napa city. Annual production of 18,000 cases also includes Gamay Blanc, Merlot, Muscat de Frontignan, Sauvignon Blanc, plus generic red and white under a second label, Vinmark. Prices $5.25–$12.85 for Markham, $4.25 for Vinmark.

Marsala
Extremely sweet, dark-hued dessert wine type with flavors much akin to those of raisins. A seldom-seen generic type, usually blended of "Mission" and "Grenache" or similar grapes.

Martin Brothers San Luis Obispo T nyr
Winemaker-partner Domenic Martin is one of several who itches to make Nebbiolo into a wine to be reckoned with in

the Paso Robles area, as it is in Barolo, Ghemme, and other Piemontese districts. The debut vintage—from Shenandoah Valley grapes while their own plantings mature—was released in 1984. The Martins' family-owned winery, meanwhile, has begun to make a name for itself with Chenin Blanc (richly aromatic of its grape), Sauvignon Blanc (uncommonly tart, distinctly varietal). The winery e. of Paso Robles town also offers Chardonnay and a lighthearted Zinfandel. Prices $5–$10. Annual production is about 7,000 cases. The inaugural vintage was '81.

Martini, Louis M. Napa T, D **/***

One of the Napa Valley's great keepers of the faith since 1933, especially in reds. The combined careers of Louis M., his son, Louis P., and Louis P.'s son, Michael, have a constant thread: their red wines have been dismissed early as too light, then hailed for the next two (or three, or four) decades as beautifully balanced demonstrations that distinctive character is not synonymous with raw power. The winery draws heavily upon 850 acres of family-owned vineyard in the Russian River Valley, Sonoma Valley, Carneros, and Chiles Valley, but also buys from independent growers throughout Napa and Sonoma counties, and, occasionally, elsewhere. Annual production hovers around 300,000 cases. Prices $3.50–$7.50, and to $15 for individual vineyard selection wines (just beginning to appear in 1984). The higher price also covers library wines available only at the cellars just s. of St. Helena.

• Cabernet Sauvignon. A bit more firmly varietal under Michael's direction, but still as supple and approachable as ever. '70 '74 '77 '78 '80 '81

• Merlot. Soft and smooth as silk. '80 '82

• Pinot Noir. Californian first, Martini second, varietal third. '75 '79

• Barbera. Named grape often has spine stiffened with a dollop of Petite Sirah. May be best ager of them all; '55 now splendid. '78 '80

• Zinfandel. Soft, easy, sunny-ripe. '78 '80

• Gewürztraminer. Unbeatable for varietal character, and dry. Ages well to 5 years in bottle.

Also: Chardonnay, Folle Blanche (from the old Cognac grape variety, unique to Martini in California), Johannisberg Riesling (dry, with floral scents), Burgundy (fine value), Cream Sherry (one of California's finest old dessert wines).

Martini & Prati Sonoma T, D *

An old-line bulk winery w. of the city of Santa Rosa, it also produces about 20,000 cases a year of generic table wines and dessert wines under the Martini & Prati label, and varietal table wines under the Fountaingrove label. Only the latter mark is distributed outside the immediate area. Cabernet Sauvignon is its mainstay. Many of the wines tend to have an earthy note from aging in ancient casks. Prices $2.50–$5.

Masson Vineyard, Paul Monterey/Madera T, S, D [**]
With the exception of their excellent Rare Souzao Port and one or two other dessert wines, the emphasis from one end of the long Masson list to the other is youthful freshness and easy affability. Even the Cabernet Sauvignon comes out with the bloom of youth still on it. The varietal whites come primarily from 4,512 acres of Masson-owned vineyards in Monterey County. Choice lots appear as Pinnacles Estate selections. Their red counterparts have come, since 1983, from purchased grapes from Sonoma County. Table wine-types of particular note are Pinnacles Estate Fumé Blanc (sometimes with startling similarity to Pouilly Fumés), Pinnacles Estate Gewürztraminer (fine varietal), and a lighthearted Zinfandel. The Seagrams Wine Company–owned winery has its major fermenting cellar in Monterey County, a separate winery for dessert types (and some generic table wines) in Madera County. Masson's transfer-process Champagne house is near the fermenting winery in Monterey County. Annual production is 8 million cases. Prices $3.15–$7.99.

Mastantuono San Luis Obispo T **
Pasquale Mastan started in 1977 as a specialist in Zinfandel. He since has branched out to include Cabernet Sauvignon, Chardonnay, Pinot Noir, and Sauvignon Blanc, but still has six Zinfandels (ranging from White to Nuovo to deep, dark, and tannic). The richest of the Red Zinfandels remain the strength of the house. All of an annual production approaching 8,000 cases comes from Paso Robles–area grapes. Prices $5.75–$15, and to $20 for special lots of Zinfandel.

Matanzas Creek Winery Sonoma T ***/****
The considerable fame of Sandra and William MacIver's 6,000-case, Sonoma Valley winery rests on its two Chardonnays (Sonoma Valley and Estate). However, all of the winemaking has been as skillful as it has been dramatic since the first vintage, '78. (David Ramey, ex-Simi, replaced Merry Edwards as winemaker late in 1984, which may change the style, but not the quality.) Prices $9.50–$18.

• Chardonnay. Powerful aromas of ripe fruit neatly balance bouquets from fermenting and aging in French oak. The best vintages age well. '79 '81 '82
• Merlot. Dark, more tannic than most, a bit heady . . . and redolent of the grape.

Also: Sauvignon Blanc (well marked by wood), Cabernet Sauvignon (same style as Merlot), Pinot Noir (tends to be heady).

Matrose
A label owned by Paulsen Vineyards winemaker Jamie Meves goes only on an Alexander Valley Gewürztraminer of impeccable varietal character and great charm. Remarkably, it is barrel-fermented. The first vintage was '82. Meves makes but 750 cases. Price $7.

Mayacamas Napa T ***/****
From "Chardonnay" vines on one rocky rib of Mt. Veeder and "Cabernet Sauvignon" on two other slopes, Bob Travers nurses spare but gloriously flavorful crops of the two grape varieties for which Napa is most famous, and from them makes two of the region's most distinctive wines. The winery dates to the 1940s; it has been his since 1968. Annual production hovers near 6,000 cases. Prices $10–$18.
• Cabernet Sauvignon. The prototypical Napa mountain Cabernet—dark, tannic, and packed with flavor. Ages almost infinitely. '69 '70 '74 '78 '79 '80
• Chardonnay. Deep gold, austere, marked but not overwhelmed by oak. '79 '80 '81
Also: Sauvignon Blanc, Pinot Noir, and—when opportunity knocks—late-harvest Zinfandel.

Mendocino
An AVA encompassing most of Mendocino County. See maps.

Mendocino Winery
A second label for Cresta Blanca Winery.

Menghini Winery San Diego T nyr
Founded in 1983 by long-time winemaker Mike Menghini, the winery and the beginnings of its vineyard are high in coastal hills e. of San Diego city. The label began with '82s made in leased space. Menghini's roster includes Chardonnay, Chenin Blanc, Sauvignon Blanc, a blush wine from "Gamay," and Cabernet Sauvignon, all from Temecula and San Diego grapes. Prices $4–$8. Production is about 2,000 cases.

Merced
Proposed AVA in the San Joaquin Valley, extending from Merced into Fresno County.

Merlot
A black grape variety and its wine (see p. 22).

Merritt Winery, John B.
A label belonging to California Wine Co.

Merry Vintners, The Sonoma T nyr
After earning high marks for her work at Mount Eden Vineyards and Matanzas Creek Winery, Merry Edwards started her own winery in 1984 with husband Bill Miller and her parents, Charles and D. J. Edwards. The cellar is in the Russian River Valley e. of Forestville, and will produce two Chardonnays, a lighter one for sale only to restaurants, one much in the vein for which she is known. Edwards is buying grapes throughout Sonoma County. Total production is 3,000 cases, with a planned peak of 5,000.

Merryvale Vineyards Napa T nyr
Four partners with deep roots in the Napa Valley are making 1,200 cases of Red Table Wine (a Bordelais blend based in "Cabernet Sauvignon") and Chardonnay. The first vintage, '83, was made in leased space. The Chardonnay is due for release in 1985 at $15; the red will be out in 1986 at a similar price.

Mesa Verde Vineyards and Winery Temecula T nyr
After a tentative start in 1980, the winery got up to commercial size with 8,000 cases of '84s. The long-term plan is to level off at 30,000 cases. Most of the wines come from Temecula grapes, but winemaker Keith Karrup buys as far away as Monterey County. The roster includes Chardonnay (Temecula and Monterey bottlings), Sauvignon Blanc, and Cabernet Sauvignon. Prices $4.50–$14.

méthode champenoise
This traditional way of making sparkling wine requires that the secondary fermentation take place in the bottle in which the wine goes to market, and that the sediment be removed by riddling. Use of the method may be noted on labels by the French term or by the words "fermented in this bottle."

Michtom Vineyard
The principal label of Jimark Winery.

Mihaly Winery, Louis Napa T nyr
A 10,000-case winery makes Chardonnay, Sauvignon Blanc, and Pinot Noir from its own 34 acres just n. of Napa city, and sells the wines only to restaurants and clubs. Essentially the same management operated briefly as Pannonia; some '80s from that firm have been relabelled as Mihaly.

Milano Winery Mendocino T */**
Chardonnays have earned Jim Milone and family their most favorable notices. They also make Cabernet Sauvignon (very ripe, woody), Gewürztraminer, Sauvignon Blanc (curiously perfumey), Pinot Noir, and Zinfandel (always ripe, ofttimes

heady), mostly with vineyard-designating labels. The fruit comes from their own Sanel Valley Vineyard on slopes near Hopland, plus independent growers in Mendocino and Sonoma counties. Annual production is fairly steady at 12,000 cases. Prices $5.50–$18, and to $25 per half bottle for a late-harvest Zinfandel.

Mill Creek Vineyards Sonoma T **/***
Year in, year out, the Charles Kreck family makes pleasing wines across-the-board. Quite a few are stylish. Several are aging well. All of the grapes come from their 65 acres of vines just w. of Healdsburg in the Russian River Valley. The first vintage for the label was '74. Prices $5–$11.
• Chardonnay. Round textures and ripe flavors give it immediate appeal, but it has improved for several years in bottle. '80 '81
• Cabernet Sauvignon. Thoughtfully modulated tannins and ripe Cabernet aromas suggest the consistent style of winemaker Jim Kreck. '77 '79 '81
Also: Merlot, Gewürztraminer, Sauvignon Blanc, Cabernet Blush.

Mirassou Vineyards Santa Clara/Monterey T, S **
Mirassou is both a rear-guard preserver of vines in northern Santa Clara County (300 acres at the winery s. of San José) and a pioneer grower in Monterey County (1,000 acres in two blocks on either side of a town called Soledad), but times and climates also have them buying additional grapes, mostly black, in Amador, Napa, San Luis Obispo, Sonoma, and elsewhere. Their annual 300,000 cases spread across a broad line of sound varietal and generic table wines and four styles of *méthode champenoise* sparklers. Prices $3.50–$8.50 for regular bottlings—among which a flowery Gewürztraminer is notable—and to $11 for special "Harvest" bottlings of Chardonnay (wispy varietal character begs early drinking), Sauvignon Blanc, and Cabernet Sauvignon. Top is $17 for a late-disgorged Champagne (can be stylish, as can the Brut).

Mission
A pale red grape variety and, infrequently, its wine (see p. 23).

Mission Sonoma
Label belonging to Montali Winery, R.

Mission Valley
Label belonging to La Mont Winery, M.

Mondavi Winery, Robert Napa T ***/****
Robert Mondavi is a ceaseless experimenter and, better, brilliant innovator. His ultra-modern winery n. of Oakville is

dedicated to turning out wines on a large scale, but with as much or more distinction than counterparts from tiny cellars. Strikingly frequent success comes from diligent attention to everything . . . Teflon edges on crusher paddles, fermentation temperatures, the techniques of coopers . . . everything. A long third of the fruit for varietals comes from 1,050 acres of family-owned grapes around the winery and in a separate block s. e. of Yountville. The rest is bought from local growers. Total production exceeds 1 million cases, but a good chunk of that is generics made in a separate Mondavi winery at Lodi. Prices $3.75 for the generics (offered under a different label design, and known affectionately by the staff as Bob White, Bob Red, and Bob Rosé), $6.25–$10 for the varietals, and to $25 for reserve bottlings.

• Fumé Blanc. Mondavi coined the name. His approach—barrel fermentation and a dollop of Sémillon—makes some observers call the wine "poor man's Chardonnay." It is, but not as pronouncedly so since '83 as before.

• Chardonnay. Elegantly polished, with just enough oak to deepen already complex flavors. '80 '81

• Cabernet Sauvignon. Seems to draw extra dimensions from "Cabernet Franc" and aging in new French barrels. Reserve bottlings stronger than regulars in both fruit and wood flavors, but not always more age-worthy. '70 '73 '75 '78 '79 '80

Also: Chenin Blanc (sipper), Johannisberg Riesling (distinctly sweet), Pinot Noir (good, occasionally outstanding; needs five years), Moscato d'Oro (splendidly fresh sipper from "Muscat Blanc" sold only at the winery).

Mondeuse

Black grape alternatively named "Refosco," and its wine.

Mont St. John Cellars Napa T **

The winery dates only from 1979, but owner Louis Bartolucci has been a grower and winemaker in Napa since the 1940s, and the label has been in existence almost as long. Most of the current wines come from a 160-acre, Bartolucci-owned vineyard near the cellars in the Carneros area. All come from Napa grapes. The roster includes Chardonnay, Sauvignon Blanc, Johannisberg Riesling, Gewürztraminer, Pinot Noir, Petite Sirah, and Zinfandel, plus generics called Wine Country White and Wine Country Red. Annual production is about 20,000 cases. Prices $2.75–$12.

Montali Winery, R. Alameda T nyr

For the R. Montali label, the proprietors truck grapes to Berkeley from Napa, Sonoma, Santa Barbara, San Luis Obispo, and Amador counties. An annual production of 20,000 cases covers Chardonnay (three separate appellations), Sauvignon Blanc, Cabernet Sauvignon, and the rest of the major varietals. Prices $6.50–$9.50. The volume end of the business goes under the Mission Sonoma label, with most of the wine bought in bulk for blending and finishing. Types include Chardonnay, Sauvignon Blanc, Chenin Blanc, a White Zinfandel called "Caprice," Petite Sirah, Zinfandel, and generics. Current volume is 60,000 cases, with plans to double the figure soon. Prices $2.99–$6.50. Both labels date from 1981.

Montclair Winery Alameda T **
Winemaker-proprietor Richard Dove makes about 1,500 cases a year of varietal wines from Napa and Sonoma grapes hauled to an East Bay warehouse-cum-winery. The emphasis is on heady Zinfandels. Cabernet Sauvignon and Petite Sirah round out a line which manages to ignore the white wine boom. Prices $5–$7.

Monterey
An AVA covering all of the vines in Monterey County. See maps.

Monterey Peninsula Winery Monterey T **
In the labyrinthine understory of a one-time restaurant on the road between Salinas and Monterey town, Roy Thomas and Deryck Nuckton preside over the making of 20 or more wines a year, counting all of the vineyard-designated bottlings. Most of the fruit comes from Monterey County, save for the Zinfandels, which are from Amador and San Luis Obispo. Annual production is 20,000 cases. Chardonnay is the mainstay white in a winery much given to sturdy reds. Prices $4.25, to $35 (for a special lot of Cabernet Sauvignon the owners wish to sell slowly), and to $111 for a late-harvest Zinfandel.

Monterey Vineyard, The Monterey T, S **
What started out as a large winery dedicated entirely to Monterey wines has grown, slowly, into a smallish one producing wines from other parts of the Central Coast, as well as Monterey. The principal wines among 55,000 cases of varietals are Chardonnay, Sauvignon Blanc, Fumé Blanc, Gewürztraminer (showy varietal aromas). The most intriguing ones are a botrytized Sauvignon Blanc and a December Harvest Zinfandel. Two programs just getting under way in 1984–85 are vineyard-designated table wines and *méthode champenoise* sparkling wines (the latter a second effort). Winemaker Richard Peterson and his staff also make 90,000 cases per year of generics subtitled "Classic." Prices $3.99–$7.99, and to $10.99 for botrytized Sauvignon Blanc.

Montevina Amador T **/***
The pioneer in bringing the Shenandoah Valley area of the Sierra Foothills to prominence among modern Zinfandel drinkers continues as one of that region's most substantial wineries. And Zinfandel remains the mainstay, though with strong company from similarly styled Barbera, Cabernet Sauvignon, Sauvignon Blanc (and a paler echo called Fumé Blanc). After 1988, Chardonnay will join the ranks. Annual volume of W. H. Fields's winery approaches 30,000 cases, all from estate grapes. Prices $3.70–$9.
• Zinfandel-Montino. The lightest one puts fruit flavors at the forefront, but still has plenty of the sort of stuffings that made the region famous. It is best early, before the heady flavors overtake the fruity ones.
• Zinfandel. There is more of everything in the regular bottlings, especially flavor notes from wood.
• Zinfandel-Winemaker's Choice. If the regular is Montino^2, the Reserve is Montino^3.

Monticello Cellars Napa T nyr
The 18,000-case-a-year winery got its name because owner Jay Corley is a Jefferson scholar, not because it lies near the end of Monticello Road, close to Napa city. From the debut '81s on, Monticello's wines have been subtle and balanced. The whites come from owned vineyards surrounding the winery; the reds are bought from farther n. in Napa. The regular Chardonnay puts fruit aromas out front; a barrel-fermented edition is typically toasty. Also: Sauvignon Blanc (in '81 the star of the show), Gewürztraminer (dry and restrained enough to go well with meals), Cabernet Sauvignon (approachable early). A Pinot Noir is in the works. Prices $8.50–$16. The winery also has labels called Cranbrook Cellars (for experimental lots priced $4.95–$7.99) and Jefferson Cellars (for excellent red and white table wines priced $4.95).

Morgan Winery Monterey T nyr
Dan Lee takes a busman's holiday from his duties as winemaker at Durney Vineyards to make about 7,000 cases of Monterey Chardonnay and Alexander Valley Sauvignon Blanc at his cellar in Salinas. The first crush, '82, yielded a lean, tart Chardonnay. The first Sauvignon Blanc was due for release in spring, 1985. Prices $8–$12.50.

Morris Winery, J. W. Sonoma T, D nyr
What started in 1975 as a specialist in Port-types in Emeryville evolved into a winery that paid equal attention to dessert and table wines before one of its independent growers bought it and moved it near his vineyard at Healdsburg. Vineyardist

Ken Toth kept the original name when he purchased the label in 1982, but has made his own vineyard the prime source of all but the non-vintage Ports. Chardonnay, Sauvignon Blanc, and Cabernet Sauvignon are the mainstay table wines, along with generic red and white table wines. The Ports (Founders, Vintage, and Late-Bottled Vintage) are still important and still appetizing. Annual production is 30,000 cases, and growing slowly toward a maximum 75,000. Prices $2.95–$7.50 for the table wines, and $4.50–$25 for the Ports.

Moscato Amabile
One name for a light, sweet, sometimes petillant white wine from Muscat (usually "Muscat Blanc" grapes.

Moscato d'Oro
Another name for a light, sweet Muscat.

Mount Eden Vineyards   Santa Clara   T   ***
The winery and 22 acres of vines in steep hills of the Santa Cruz Mountains originally belonged to Martin Ray, but became a separate property in a legal action in the mid-1970s. Merry Edwards (now Merry Vintners) set a style of pungently toasty, big-bodied Chardonnay and equally intense Pinot Noir then. Subsequent winemakers have sustained her original thoughts while adding Cabernet Sauvignon to the regular roster. Annual production from the estate is about 2,000 cases. Price $18. A second label, MEV, covers about 1,000 cases per year of Chardonnay bought from Monterey County. Price $12.50.

Mount Palomar Winery   Temecula   T, D   */**
Owner John Poole draws from 125 acres of vineyard he planted in the late 1960s to make an annual 13,000 cases of sound, straightforward Chardonnay, Sauvignon Blanc, Fumé Blanc (sweeter than the wine labelled as Sauvignon), Cabernet Sauvignon, Petite Sirah, and Shiraz. There are, also, a Cabernet Port and a pair of Sherry-types. The first vintage was '75. Prices $4.25–$5.95.

Mt. Veeder Vineyard   Napa   T   **/***
Henry and Lisille Matheson bought Mt. Veeder in 1982, when it was 9 years old and well established as a source of the sort of dark, tannic Cabernet Sauvignons for which Napa's mountainous vineyards are famous. They have added Chardonnay to the list (the first vintage is to be released in spring 1985), and are dropping Zinfandel ('82 was the last in the series). Annual production is 5,000 cases, all from their 22 acres of vines. Price $13.50.

• Cabernet Sauvignon. Though dark and tannic, the wine is balanced and ages harmoniously.   '79

Mountain Gold
A label belonging to La Mont Winery, M.

Mountain House Winery Mendocino T nyr
Reformed lawyer Ron Lipp reaches out from a cellar almost on the Mendocino-Sonoma line to buy grapes from both counties for his short list of table wines. The production includes Sonoma and Mendocino Chardonnays (both honed smooth, but with appealing fruit flavors in the forefront), Sonoma Cabernet Sauvignon, and a pair of proprietaries called Mendocino Gold and Vermillion. He makes 2,500 cases a year. The debut vintage was '80. Prices $5.25–$11.

Mountain View Winery Santa Clara T nyr
Like many wineries in Santa Clara, this one in the Silicon Valley community of Mountain View is mildly misplaced. All of the grapes for its Chardonnay, Cabernet Sauvignon, and Zinfandel come from Sonoma-Green Valley and Chalk Hill in Sonoma County. Owner-winemaker Patrick Ferguson makes about 750 cases a year, sold primarily in the San Francisco Bay Area. Prices $9–$12. The first vintage was '82.

Muscat Blanc, Muscat Canelli, Muscat de Frontignan
Three alternative names for a white grape and its wines (see p. 19).

Muscatel
Fortified sweet wine from grapes of the Muscat family. Usually inexpensive and sold for immediate, even curbstone drinking, it can age into elegant old wine if the producer has taken some trouble.

Napa Cellars Napa T nyr
The winery dates from 1976, but new management in 1981 revamped the style and the sources of grapes. Now, under the direction of Aaron Mosely, the annual 13,000 cases of Chardonnay (discreet hint of oak plays against appealing fruit flavors), Sauvignon Blanc (good varietal character, matures swiftly), Cabernet Sauvignon (tannic, somewhat heady), and Zinfandel all will come from Napa grapes, after some years of drawing also from the Alexander Valley. Prices $8–$16.

Napa Creek Winery Napa T nyr
Jack Schulze founded the winery in 1980. It produces sound, usually rather heavy Chardonnay, Napa Fumé, Gewürztraminer, Cabernet Sauvignon, and Merlot, among others. All are from purchased Napa grapes. Annual production approaches 15,000 cases a year. Prices $7–$12.50, and to $18 for older vintages only at the winery.

Napa Gamay
The black grape and its wine (see p. 22).

Napa Valley
An AVA encompassing much of Napa County. The valley is one of California's oldest wine districts, and by all odds its most famous source of fine wine. See maps.

Napa Vintners
A label belonging to the Ross Winery, Donald C.

Natural (or Naturel)
The term is beginning to have two meanings. The original definition describes a Champagne or other sparkling wine finished without dosage. A newer, unofficial usage covers wines made without SO_2 or other additives, from organically farmed vineyards.

Navarro Vineyards Mendocino T, S **
Ted Bennett started his Anderson Valley winery in 1975 to produce Germanically styled Gewürztraminer. That remains an annual goal, but the roster has broadened to include Chardonnay (regular and Reserve, both tart and nicely tinted by French oak), Sauvignon Blanc, Cabernet Sauvignon (definite bouquets of oak), and Pinot Noir (velvety texture, appealingly eccentric fruit flavors). A sub-specialty is Edelzwicker, in the Alsatian tradition. Annual production is 1,200 cases, almost all from the owner's vineyard, nearly all sold directly from the winery. Prices $4.95–$12, and to $10 a half bottle for late-harvest Johannisberg Riesling or Gewürztraminer.

Nebbiolo
The black grape and its wines.

Nervo Winery
An old name in Sonoma County, now owned by Geyser Peak and sold only from the old Nervo cellar in the Alexander Valley s. of Geyserville.

Nevada City Winery Placer T, S. nyr
Among an annual 5,000 cases of wines from Sierra Foothills grapes there is a unique bit of Douce Noir, an old Rhônish variety. More conventional entries on a long list include Chardonnay, White Riesling, Petite Sirah, and, of course, Zinfandel. There begins to be a bit of White Zinfandel Champagne. The first crush was '80. Prices $4.50–$9, and to $20 for what the owners feel is a breakthrough Pinot Noir.

Newlan Vineyards and Winery Napa T **
Bruce Newlan makes a bit more than 3,000 cases a year of Chardonnay, Sauvignon Blanc (subtle, nicely made), Cabernet Sauvignon, and Pinot Noir (fragrant, almost floral) from his

two small vineyards just n. of Napa city. In favorable seasons he adds a late-harvest Johannisberg Riesling from purchased grapes. Prices $7–$12, and to $20 per half bottle of the sweet Riesling.

Newton Vineyards Napa T **/***
Peter and Su Hua Newton have planted a few more than 60 acres of slopes that plummet down to St. Helena from the w. Their Sauvignon Blanc (weighty, full of flavor), Cabernet Sauvignon, and Merlot (soft, well marked by wood) come from these hillsides. A Chardonnay (rich, ripe, subtly toasty) that rounds out an annual 12,000-case production is from purchased Napa grapes. The first vintage was '79. John Kongsgaard joined as winemaker in time to make the '83s. Prices $9.50–$14.

Neyers Winery Napa T nyr
Cabernet Sauvignon and Chardonnay are the beginning and end of the list for Bruce Neyers, who plans to build his own cellar in 1985 after four vintages of working in leased space. All of the grapes for his annual 4,500 cases are purchased in Napa. Price $11.

Nichelini Vineyards Napa T *
In hills e. of Rutherford, where Chiles Valley bends down toward the main body of the Napa Valley, an old-line family cellar upholds the worthy tradition of buy-at-the-door country wineries. It is the last of its kind in Napa. Proprietor Jim Nichelini makes about 5,000 cases a year of honest, unpretentious Cabernet Sauvignon, Zinfandel, and Sauvignon Vert from family vineyards. Prices $2.50–$6.

Niebaum-Coppola Estates Napa T nyr
The first wine from Francis Ford Coppola's cellar at Rutherford is advancing to market at an even slower speed than the director's tardiest film. Coppola has but one wine, called "red table wine" in yet another rejection of tightened requirements on varietal wines. It is made from "Cabernet Sauvignon," "Cabernet Franc," and "Merlot." The debut '78 is scheduled for release sometime during 1985, but it may come later, following the '79. Annual production ranges around 3,500 cases, all from the vineyard planted by Gustave Niebaum to launch the original Inglenook. Probable price, about $20.

noble mold
The romantic name for *Botrytis cinerea.*

Nonini Winery, A. Fresno T *
Old-line family firm w. of Fresno city hews to the earthy, thoroughly ripe style that has long made it a favorite of local

Basque shepherds. The prides of the house are Barbera, Grenache, and Zinfandel, all from the owners' 200-acre vineyard. Annual production is 30,000 cases. Prices $1.58–$2.64.

North Coast
An AVA encompassing all or most of the counties of Lake, Mendocino, Napa, Solano, and Sonoma. See maps. In literature pre-dating the 1980s, it may refer to 14 counties stretching as far s. as Santa Barbara.

North Coast Cellars
A second label for Souverain.

Novitiate Wines   Santa Clara   T, D   */**
The winery belongs to the Jesuits, who use it primarily to make sacramental wine but have also developed a small but thriving market for commercial wines. All of the familiar varietal table wines are on the lists, but the label covers some unusual specialties. Black Rose table wine and Black Rose Champagne (Charmat) are made from the rarely encountered "Muscat Hamburg." Flor Dry Sherry (see: flor) is perhaps the most intriguing type in the roster, unless that honor goes to the '73 Angelica. Annual production is 30,000 cases. Prices $3.25–$9.

Oak Ridge
Principal table wine label for East-Side Winery.

Obester Winery   San Mateo   T   **
The winery is in a coastside fishing and farming village called Half Moon Bay, where grapes will not grow. Paul and Sandy Obester reach n. to Mendocino County for Sauvignon Blanc (consistently appealing as an oaky poor man's Chardonnay) and Sonoma County for Cabernet Sauvignon. They look s. to Monterey for Johannisberg Riesling. And they look in both directions for Chardonnay. The first vintage was '77. Annual production is 8,000 cases. Prices $4.95 (for a blush wine from Cabernet)–$12.

off-dry
Term sometimes used on labels or back labels to indicate wine that is neither technically dry (see: dry) nor dessert sweet. Usually the r. s. is .5% to 1.5%, but no regulation governs the limits.

Old Creek Ranch Winery   Ventura   T   nyr
A restoration of an historic winery, the 800-case cellar began with '81 to make several varietals from Santa Maria Valley grapes, and Chenin Blanc from a 5-acre vineyard of its own. Sales are mostly local. Prices $4.50–$9.

Olson Vineyards Mendocino T nyr
A veteran grower in Redwood Valley opened his own winery in 1982. The roster of wines—part from his own vines, part from locally purchased grapes—includes Chardonnay, Sauvignon Blanc, French Colombard, Petite Sirah, and Zinfandel, plus a pair of blush wines. Production approaches 10,000 cases, on the way to 20,500. Prices $4–$9, and to $10 per half bottle for a *Botrytis*-affected Chardonnay.

Opici Winery Cucamonga T *
A family business headquartered in this old district e. of Los Angeles leases cellar space in other regions to make a broad range of varietal and generic wines sold mostly along the Atlantic seaboard.

Opus One Napa T nyr
The already legendary joint venture of Napa's Robert Mondavi and Bordeaux's Baron Philippe de Rothschild makes only one wine, a blend of traditional Bordelais varieties called Opus One. The first vintage was '79. It and the '80 were released in 1984 amid great hoopla—and to substantial acclaim. At present, the winemaking goes on in Mondavi's winery, using Mondavi grapes. A separate vineyard has been planted, and plans are under way for construction of a cellar. Price $50.

Orleans Hill Vinicultural Association Yolo T nyr
The name celebrates an early winemaking endeavor not far from what is now the University of California-Davis campus and its famous winemaking school. Winemaker-partner Jim Lapsley is whimsical enough to call his White Zinfandel "Noel Blanc," releasing it in time for Christmas. Also on the list: Chenin Blanc, French Colombard, Sauvignon Blanc, and Zinfandel. All of the annual 5,000 cases are sold in the Sacramento area. Prices $4–$5.

Pacheco Ranch Winery Marin T **
Marin's first estate winery in modern times grows only Cabernet Sauvignon, but makes a Sonoma Chardonnay as well. Two generations of the Herbert Rowland family have 15 acres of vines and a 1,500-case cellar on rolling hills n. of San Rafael. From '79 onward, the Cabernets have been distinctly varietal and smoothly polished. Their balance promises some age-worthiness. The debut Chardonnay was an '82. Prices $8.50–$9.50.

Page Mill Winery Santa Clara T **/***
The winery of Dick and Ome Stark in the Santa Cruz Mountains town of Los Altos Hills makes 3,000 cases a year of vineyard-identified Cabernet Sauvignon, Chardonnay, Sauvi-

gnon Blanc, and Zinfandel. The great majority come from the Napa Valley. Most types have tended to be strongly marked by the flavors of oak in recent vintages. Prices $9–$12.50.

Paicines
An AVA in San Benito County running along the e. side of the San Benito River valley. See maps.

Palomino (alias Golden Chasselas)
The white grape and, rarely, its wine.

Panache
The label of a *ratafia*-type (sweetened, fortified wine from Pinot Noir press juice) owned by Domaine Chandon.

Papagni Vineyards Madera T, S, D **
Angelo Papagni's family has grown grapes since the 1920s, but Angelo turned to winemaking only in 1975. He won instant critical acclaim on two fronts—first for deliciously fresh light Muscats, second for dry, oak-aged red wines from San Joaquin Valley grapes. These continue to win steady praise, especially the Spumante d'Angelo (styled much as Asti Spumantes of Italy), Moscato d'Angelo (beautifully delicate sipper), Barbera, Charbono, and Zinfandel. All of these and most other wines under the Angelo Papagni and Papagni Vineyards labels come from family vineyards in Madera and Fresno counties. Papagni no longer releases production figures, but had surpassed 130,000 cases in 1980. Prices $2.66–$9.50.

Parducci Wine Cellars Mendocino T [**]
John Parducci kept Mendocino alive as a recognizable wine district for years. His sound, consistently appealing wines now reap substantial rewards for his diligence. Most come from 400 acres of winery-owned vineyards in three parcels: around the cellars n. of Ukiah, s. e. of town at Talmage, and several miles s. of there. The name is best known for: French Colombard (richly flavored, off-dry sipper that sets the pace for everybody else), Petite Sirah (a red wine drinker's red), Zinfandel (fine berryish flavors, well balanced), and Barbera (less tannic alternative to the Petite Sirah). Parducci is often underrated as a source of Cabernet Sauvignon (distinctive varietal flavors, well balanced to age, as the '75 still proves) and Chardonnay (more fruit than oak, has aged well). Production has eased past 300,000 cases. Prices $3.75–$6.75, and to $12 for special selections identified as "Cellarmaster" bottlings. Some library wines are available only at the winery.

Parsons Creek Winery Mendocino T, S [**]
Partner-winemaker Jesse Tidwell started the notion of leaving a barely detectable amount of r. s. in French oak-aged Char-

donnay with his debut '79, and succeeded so well at melding the sweet flavors of fruit and new French oak that he now has dozens of imitators. There are separate Mendocino and Sonoma bottlings. The other table wine on the list is a frankly sweet Mendocino Johannisberg Riesling. The winery has added a non-vintage Mendocino Brut (on average 70% Pinot Noir, 30% Chardonnay), first made in '81. It is the driest wine on the list at .5% r. s. Annual production at the Ukiah winery approaches 15,000 cases. Prices $6.75–$9.50, and to $13.50 for the sparkler.

partridge eye
Descriptive term for wine made as Blanc de Noir, but retaining a pale blush similar in color to the bird's eye. Sometimes appears in the original French, *Oeil de Perdrix*.

Paso Robles
A sprawling AVA in San Luis Obispo County. It reaches a short way w. of the town of Paso Robles, and a long way e. See maps.

Pastori Sonoma T *
The Pastoris make sound, rustic Cabernet Sauvignon, Chenin Blanc, Zinfandel, and generics from their own 50-acre vineyard near the winery at Geyserville in Alexander Valley, and sell all they make from their cellar door. Prices $2.50–$5.50.

Paul Masson Vineyards
See: Masson, Paul.

Paulsen Vineyards, Pat Sonoma T **/***
The television comedian is indeed the owner of the winery and its vineyard s. e. of Cloverdale, at the upper end of Alexander Valley. A bit less than half the grapes come from the home vineyard; the rest are bought from independent growers in Sonoma. Production is at 14,000 cases on the way to 25,000. Prices $7–$10.50.

- Sauvignon Blanc. More austere than most; distinctive for subtle note of American rather than French oak.
- Cabernet Sauvignon. Subtle, polished. Appears able to take some age. '79 '81
- Muscat Canelli. Superb rendition of varietal flavors. Barely off-dry (.7% r. s.).

Also: Chardonnay, Gewürztraminer (new in '84).

Pecota Winery, Robert Napa T **
Having replanted 40 acres n. of Calistoga, Pecota is shifting over from producing an acquired miscellany of varietals (Flora, Gray Riesling, Petite Sirah) to become a specialist in estate Cabernet Sauvignon and Sauvignon Blanc (fat, dis-

tinctly marked by oak). Also on the list: a Muscat Blanc called Moscato di Andrea (superior sipper), Chardonnay, and carbonic maceration Gamay Beaujolais, all from purchased Napa grapes. The winery dates from 1978. Production is 15,000 cases. Prices $5.50–$12.

Pedregal
A second label for Stag's Leap Vintners.

Pedrizzetti Winery   Santa Clara   T   *
A family winery e. of Morgan Hill has a long track record as a producer of generic jugs, and a more recent one as a maker of vintage-dated, vineyard-identified varietals, including Barbera, Petite Sirah, Zinfandel, French Colombard, and Gewürztraminer along with the inevitable Cabernet Sauvignon and Chardonnay. The wines remain unpretentious. Annual production is in the 30,000-case range. Prices $1.99–$6.75, and to $10 for library wines.

Pedroncelli Winery, J.   Sonoma   T   [**]
Family-owned cellar above Geyserville on the ridge separating Dry Creek Valley from Alexander Valley draws on its own 120 acres plus independent growers in the two appellations to make 120,000 cases a year of always understated, often underestimated varietal and generic wines. Of particular note: Cabernet Sauvignon (gentle regular bottling, darker and more tannic Reserve lots), Chardonnay (reliably good, sometimes much ahead of costlier peers), Sauvignon Blanc (fine varietal), Zinfandel (subtle, restrained, balanced regular bottling; huskier Reserves), Zinfandel Rosé (dry, vinous), Gewürztraminer (soft, but lovely varietal flavors). Generics available in jugs offer good value. Prices $3–$7.75, and to $12 for Reserves.

Peju Province   Napa   T   nyr
The plan is ambitious: from 4,000 to 50,000 cases in five years. Tony Peju began with '82 Cabernet Sauvignon from his own 30 acres s. of Rutherford, but will buy grapes to build toward his goal. The only wines are Sauvignon Blanc (beginning with '83) and Cabernet Sauvignon. Prices $7–$10.

Pendleton Winery   Santa Clara   T   **/***
Many small wineries start as specialists and end up with a general line to survive in business. Brian Pendleton managed to start as a generalist and end up with one wine that brought him considerable critical acclaim. That means a dark, deep, toasty Chardonnay, usually from Monterey, but in two recent vintages from vineyards in San Luis Obispo. Annual production approaches 4,000 cases. Price $12.50.

Pepi Winery, Robert Napa T nyr
Long-time Napa growers built a winery on their 70-acre vineyard n. of Oakville to specialize in estate Sauvignon Blanc (fine in its first outing, finer and better balanced in the next), and to make smaller lots of Sémillon, Chardonnay, and Cabernet Sauvignon. The latter is from grapes purchased from a neighbor. The first crush was '81. Production approaches 18,000 cases, 70% of that Sauvignon Blanc. Prices \$8–\$11. The first Cabernet is to be released in mid-1985, probably at \$13.

Pepperwood Springs Vineyards Mendocino T nyr
The Anderson Valley winery introduced itself with an impressive '81 Chardonnay (tart, underplayed, with flickering hints of asparagus—typical of cool-season grapes of this variety). The following vintage appealed every bit as much. The rest of the regular roster is Pinot Noir. Owner-winemaker Larry Parsons also has made fine *Botrytis*-affected Chardonnay ('82) and Gewürztraminer ('84). Annual production is about 1,300 cases. Price \$9 for dry wines. (The Braille is on the label because Parsons is blind.)

Perret Vineyards Napa T nyr
From Paul Perret's 20-acre vineyard in Carneros comes only one wine, Chardonnay. The debut vintage was '82. Annual production, in leased space for the time, is 2,200 cases on the way to a peak 3,500. Price \$14.50.

Pesenti Winery San Luis Obispo T, S, D *
The family-owned winery's traditional role has been as a supplier of rustic Zinfandel and generics to a local market in and around Paso Robles town. In recent years it has broadened its line to include most of the familiar varietals, without changing the style or audience. Most of the grapes come from its 65-acre vineyard at Templeton; all are from the Paso Robles area. Annual production is about 30,000 cases. Prices \$4.98–\$6.95.

Petite Sirah
The black grape and its wine (see p. 23).

Petri
Label belonging to Italian Swiss Colony.

Phelps Vineyards, Joseph Napa T ***/****
In one of the substantial demonstrations that fame can come quickly in California, Phelps launched its lofty reputation with a splendid late-harvest '75 Johannisberg Riesling. It was identified as an old master at the type by the time its even better '79 rolled around. Overall the cellar has developed a slightly schizoid style, making delicate whites and emphati-

cally dark, tannic reds. A considerable portion of the annual 65,000 cases comes from 250 acres Joseph Phelps owns at locations scattered throughout the valley, but he buys in both Napa and Sonoma counties. The main vineyard and winery are just e. of St. Helena. Prices $4.75–$14, and to $25 for Insignia, $35 for older vintages.
• Johannisberg Riesling. Nobody does it better. Subtle, polished, invites second, third, fourth glass alone or with cold cracked crab. *Botrytis*-affected late-harvest bottlings of Riesling and closely related Scheurebe also are models of their kind. '76 '78 '82
• Chardonnay. Polished, silky, with complex enough fruit flavors to permit underplaying the oak. '78 '79 '80
• Insignia. Blockbuster.
Also: Sauvignon Blanc (fine varietal, beginning with '83 to be rich, complex), Cabernet Sauvignon, Syrah, Zinfandel.

Phillips Vineyards, R. H. Yolo T nyr
Founded just in time to make '83s, the winery offers 9 wines, most styled to show off the quality of the owning Giguiere family's 230-acre vineyard w. of Woodland. The first releases were attractive, and included Chenin Blanc (dry and off-dry), French Colombard, Sauvignon Blanc, White Zinfandel, and Zinfandel, plus generic white and red. Yet to come, a Sémillon for which the proprietors have particularly high hopes. Volume approaches 30,000 cases. Prices $3.75–$6.

Piconi Winery, Ltd. Temecula T nyr
The label began with an '80 Petite Sirah made in leased space. The winery was built in time to make the '82s. Dr. John Piconi's roster of wines—Johannisberg Riesling and Merlot from Santa Maria Valley, Chardonnay, Chenin Blanc, Fumé Blanc, Cabernet Rosé, and Petite Sirah from Temecula—all come from purchased grapes. Production is 6,000 cases. The debut Petite Sirah appears sound, and a bit stylish. Prices $5.50–$8.

Pigeon Creek
A grower-owned label devoted mainly to Sauvignon Blanc from a vineyard named Clockspring, in Amador County's Shenandoah Valley.

Piña Cellars Napa T nyr
The winery is e. of Rutherford. From locally purchased grapes, the owning Piña family makes 750 cases per year of Chardonnay (very ripe, well marked by wood) and Zinfandel (first bottling scheduled for release in spring 1985). The first crush was '79. Price $9.50.

Pine Ridge Napa T **/***
Gary Andrus has shown a steady, sometimes inspired touch since the inaugural vintage, '78. The winery, s. e. of Yountville, draws grapes from its own neighborhood and n. to Rutherford to make consistently attractive wines. Annual production is 25,000 cases. Prices $6.75–$20, and to $35 for a Reserve Cabernet Sauvignon.
• Chardonnay. Lightly kissed with oak, it keeps subtle but complex varietal character at the forefront. Apparently able to age. '81
• Cabernet Sauvignon. Leans a bit in the direction of dark and tannic. Even so, the wines are attractive early. Seems able to age. '78 '79
Also: Chenin Blanc (just off-dry, subtle varietal character), Merlot (a bit more tannic spine than most).

Pink Chablis
Generic label term for ordinary, off-dry rosés; name has been bastardized from French commune making only whites.

Pink Champagne
Generic label term for pink sparkling wines. Nearly all are sweet and inexpensive. The closest California counterparts to French Champagne rosés would be partridge-eye Blanc de Noirs.

Pinot Blanc
A white grape and its wines (see p. 19).

Pinot Chardonnay
A longstanding botanic misidentification of Chardonnay now nearly disappeared from varietal labels.

Pinot Noir
A black grape and its wines (see p. 23).

Pinot Noir Blanc
See Blanc de Noir

Pinot St. George (alias Red Pinot)
A black grape and, rarely, its wines.

Piper-Sonoma Sonoma S nyr
The joint venture of Piper-Heidsieck and Sonoma Vineyards got off to a swift start with a set of fine, complex *méthode champenoise* '80s—a Brut (80% "Pinot Noir," 20% "Chardonnay") a Blanc de Noir (100% "Pinot Noir"), and a Tête de Cuvée (100% "Chardonnay"), all from Sonoma grapes. Brut anchors an annual production of 80,000 cases. The other two are made in much smaller amounts. Prices $12.95–$30.

Point Loma San Diego T nyr
Former "serious home winemakers" Kurt Mengel and Ron

McClendon launched their urban commercial winery in '80. They make 1,000 cases a year of Cabernet Sauvignon-Napa Valley, Chardonnay-Edna Valley, and Gamay Beaujolais and Sauvignon Blanc from Temecula. Prices $5–$10, only in California.

Pommeraie Vineyards Sonoma T nyr
The Cabernet Sauvignon and Chardonnay made by partner-winemaker Ken Dalton appear to have settled into stride since the first vintage, '79. Both wines have become steady and begin to be stylish, especially the Cabernet ('80). They are from purchased, mostly Alexander Valley grapes. The 2,000-case winery is w. of Sebastopol. Price $8.

Port
A generic term for dessert wines of 17 to 19% alcohol, and 4–10% r. s. The tribe subdivides into white, tawny, ruby, vintage, and late-bottled vintage among purely generic bottlings. There also are semi-varietal and varietal types including Tinta, Tinta Madeira, Cabernet Sauvignon, Pinot Noir, and Petite Sirah. Most but not all of the varietals are vintage or late-bottled as well.

Posson, Phillip
A brand for dry flor Sherry belonging to Sierra Wine Corp.

Potter Valley
An AVA in Mendocino County. See maps.

Potter Valley Winery
A label belonging to California Wine Co.

Prager Winery Napa T, D nyr
Jim Prager settled on the s. side of St. Helena in 1980 with the still singular notion that the Napa Valley might be a good place to make Port-types. To that end he works at developing Noble Companion (a Cabernet-based Port), Petite Sirah Port, and Pinot Noir Port, all drier than most at 4–5% r. s. Prager also makes Cabernet Sauvignon and Chardonnay table wines in a heavy style Port fanciers might prefer. Annual production is 3,000 cases. Prices $9.50–$15.

Preston Vineyards & Winery Sonoma T **/***
Sauvignon Blanc and Zinfandel are the mainstays for Louis Preston, and have been since the outset, in 1975. His 23,000-case winery also will begin to offer a fresh, youthful Gamay (not a Nouveau) and a traditional Cabernet Sauvignon in 1985. All of the wines come from Preston's 120-acre vineyard some miles w. of Healdsburg in Dry Creek Valley. Prices $5–$12.

• Sauvignon Blanc. Perfect evocation of the grassy Sonoma

regional character for this variety. Nicely balanced, well made. '80 '82
• Cuvée de Fumé. A proprietary wine in which a dollop of "Chenin Blanc" tempers the varietal character of "Sauvignon Blanc."
• Zinfandel. Heady, but strikingly clear example of berryish or briery flavors of the variety. '83

Quady Winery Madera D **/***
In 1975 Andrew Quady set out in a small cellar near the town of Madera to become a specialist in Port-types, which he has done. Along the way he also has become fascinated with dessert wines of Muscat, to equally admirable effect. Annual production is edging up on 8,000 cases. Prices $12–$12.50.
• Vintage Port. The main bottling is made from Amador "Zinfandel" grapes, aged two years in wood in the classical tradition of Oporto. The oldest ones have not been in bottle too long. '79 '81 '82
• Essencia. Splendid evocation of the varietal flavors of "Orange Muscat" in a wine that somehow manages to be austere at the same time it is sweet.
Also: Vintage Port-Frank's Vineyard ('82 yielded tiny first crop of traditional Portuguese grape varieties grown in a young vineyard in Amador; future production will become major factor); Elysium (from "Black Muscat," the grape of the great Muscats of yore from Constantia; focused here on grape flavors); Port of the Vintage (lighter than Vintage Port, ready to drink on release).

Quail Ridge Napa T **/***
The winery evolved out of a particularly well-received lot of homemade Chardonnay. Its first commercial vintage, '78, went over just as well. Elaine Wellesley and Leon Santoro limit production to Cabernet Sauvignon, two Chardonnays, and a curiosity—a barrel-fermented, bone-dry French Colombard. Much of the Napa Chardonnay comes from a winery-owned vineyard well up in the w. hills of Napa; the Sonoma Chardonnay and Napa Colombard are from bought grapes. Annual production is about 7,000 cases, with a planned maximum of 10,000. Prices $5.50–$14.
• Chardonnay. The Napa edition is toastier than most after barrel fermentation. The steel-fermented Sonoma one is a bit crisper and lighter. '81
Also: Cabernet Sauvignon (debut '83, not yet released).

Qupé Santa Barbara T nyr
Bob Lindquist makes 3,000 cases a year of Santa Maria Valley Chardonnay and *vin gris* ("Pinot Noir" with some "Chardon-

nay"), and Paso Robles Syrah, all from purchased grapes. The label dates from 1982. Winemaking is in leased space pending construction of a small cellar in Santa Barbara County. Prices $6–$10.

r. s. (residual sugar)
Precisely controllable proportions of natural grape sugar can be left unfermented to make off-dry to sweet wines. The usual range is from .5% (threshold of recognition) to 35% (in the richest *Botrytis*-affected wines). See also: dry.

racking
Oldest method of clarifying; the process of moving wine from one barrel or tank to a clean one in order to leave precipitated solids behind. Practice sometimes noted on back labels.

Rafanelli Winery, A. Sonoma T [**]
Family-owned cellar of a veteran grower in Dry Creek Valley produces a shade more than 3,000 cases a year of Gamay Beaujolais and Zinfandel. Americo Rafanelli hand-tends every step from pruning vines to bottling wines. His attention to detail shows in soft, balanced wines richly flavorful of ripe grapes. Prices $4.50–$6.25, mostly in California.

Ranchita Oaks San Luis Obispo T nyr
Primary wines are Chardonnay and White Zinfandel from owner Ron Bergstrom's 44-acre vineyard in Paso Robles area e. of the mission town of San Miguel. Petite Sirah is also regular on the roster. Annual production peaked at 10,000 cases. First vintage was '79. Prices $4–$6.

Rancho de Philo Cucamonga D **
Tiny cellar of Philo Biane makes only a few hundred cases per year of Cream Sherry, mainly to demonstrate Biane's belief that Cucamonga-district grapes can make dessert wines of real interest. Sold only at the winery. Price $8.25.

Rancho Sisquoc Winery Santa Barbara T **
James Flood's 3,000-case winery is dwarfed by his 210-acre vineyard, which in turn is dwarfed by his 38,000-acre ranch at the e. end of the Santa Maria Valley. Production is divided among Chardonnay, Sauvignon Blanc, Franken Riesling, Johannisberg Riesling, Cabernet Sauvignon, and Merlot, all of them sound and straightforward. The first vintage was '77. Prices $5–$8.50, mostly to regular subscribers to a mailing list.

Rapazzini Winery Santa Clara T *
The winery is in Gilroy, Garlic Capital of the World, in tribute to which fact it has a Garlic Wine that renders the aromas of the stinking rose to perfection. The rest of the list is conven-

tional varietals soundly made for immediate drinking. They are sold only at the tasting room. Annual production is 10,000 cases. Prices $5–$8.

Ravenswood Sonoma T *
Joel Peterson makes only red wines—Cabernet Sauvignon, Merlot, and Zinfandel—from grapes bought in Sonoma and Napa counties. There are several separate bottlings of Zinfandel in most years. The general approach is pruney-ripe and heady. Annual production is 4,500 cases. Prices $6–$11. The first crush was '77.

Ray Vineyards, Martin Santa Clara T, S **/***
Most of the vineyards planted by Martin Ray, the man, now belong to Mt. Eden Vineyards. Ray's successors at the mountain winery n. w. of Saratoga make an estate Chardonnay from a remaining patch of Santa Cruz Mountain vines. The other Chardonnays plus Cabernet Sauvignon, Merlot, and Pinot Noir come from purchased Napa and Sonoma grapes. In Ray's time, the wines varied wildly in quality and character. If swings are far less at both ends of the pendulum these days, the tendency is to stay on the plus side oftener. Most bottlings are vineyard-identified. Annual production is 4,000 cases. Prices $12.50–$18.
• Chardonnay. Distinctly toasty after barrel fermentation, but fine fruit flavors make their presence felt. '81 (Dutton Ranch) '82 (Winery Lake)

Raymond Vineyard & Cellar Napa T [***]
Family-owned 90-acre vineyard and 60,000-case winery on Zinfandel Lane s. of St. Helena burst on the scene with a fine first vintage, '74. The beginnings were not by novices. Roy Raymond, Sr., has been a grower and winemaker in Napa since the repeal of Prohibition; his sons, Roy, Jr., and Walter, grew up in vineyard and cellar. All wines with Napa appellations come from vines owned or managed by the family. Prices $4.25–$12.
• Chardonnay. Napa bottling is richly textured, redolent of ripe fruit, with a subtle touch of oak for support. The California bottling (Napa, Sonoma, Mendocino, Monterey grapes) is a kid brother. '80 '81
• Cabernet Sauvignon. Can age, but has relatively early appeal as a fat, ripe, even plummy wine. '75 '79 '80
• Johannisberg Riesling-Late-Harvest. Beautiful rendition of varietal fruit flavors in a neatly balanced nectar. '81 '82
Also: Chenin Blanc, Fumé Blanc, Johannisberg Riesling (pleasing in a ripe style), generic red and white.

Redwood Valley
Well-defined area in Mendocino County, between Ukiah to the s. and Potter Valley to the e. Not an AVA.

Rhine
Generic label term for white wine made off-dry (usually 1–3% r. s.). Typically inexpensive, often sold in jugs. The name has many proprietary variations, among them Rhinegarten, Rhine Castle.

Richardson Vineyards Sonoma T nyr
Dennis Richardson's cellar s. of Sonoma town in Sonoma Valley has been the source of bold but balanced, intriguing reds in its early vintages, beginning with the '80s. The first Zinfandel was especially notable (plummy-ripe, bouqueted after wood aging), but that variety has become a minor part of production behind Sonoma-Carneros Pinot Noir and Sonoma Valley Cabernet Sauvignon (fat, ripe, rich with spicy overtones). Early whites were less sure-handed. Annual volume approaches 2,000 cases. Prices $6.75–$11.75

Ridge Vineyards Santa Clara T ***/****
From a ridge-top site in the Santa Cruz Mountains high above the town of Cupertino, Ridge reaches far and wide for red wine grapes to make area- and vineyard-designated Cabernet Sauvignons, Zinfandels, and one Petite Sirah. The wines, mostly from steep hillside vineyards, have natural power, but winemaker Paul Draper also imbues them with subtle balance that has caught the attention of knowledgeable drinkers everywhere. Annual production is about 40,000 cases. Prices $6–$30, and more for library vintages only at the winery.

• Cabernet Sauvignon. From the winery's own Montebello vineyard, strongly flavored and steely hard, but rigged to outlive the tannins. In cool years, can taste a bit underripe. York Creek Vineyard bottlings from Napa Valley have a little more flesh on the bones, but remain more austere than most California Cabernets. '70 '73 '75 '78 '79

• Zinfandel. Dark, powerfully scented of the grape, but balanced for drinking at 4–10 years, usual for the variety. As many as a dozen bottlings may be on hand at the winery. Main ones are labeled Geyserville (Alexander Valley), San Luis Obispo (from Paso Robles area, usually the headiest of the lot), and Howell Mountain and York Creek from Napa. '78 '79 '80

• Petite Sirah. From York Creek. Not a wine to be served with quiche or Brie. '74 '78

Riesling
Rarely used in California as a label for wine of "White Ries-

ling." Historically has identified a semi-varietal made from any blend of "White Riesling," "Emerald Riesling," "Sylvaner."

Ritchie Creek Napa T **
Richard Minor makes only Cabernet Sauvignon and Chardonnay from his 8-acre vineyard high on Spring Mountain, to the w. of St. Helena. From a steep, hillside planting, Minor's Cabernet has been very consistent as an intensely flavored, firmly structured wine since his first vintage, '74. A loyal following buys most of the annual 450 cases. Chardonnay is a recent addition; there were 300 cases of '84. Price $12.50.

River Bend
Label belonging to the Bynum Winery, Davis.

River Oaks Vineyards Sonoma T [**]
The ownership has substantial overlaps with Clos du Bois—the two labels share some cellar facilities and vineyards—but the styles of the two labels are a couple of leagues apart. River Oaks wines are meant to please as soon as they are released. In general, they do. The list includes Chardonnay, Cabernet Sauvignon, and Zinfandel, as well as the predictably affable Johannisberg Riesling, Gewürztraminer, and Gamay Beaujolais. All come from 700 partner-owned acres in Alexander Valley. There also are red, white, and rosé generics. Annual volume fluctuates around the 175,000 case level. Prices $3.50–$7.

River Road Vineyards Sonoma T */**
Proprietor Gary Mills makes Chardonnay, Fumé Blanc, and White Zinfandel from his own vineyard in the Russian River Valley near Forestville, and buys Cabernet Sauvignon. Prices $5–$7. The same roster of wines is offered under a second label, Sandy Creek, using mostly purchased grapes. Prices $3.99–$4.99. Annual production approaches 9,000 cases, all in leased space. Mills's first wine was a '77; his first full vintage was '78.

River Run Vintners Santa Cruz T nyr
The J. P. Pawloski family in 1982 bought a 1,500-case winery founded in 1978 in a little corner of Santa Cruz County which is but a hop from Santa Clara, a skip from San Benito (one source of Zinfandel), and a jump from Monterey (from whence Chardonnay and Riesling). Pawloski reaches farther, to San Luis Obispo for more Zinfandel, and to Mendocino for Cabernet Sauvignon. Prices $4–$9.50.

Riverside Farms
A label of the Foppiano Winery, Louis J.

Robert Keenan Winery
See: Keenan Winery, Robert.

Robert Mondavi Winery
See: Mondavi Winery, Robert.

Robert Pecota Winery
See: Pecota Winery, Robert.

Robert Pepi Winery
See: Pepi Winery, Robert.

Rochioli Vineyards Sonoma T nyr
Tom Rochioli is producing an annual 1,200 cases of Chardonnay, Fumé Blanc, Cabernet Sauvignon, and Pinot Noir from his sizable vineyard toward the w. end of the Russian River Valley. The first reds are '82s, the first whites '83s, though Rochioli had wines made from his property beginning in 1976 under another label, Fenton Acres. Volume is planned to increase to 5,000 cases as a new winery is completed. Prices $7.50–$12.

Roddis Cellars Napa T **
From a bit less than 10 acres of vines at the base of Napa's west hills near Calistoga, William Roddis makes an annual 500 cases of sturdy, straightforward, well-balanced Cabernet Sauvignon. The first vintage, '79, is aging well. Price $12.50. Most sales are local. Volume will increase to 1,000 cases as new plantings mature.

Roederer Mendocino S nyr
When the *méthode champenoise* wines finally get to market, in 1988 or thereabouts, they will not be called just Roederer, but the family name is likely to figure somewhere on the label. The famous French firm has 570 acres of vineyard land in the Anderson Valley. It plans to begin by making as many as 10,000 cases of California Champagne-types, and has 90,000 cases as its first long-term goal. The first crush will be '85.

Rolling Hills Vineyards Ventura T nyr
Cabernet Sauvignon, Chardonnay, Merlot, Pinot Noir, and Zinfandel are the roster of wines under the label. Most are from Santa Maria Valley fruit. Owner-winemaker Edward A. Pagor, Jr., is making an annual 1,000 cases on the way to a goal of 3,500. The first vintage was '81. Prices $7–$11.

Rolling Ridge Winery San Luis Obispo T nyr
A trio of partners' first vintage, '83, yielded more than 4,000 cases of Chardonnay, Cabernet Sauvignon, Petite Sirah, and Zinfandel, all from Paso Robles area grapes. All are from purchased fruit and will be until a 70-acre vineyard e. of Mission San Miguel matures. The label, meanwhile, will go

back to '80s with wines brought from an earlier venture by one of the partners, winemaker Cliff Hight. Prices $5–$7.50.

Roma
Label owned by Guild Wineries.

Rombauer Vineyards Napa T nyr
The first Chardonnay for Kerner Rombauer's winery was an '82 (impressively flavorful of its grape variety, balanced, well made); the first Cabernet Sauvignon came from '80. Current production approaches 3,000 cases; the planned peak is 10,000. All of the grapes are bought in the Napa Valley. Prices $12.50–$13.50.

Rosé
Generic label term for pink wines.

Rose Family Vineyard Sonoma T nyr
Working in leased space, the Rose family makes Chardonnay (competent), Pinot Noir (distinctive varietal, well balanced, distinct oaky note), and Gewürztraminer from purchased Russian River Valley grapes. The first vintage was '81. Annual volume is 3,000 cases. Prices $6–$9.75, only in California.

Rosenblum Cellars Alameda T, S **
Most of the grapes for Kent Rosenblum's annual 5,000 cases of wine come to his Emeryville cellar from Napa and Sonoma counties. His most remarkable effort to date is a splendidly true-to-the-variety, *méthode champenoise* sparkling Gewürztraminer. Also on the list, and all consistently well made: Chardonnay, Cabernet Sauvignon, Petite Sirah, and Zinfandel. First crush for the label was '78. Prices $6–$11.

Ross Winery, Donald C. Napa T *
Don Ross makes sound, sometimes homespun Chardonnay, Sauvignon Blanc, Cabernet Sauvignon, and Zinfandel, almost entirely from grapes purchased in Napa. Annual production is around 4,000 cases, on the way to 6,000. His first wines were '78s under the Napa Vintners label, which is being revived as a companion to the Ross name. Prices $4–$8.

Ross Keller San Luis Obispo T nyr
Howard and Jacqueline Tanner started their 2,000-case winery in the Santa Barbara County town of Buellton in 1980, then moved it to their horse ranch at Nipomo in San Luis Obispo County in time to make the '83s there. (The name translates from German as "horse cellar.") The roster includes five familiar varietals and a couple of Blanc de Noirs. Prices $4–$8.

Rossi, Carlo
Label owned by E. & J. Gallo.

Roudon-Smith Vineyards Santa Cruz T ***

Winery begun as a hobby in 1972 blossomed in fairly short order into one of the more consistent and stylish cellars in the state. Partners Robert Roudon and James Smith produce well-regarded wines from varied sources, designating vineyards in many instances. Production is steady at 10,000 cases. Prices $3.50–$12, and to $16 for a Barrel Select Cabernet Sauvignon available only at the winery near Scotts Valley.

• Chardonnay. Supple, even silky in texture. Fruit flavors play off against subtle ones from oak. '81

• Cabernet Sauvignon-Steiner Vineyard. Wines from hilly planting in Sonoma are dark, tannic, lightly touched by American oak, and rigged with aging in mind. '79

Also: Pinot Noir (Edna Valley), Petite Sirah (San Luis Obispo), Zinfandel (Sonoma). A second, lower-priced label, McKenzie Creek, is used for lots of wine judged not quite up to the top standards of the owners.

Round Hill Napa T [**]

Modest prices have kept a great many people from noticing just how fine some of the wines under this label—and its companion, Rutherford Ranch—can be, given a bit of time in the cellar. All the wines by Jim Yerkes are sound, and give good value. An annual volume of 100,000 cases is divided about half and half between wines produced on the premises from Napa grapes, and others (inexpensive) bought in bulk and polished up (then identified as "House" Chardonnay, "House" Cabernet Sauvignon, etc.). Napa Chardonnay (fine varietal character, especially the Rutherford Ranch), Cabernet (firm, inviting), Zinfandel (released as a soft, mature wine), and Gewürztraminer are particular wines to watch under both labels. Also: Fumé Blanc, Petite Sirah. Prices $2.35–$9 for Round Hill, $6–$12 for Rutherford Ranch.

Ruby Cabernet

The U. C.-Davis hybrid black grape and its wines (see p. 24).

Ruby Port

Generic label name for Port-types made of black grapes; no requirement as to variety. See: Port.

Rudd Cellars, Channing Lake T */**

After several years in a small, basement-sized winery in Alameda, Rudd moved to a remote, hilly site in Lake County, where he has planted the first half of a 25-acre vineyard, and is making an annual 1,000 cases, with plans to grow to 5,000. The current wines are all red: Cabernet Sauvingon, Petite Sirah, and Zinfandel, from a variety of Napa, Lake, and Amador county vineyards. The style leans toward ripe, and tannically rough. Prices $7–$14.

Russian River Valley
An AVA in Sonoma County, extending w. from Santa Rosa and Windsor. See maps.

Rutherford Hill Winery Napa T **/***
From some 800 acres of Napa Valley vineyards belonging to its owning partners, winemaker Phil Baxter draws grapes to make an annual 150,000 cases of ofttimes underrated wine. There is room to grow to 200,000 cases. Emphasis is on Chardonnay, Sauvignon Blanc, Cabernet Sauvignon, and Merlot, with smaller amounts of Gewürztraminer and Pinot Noir. The first crush for the label was '76. Prices $7.50–$12. Some library wines are available at the cellars, in the first roll of hills e. of Rutherford.
• Chardonnay. Excellent varietal character backed by a light touch of oak in a deftly balanced wine. '80 '81
• Cabernet Sauvignon. Red counterpart to the Chardonnay. '77 '79 '80
• Gewürztraminer. Just off-dry, distinctly varietal.
• Merlot. Superior varietal flavors, fine backbone. '78 '80

Rutherford Ranch
A label belonging to Round Hill Winery.

Rutherford Vintners Napa T **
Bernard Skoda goes a quiet way in his 12,000-case cellar just n. of Rutherford, making well-balanced, polished, age-worthy wines, much like the ones he worked with for years while he was at Louis M. Martini. The list includes Cabernet Sauvignon (good varietal with a distinct overtone of oak, from Skoda's own 24-acre vineyard), Merlot (same style as Cabernet), Pinot Noir, Chardonnay, and Johannisberg Riesling (dry, bouqueted). Prices $7.50–$12, and to $17.50 for older vintages of the reserve Cabernet, called Chateau Rutherford.

Saddleback Cellars Napa T nyr
Saddleback is a 1,500- to 2,500-case busman's holiday for Nils Venge, the winemaker at Groth Vineyards. Venge began making Cabernet Sauvignon, Chardonnay, and Pinot Blanc from his 17-acre vineyard near Oakville with the '82s. No wines are to be released before 1985.

Sage Canyon Winery Napa T nyr
Tucked away in hills e. of Rutherford, the winery produces White Zinfandel and a dry, barrel-fermented proprietary white from "Chenin Blanc," the '82 labelled as Aurora Blanc, the '83 most likely as Auroral (the change is to avoid confu-

sion with the French-American hybrid grape called "Aurora"). Gordon Millar's first wine was an '81. Production is about 1,800 cases on the way to 5,000. Price $5.50.

Sage Creek Vineyard
A label belonging to California Wine Co.

St. Amant T nyr
Grower Tim Spencer launched his own label with an '82 Zinfandel. The early wines were sound, typical of their warm growing region.

St. Andrews Winery Napa T nyr
Chardonnays are the main event at Imre Vizkelety's 6,000-case winery just n. of Napa city. The principal bottling comes from St. Andrews Vineyard, 63 acres at the winery (polished, superior, maintains intriguing balance between fruit and wood flavors). Two others, of bought grapes but similar virtues, come from Napa Valley and Edna Valley. Napa Sauvignon Blanc and Cabernet Sauvignon round out the list. The label first appeared on '80s. Prices $6.75–$12.50.

St. Carl
A label belonging to Brander Vineyard.

St. Clement Vineyard Napa T ***
The winery has carved out an enviable reputation for each of its three varietal wines since the first vintage, '75. All of the wines are from purchased Napa grapes. Dr. William Casey's cellar is producing at a steady 10,000 cases a year under the direction of winemaker Dennis Johns. Prices $9–$14.50.
• Chardonnay. Always a distinct smack of oak from barrel aging, but favorable vintages provide enough fruit to balance against it. '82
• Sauvignon Blanc. First-rate varietal flavors, including the pleasing melon-like flavors typical of much of Napa. '81 '82 '83
• Cabernet Sauvignon. Of the dark, tannic school. '78 '79

St. Francis Sonoma T, S **
Most of the wines come from proprietor Joe Martin's 100-acre vineyard, flanking the cellars in the Sonoma Valley town of Kenwood, but some are from bought grapes. The wines are steady right across the list. Occasionally the estate-grown Gewürztraminer and Merlot are well above average. Also: Chardonnay, Pinot Noir, Johannisberg Riesling, and sparkling wine blended of "Gewürztraminer" and "White Riesling." Capacity is 20,000 cases. Prices $4.50–$14.

Saintsbury Napa T nyr
The old professor would be unlikely to complain about Rich-

ard Ward and David Graves borrowing his name for their Carneros-district winery, which produces only Chardonnay and Pinot Noir (two bottlings of the latter, one bouquetish but still richly varietal after wood aging, the other, subtitled Garnet, much fruitier), only from Carneros grapes. The debut '81 Pinot Noir earned the accolades heaped upon it; the '82 held that pace. Annual production is at 15,000 cases on the way to 25,000. Prices $8–$11.

San Antonio Los Angeles T, S, D */**
An old-timer in Los Angeles, the winery long made its way selling a lengthy list of everyday wines (sound, off-dry to outright sweet) only through its own outlets in Los Angeles. In recent seasons it has added sound, often better than average varietal wines under the Maddalena Vineyard label. The latter come from vineyards as close as Santa Barbara, as far n. as Mendocino. Among them: Chardonnay, Gewürztraminer, Johannisberg Riesling, Sauvignon Blanc (steady, appealing fruit), Cabernet Sauvignon, Zinfandel. Annual volume is about 300,000 cases. Prices $1.95–$2.55 for San Antonio, $3.90–$6.90 for Maddalena Vineyard.

San Joaquin Valley
The great interior valley of California extends from San Joaquin County on the n. to Kern County on the s. Its warm, dry climate is responsible for much of the state's everyday table wine, and nearly all of its dessert wine.

San Martin Santa Clara T, D **
In the course of evolving from a country jug and fruit wine operation to a substantial producer of vintage-dated varietals, San Martin earned a reputation for producing sound, appealing wines—partly for the varietals, but also for well-made, even stylish generics. They have not held quite the level of the late '70s, but remain priceworthy. Whites have the edge, especially Chardonnay (ripe varietal flavors plus a distinct note from oak aging), Sauvignon Blanc (straightforward, easy), and Chablis. Volume is in the 500,000-case range. Prices $3.99–$7.25, and to $9.95 for a dessert specialty called Montonico.

San Pasqual
Tiny, one-winery AVA in San Diego County. See maps.

San Pasqual Vineyards San Diego T, S **
In an easterly suburb of San Diego called Escondido, winemaker Kerry Damskey consistently turns out agreeable whites (especially a fragrant Muscat Canelli), and an affable Gamay. With '81, he added a remarkably floral *méthode champenoise* sparkler made from "Gamay," "Sauvignon Blanc," and

"Chenin Blanc." Most of the wines come from winery-owned vineyards in the San Pasqual AVA, but the winery began buying Santa Maria Valley grapes for Chardonnay and Pinot Noir in '83. Production has grown to 25,000 cases since the 1972 startup. Prices $5–$8 for still wines, $12 for the Champagne.

Sanford & Benedict Vineyards Santa Barbara T */**
Michael Benedict pursues the ideals of Burgundy at his 110-acre vineyard and 8,000-case winery some miles w. of Buellton in the Santa Ynez Valley. Chardonnay and Pinot Noir are the mainstays, supplemented by Cabernet Sauvignon and a trio of proprietary types. The character of the wines has been somewhat uneven throughout the winery's career. The label first appeared with the vintage of '76. Prices $4–$9.

Sanford Wines Santa Barbara T nyr
Richard Sanford, once a partner in Sanford & Benedict, launched his own firm with a handsome set of '81s. The style for both Chardonnay and Sauvignon Blanc is distinctly toasty (from barrel fermentation and malolactic fermentation). The Pinot Noir is well marked by wood. Also in the roster is a Pinot Noir-*vin gris*, a blush wine made dry and, again, distinctly oaky. All of the grapes are bought at present, primarily in Edna Valley and Santa Maria Valley. The winery, under construction in 1984 amid young vines, is 5 miles w. of Buellton in the Santa Ynez Valley. Annual production is 18,000 cases. Prices $6.50–$12.50.

Santa Barbara Winery Santa Barbara T **
What began in 1962 as a neighborhood source of jug wines for Santa Barbarans has evolved into a producer of consistently appealing varietals, some from a winery-owned 50-acre vineyard in the Santa Ynez Valley. Owner Pierre Lafond offers all of the major varietals with the exception of Pinot Noir. Of note: Chardonnay, Zinfandel. Annual production is 10,000 cases. Prices $5.50–$12.

Santa Cruz Mountain Vineyard Santa Cruz T **
One of a considerable and still growing number of seekers of the perfect Pinot Noir, which is to say a close approximation of Burgundy. The results from owner Ken Burnap's 12-acre vineyard high in the Santa Cruz Mountains have been something different—heavy, almost raisiny-ripe, and heady (to 14.8% alcohol)—but fascinating nonetheless. There are in addition a Cabernet Sauvignon (also extra-ripe) from a nearby property, and a third wine which varies by type and source from year to year. Production is about 3,000 cases. Prices $12.50–$15, mostly to a mailing list.

Santa Cruz Mountains
An AVA covering parts of San Mateo, Santa Clara, and Santa Cruz counties. See maps.

Santa Lucia Cellars
A label belonging to HMR.

Santa Maria Valley
An AVA extending inland from the town of Santa Maria in northern Santa Barbara County. See maps.

Santa Ynez Valley
An AVA centered on Solvang, in central Santa Barbara County. See maps.

Santa Ynez Valley Winery Santa Barbara T **/***
The enduring fame of the place since its founding in 1976 has rested with its Sauvignon Blanc, but several other wines have been consistently appealing, especially the Chardonnay (ripe, subtly enhanced by wood flavors), and Johannisberg Riesling (adroitly balanced as a sipper). Also: Gewürztraminer, Blanc de Cabernet, Sémillon. Annual production is 10,000 cases, much of it from winery-controlled vineyards near the winery in the Santa Ynez Valley at the village of Santa Ynez. Prices $4–$8.50.
• Sauvignon Blanc. Tart. Splendid varietal flavors, but without the sometimes over-bold regional flavor of cooked asparagus. Reserve de Cave bottlings, with slightly more perceptible wood flavors, have aged well. '79 '81 '82

Santino Winery Amador T */**
In the long run, Nancy Santino means hers to be a red Zinfandel winery. To that end it has separate bottlings from Shenandoah Valley and Fiddletown (both typically weighty, ripe). In the short run, it has grown quickly to 20,000-case production by anticipating, then riding the fad for White Zinfandel (made by German-schooled winemaker Scott Harvey to balance betwixt 2.5% r. s. on the one hand and .7 to .8 t. a. on the other, and called White Harvest Zinfandel). Also: Sauvignon Blanc, Fumé Blanc (the latter gets less time in wood than the former), and Cabernet Sauvignon—all from Sierra Foothills grapes. Prices $4–$8. The first vintage was '79.

Sarah's Vineyard Santa Clara T **
Marilyn Otteman makes Chardonnay from Ventana Vineyards in Monterey, Johannisberg Riesling from the Mattheu vineyard in Mendocino's Potter Valley, and a red "of Sarah's choice" ('81 Zinfandel, '82 Cabernet-Merlot blend, '83 Merlot). Her basic goal is to keep the fruit flavors foremost in

whites (no SO_2, no barrel fermentation) and reds alike. The winery, w. of Gilroy, produces about 2,000 cases per year. Prices $8.50–$17. The first crush was '78.

Sattui Winery, V. Napa T, D **/***

Daryl Sattui sells all of his annual production direct from his swiftly growing winery on the s. side of St. Helena, and still manages to gather acclaim from a broad spectrum of critics. Production was at 15,000 cases in 1984, and climbing. Prices $5.75–$11.75.

• Cabernet Sauvignon. Always well marked by wood, polished, even mature at release. '79 '80

• Johannisberg Riesling. One dry, one just off-dry, both distinctly varietal and fresh.

• Madeira. Complex, close to dry.

Also: Zinfandel (reliably well balanced, subtle), Sauvignon Blanc (easy, friendly), Chardonnay.

Saucelito Canyon Vineyard San Luis Obispo T nyr

After 10 years as a grower, Bill Greenough built a 1,000-case winery in 1982 on his 25-acre property e. of Edna Valley. The roster includes White Zinfandel, Zinfandel, and Cabernet Sauvignon, all from his own vines. Prices $5.25–$9.

Sausal Winery Sonoma T **

After a long, honorable career in the bulk trade, the owning Demostene family began making wine for its own label with a fine '74 Zinfandel. Winemaker David Demostene has followed his original success with a long string of others (ripe, fleshy, heaped with berryish fruit even when they are a bit heady). He also produces a Chardonnay (barrel-fermented but rich in fruit flavors nonetheless), Cabernet Sauvignon, White Zinfandel, Pinot Noir-Blanc, and a proprietary white called Sausal Blanc (10% Chardonnay, the rest French Colombard). Annual production is 8,000 cases and growing slowly. Prices $4–$8.50, and to $10 for a Private Reserve Zinfandel.

Sauterne

A generic label term borrowed from the French and applied to a range of dry to off-dry to distinctly sweet (but rarely, if ever, *Botrytis*-affected) wines. Sometimes modified to read Dry Sauterne, Sweet Sauterne, or Haut Sauterne. Not much in use now.

Sauvignon Blanc

The white grape and its wines. Often identified by an alternative name, Fumé Blanc (see p. 19).

Sauvignon Vert

A white grape and, rarely, its wines.

Scharffenberger Cellars Mendocino S, T nyr
John Scharffenberger draws from a broad range of sources in Mendocino County to make *méthode champenoise* sparkling wines. The mainstay in his 15,000-case production is Brut (80% "Pinot Noir," 20% "Chardonnay"). There is a smaller amount of Blanc de Blanc (all "Chardonnay"). The first vintage, '81, yielded well-made, very tart wines. Prices $13.50–$14.50. Scharffenberger also offers 4,000 cases of still wines under his Eaglepoint label. The early vintages of Blanc de Pinot Noir and Chardonnay were bracingly crisp, only lightly touched by wood. Prices $4–$9.50.

Schramsberg Napa S ****
Since 1965, historic hillside cellars s. w. of Calistoga have been the most stylish *méthode champenoise* sparkling wine producer in California. Purchased grapes from the s. half of the Napa Valley outweigh the winery's own 40-acre vineyard in all of the types. Under the skilled direction of Jack L. Davies, the winery has grown to an annual volume of 31,000 cases, divided among five types, all vintage-dated. Prices $15.40–$19.85, and to $25.70 for Reserve.
• Blanc de Blanc. "Chardonnay" dominates and "Pinot Blanc" complicates, though there is nothing of varietal character in a subtle, complex, properly austere wine finished as Brut.
• Blanc de Noir. Rich, creamy textures reveal the presence of a majority of "Pinot Noir" in the cuvée as soon or sooner than a scintilla of color does. It is finished as a Brut.
• Reserve. Has shifted in recent times from essentially a Blanc de Blanc to a Blanc de Noir. It is made of lots chosen specifically for their apparent ability to age.
• Cuvée de Pinot. Rare in California, a pink Champagne as French stylists make them—dry, and closer to partridge eye than pink in color and flavors. The cuvée is principally "Pinot Noir," with an enlivening dollop of "Gamay."
• Crémant. For dessert. Flowery flavors of "Flora" mate with 3.8% r. s. Less bubbly than conventional sparklers so sweetness is easy to find. Similar to but much subtler than sparkling Muscats patterned after Asti Spumantis.

Schug Cellars Napa T nyr
Walter Schug (ex-Joseph Phelps Vineyards) established his own winery in 1981 to focus on vineyard-designated Chardonnays and Pinot Noirs (uncommonly dark and tannic for the variety), mostly from Napa-Carneros, but some from the upper Napa Valley and others from Sonoma Valley. Schug also makes occasional Sauvignon Blanc and Cabernet Sauvi-

gnon. Production is at 8,000 cases on the way to a planned maximum of 10,000. Prices $8.25–$12.75.

Searidge Winery Sonoma T nyr
Partner-winemaker Daniel Wickham is a marine biologist, which explains the seashell motif of the label, but not the seaside location of the winery and the vineyards from which it buys. That owes to the belief of Wickham and Tim Schmidt that there is no other climate in California to grow "Chardonnay" and "Pinot Noir" cool enough to echo Burgundian counterparts. The first vintage, '80, yielded strongly woody, toasty wines of both types. Production is 4,000 cases. Prices $6.25–$15.

Sebastiani T, S, D **
Under the direction of Sam Sebastiani, the third generation, this venerable family-owned winery has taken its third turn, from jug to fine varietal, having earlier gone from bulk to jug. In moving toward fine varietals, Sebastiani also is focusing sharply on Sonoma Valley, even vineyard-designated varietals —including some from the winery's own 300 acres. Several of the new wines suggest it is getting ready to compete with the best. Of particular note in the long list of varietals: Gewürztraminer (flawless evocation of varietal flavors), Cabernet Sauvignon (the Proprietor's Reserves since '79 have been polished, distinctive in fruit flavors). This always was as good a place to turn as any for Zinfandel (echoes of fruit amid pleasing overtones from long aging in old wood) and Barbera (husky, designed to go with venison by somebody who knew the tastes of both). The sweet Sherries command attention, too. A *méthode champenoise* sparkler joined the lists with the vintage of '81. Annual production 2.5 million cases. Prices $3.45–$7.25, and to $25 for Cabernet Sauvignon-Eagle Vineyard.

Sec
Label term, used mostly on sparkling wines, to indicate something distinctly sweet, even though the French word means "dry." The Brits caused the original confusion when they wanted to drink sweet Champagne but pretend it was dry.

Seghesio Winery Sonoma T */**
A firm with a long, honorable career in bulk winemaking turned to producing bottled wines under the owning family's name early in the 1980s. It was able to reach back in the cellars to introduce itself with a fine '74 Zinfandel, a better '76 Cabernet Sauvignon. Also in the varietal list: French Colombard, Chenin Blanc, White Zinfandel, and Pinot Noir, all well made, all from the family's six Sonoma County vineyards

(mostly Alexander Valley), plus one in Mendocino County. Annual production is about 20,000 cases. Prices $3.25–$5.

Sellards Winery, Thomas   Sonoma   T   nyr
Since the first vintage, '80, the emphasis has been on Cabernet Sauvignon, Sauvigon Blanc, and Chardonnay, mostly from purchased Alexander Valley grapes. Production is 750 cases on the way to a planned 2,000. Prices $8–$10.50.

Sémillon
A white grape and its wine (see p. 20).

Sequoia Grove   Napa   T   **/***
Winemaker-partner James Allen has shown a sure, subtle touch in each of the several Chardonnays he has made since a debut '79. Dark, tannic, distinctly oak-tinged Cabernet Sauvignons from Napa Valley and Alexander Valley round out the short list in a 9,000-case winery located amid 22 acres of vines n. of Oakville. An affiliated "Chardonnay" vineyard in the Carneros district is just beginning to bear. Prices $9.50–$12.
• Chardonnays. Napa, Estate, and Sonoma lots trade off as front-runners from year to year, but all balance fruit and oak flavors neatly. '80   '81

Shadow Creek
A label owned by Glenmore Distillers, also the owners of Corbett Canyon.

Shafer Vineyards   Napa   T   **/***
After some years as a grower, John Shafer launched his own label with the '78s. Nearly all of the 12,000 cases each year come from his own 75 acres of vines in the Stag's Leap area e. of Yountville. Prices $8–$12.50, and to $14.50 for a Reserve Cabernet to be introduced in 1985.
• Chardonnay. Silky, polished, flavored a good deal by its fruit and only a bit by oak aging. '81
Also: Cabernet Sauvignon (promising in early vintages, but not settled into a style), Merlot. A good Zinfandel is, alas, gone, the vines for it rooted out in favor of more "Cabernet Sauvignon."

Shaw Vineyards & Winery, Charles F.   Napa   T   **
Shaw came to the Napa Valley to make the ultimate California Gamay, which he has pretty well done since the first one, a '79. He has both a Nouveau style and one patterned more after a good Fleurie, or Morgon. Recently, the winery has added Chardonnay (sound, agreeable) and Fumé Blanc (fine melon-like varietal flavors) to the list. Most of the grapes come from his 35 acres at the winery n. of St. Helena. Annual

production approaches 25,000 cases a year. Prices $5–$12.50. A second label, Bale Mill Cellars, covers the same varietal types, all from lesser lots from regular production. Prices $3–$7.50.

Shenandoah Valley-California
An AVA in Amador County. The "California" is tacked on to distinguish it from the other Shenandoah, in Virginia.

Shenandoah Vineyards Amador T, D */**
The basic roster of Leon Sobon's 14,000-case winery in the Shenandoah Valley e. of Plymouth is White Zinfandel, Sauvignon Blanc, Cabernet Sauvignon, and Zinfandel (both the Dal Porto-Shenandoah Valley and the Special Reserve-Eschen Vineyards Fiddletown are typically thick and heady). However, late-harvest Zinfandel (15% alcohol, 10% r. s.), Zinfandel Port, Vintage Port, and Mission Cream Sherry—a tiny proportion of production—contribute heftily to the winery's reputation. Prices $5–$12.

Sherrill Cellars Santa Clara T **
Cellar of Nat and Jan Sherrill in Santa Cruz Mountains n. w. of Saratoga devotes itself to burly, assertive reds from the Central Coast, many of them vineyard-designated. Principal types in 2,000-case annual production are Zinfandel, Petite Sirah, and Cabernet Sauvignon, sold mostly from the cellar door, or nearby. Prices $5–$10, and to $12 for a Chardonnay sold only at the winery.

Sherry
A generic label term for a varied roster ranging from barely dry appetizer wines to outright sweet dessert ones. Most commonly in California, the name refers to wine first fortified to 17–20% alcohol, then exposed to air in a warmed tank to produce characteristic oxidized flavors. Some more expensive bottlings, closer to Spanish models, are produced by blending younger and older wines oxidized only through long aging in wood. The degree of sweetness is controlled by the timing of fortification. The name usually is modified to describe sweetness, Dry or Cocktail Sherry (2.5% r. s. or less), Medium or Golden Sherry (2.5–4% r. s.), or Sweet or Cream Sherry (4% r. s. or more).

Shown & Sons Napa T */**
On moving in 1984 from a 70-acre winery and vineyard site e. of Rutherford to a 27-acre one s. of the same town, Richard Shown narrowed the focus of his winery from several varietals to Chardonnay and Cabernet Sauvignon. Production is running at about 8,000 cases. Prices $5.50–$13, and to $15 for

older vintages. From the debut '78s onward, the wines have been sound and straightforward.

Sierra Vista El Dorado T **
John and Barbara MacCready's winery, set amid vines that look up to some of the most scenic peaks in the Sierra, has grown from 400 cases of '77 to 5,000 cases of '84, all from Sierra Foothills grapes, all sound and agreeably rough-hewn. Cabernet Sauvignon and Zinfandel anchor the reds (though a dollop of experimental Petite Sirah sold only at the winery is of some interest). The white varietals are White Zinfandel and Fumé Blanc. Prices $4–$8.50.

Sierra Wine Corp. Tulare T, D */***
A large winery dealing mostly in bulk, Sierra's two labelled products are poles apart. One—new late in 1984—is a set of standard, off-dry generic table wines packaged in "bricks" (sort of like milk cartons) under the name of Château de la Vallée, and priced at $2.90. The other, which goes back a number of years, is Phillip Posson Dry Flor Sherry, named for the skilled winemaker who produces it. Annual production, less than 10,000 cases, sells only in California. Price $6.50.

• Dry Flor Sherry. Not as light as a Spanish fino, but getting in that direction, and just as well marked by the curiously appealing flavors of flor yeasts. It is dry by both lab analysis and taste. The wine merits recognition as one of the state's finest appetizers.

Silver Mountain Vineyards Santa Clara T nyr
Monterey Chardonnay ('80 dark, faded quickly) and Sonoma Zinfandel (strong notes of oak) are the only wines produced at Jerry O'Brien's ridge-top winery w. of Los Gatos, though an estate Chardonnay will join the roster as 12 acres of vines mature. The first crush was '79. Annual production is 2,000 cases. Prices $6.50–$11.

Silver Oak Cellars Napa T ***
The only wine is Cabernet Sauvignon, but it comes in three forms from Justin Meyer's handsome stone cellar e. of Oakville. The label dates from 1973. Annual production is 15,000 cases, the planned peak. Prices $18, and to $35 for Bonny's Vineyard bottlings.

• Cabernet Sauvignon-Alexander Valley. Polished, soft, and smacking more of the American oak in which it ages than of fresh grapes, even at release. '79

• Cabernet Sauvignon-Napa Valley. From a vineyard at Oakville, the wine has a bit more tannic austerity and more distinctive fruit flavors than its running mate from Sonoma County. '79 '80

• Cabernet Savignon-Bonny's Vineyard. The Napa style, only more so. From a winery-owned vineyard near the cellars. Gives every evidence of being an ager. '79

Silverado Vineyards Napa T nyr
Winemaker John Stuart hit the ground running at Lillian Disney's winery e. of Yountville with a fine set of '81s. If anything, he has picked the pace up a bit since with all three wines: Chardonnay (polished, a hint toasty, but with rich, ripe varietal character to play against the bouquets), Sauvignon Blanc (also silky and ripe), and Cabernet Sauvignon (just appearing in the markets; promising). Annual production approaches 25,000 cases, and will peak at 50,000, all from winery-owned grapes. Prices $8–$11.

Simi Winery Sonoma T ***/****
Winemaker Zelma Long (ex-Robert Mondavi) brought a firmly developed sense of style and superb technical skills to Simi in time to make an impressive collection of '80s. Her wines have gained steadily since, as she has homed in on vineyards she prefers. Some 175 acres of winery-owned vines are just beginning to produce. Meanwhile, Simi (under the ownership of France's Moët-Hennessy) buys all of the grapes for its annual 130,000-case production, most in Sonoma, a few in Mendocino. Chardonnay and Cabernet account for 70% of that total. Prices $6–$11, and to $30 for reserve and library wines.
• Chardonnay. Fine ripe varietal flavors are buttressed by the toasty, buttery ones that come from barrel and malolactic fermentations. '80 '81
• Cabernet Sauvignon. Subtle, silky in the way of most Alexander Valley Cabernets, but not so blunt in varietal flavors as many. '35 '74 '78 '80 '81
• Sauvignon Blanc. Splendid example of the virtues of restraint. '82 '83
• Zinfandel. Fine berryish flavors subtly buttressed with the sweet, vanillin-like flavors of new French oak. '74 '80
Also: Chenin Blanc (manages to make the charms wispy instead of blatant), Rosé of Cabernet Sauvignon.

Sky Vineyards Napa T nyr
Lore Olds produces only Zinfandel from his lofty 12-acre vineyard in the Mayacamas Mountains between the Napa and Sonoma valleys. The first vintage was '81. Planned peak production is 2,000 cases. Price $9, only in California to date.

Smith & Hook Monterey T nyr
The winery makes only Cabernet Sauvignon from its 250-acre vineyard on a steep slope in hills w. of Soledad, in the Arroyo

Seco area. Duane DeBoer's first vintage was '79. It and the '80 are powerfully regional in flavor as well as varietal, which is to say bell pepper heaped upon herbs. Annual production is steady at 10,000 cases. Price $13.50.

Smith-Madrone Napa T **/***
Since their inaugural '77s, Stuart and Charles Smith have been migrating steadily from powerful wines to subtler ones at their 38-acre vineyard and 7,000-case winery high on Spring Mountain, to the w. of St. Helena. All four varietals on the roster have been well made from the outset. Prices $7.50–$12.
• Riesling. From the grape commonly called Johannisberg, the wine has excellent varietal character and a pleasing fillip of r. s. Like most from Spring Mountain, it has an ability to improve with age for three or four years.
• Chardonnay. Distinctly but deftly marked by wood, even following shift to less ripe style after '81.
Also: Pinot Noir ('80 was and is fine evocation of ripe style; '81 is fresher and livelier), Cabernet Sauvignon ('80 well freighted with oak, but nicely balanced).

Smothers Santa Cruz T **
The most spectacular wines from entertainer Dick Smothers's 5,000-case winery in the hills e. of Santa Cruz have been late-harvest Johannisberg Rieslings and Gewürztraminers. Also on the list: regular Johannisberg Riesling and Gewürztraminer, two Chardonnays (one from brother Tom Smothers's vineyard in Sonoma), Sauvignon Blanc, Cabernet Sauvignon, and Zinfandel. All of the wines are from grapes purchased in Sonoma. The first vintage was '78. Prices $7–$12.50.

Soda Rock Winery Sonoma T **
Charles Tomka, working in a veritable museum of a winery in the Alexander Valley, produces surprisingly fresh, subtle whites (notably including a dry Gewürztraminer) as well as polished, agreeable reds (Cabernet Sauvignon, Zinfandel). Charlies Country White and Charlies Country Red give particularly good value. All are from purchased Sonoma grapes. The 7,000-case annual production is sold almost entirely from the winery. What little escapes goes only as far as Healdsburg. Prices $5–$14.50.

Solano-Green Valley
A small AVA on the boundary between Solano and Napa counties.

Soleterra
A proprietary red wine made from "Pinot Noir," but in the style of Rhônes. The name and the wine belong to Sloan and

John Upton, the owners of a northern Napa Valley vineyard called Three Palms (from whence the grapes come), and a partner. The 1,250 cases of the debut '82 were made in leased space.

Sonoma-Cutrer Vineyards Sonoma T, S nyr
Winemaker William Bonetti made a spectacular sequence of Chardonnays for Charles Krug between 1963 and 1968. Now he has a winery in the Russian River Valley that makes nothing else, and only from Sonoma County vineyards owned by Brice Jones, the owner of Sonoma-Cutrer. The three inaugural bottlings of '81s promise as much as the old Krugs did, a considerable claim indeed, and each in a different way. The Russian River Ranches bottling has the fresher, fuller fruit flavors, the Les Pierres (Sonoma Valley) a classical austerity. In between comes the Cutrer Vineyard. Production is edging past 20,000 cases. Prices $10–$15.50. To come is a Blanc de Blanc *méthode champenoise* sparkling wine 100% of "Chardonnay," and destined to spend 5 to 7 years in tirage. The first vintage of this was '82.

Sonoma-Green Valley
An AVA in Sonoma County. See maps.

Sonoma Hills Winery Sonoma T nyr
Chardonnay from hillside vineyards in the Sonoma Valley is the only wine Terry Votruba makes at her 200-case (going on 1,000-case) winery at the n. w. corner of that AVA. Her aim is for as much lightness and freshness as she can retain after partial barrel fermentation of early-harvested fruit. The first vintage was '83. On release in '85, the price will be $8–$10.

Sonoma Valley
An AVA extending from Sonoma town n. and w. toward Santa Rosa, in Sonoma County. See maps.

Sonoma Vineyards
A label and winery recently renamed Rodney Strong Vineyards after its founder-winemaker.

Sotoyome Sonoma T */**
William Chaikin makes 3,000 cases a year of Chardonnay, Cabernet Sauvignon, Petite Sirah, and Zinfandel, all from Sonoma grapes, mostly from his own hilltop vineyard in the Russian River Valley s. of Healdsburg. The results have varied somewhat in character and quality, sometimes on the side of excellence. Prices $4.75–$6.75.

Souverain Cellars Sonoma T **
The winery has gone through a succession of names and ownerships since its founding in 1972. The confusion has hidden

the fact that some excellent wines have sprung from the place, owned now by a partnership of its major growers, all of whom are in Mendocino, Napa, and Sonoma counties. Annual production is 130,000 cases. Prices $4.50–$13, and to $45 for older vintages of reserve wines. Of particular note in recent seasons: Sauvignon Blanc (spot-on varietal flavors in a light, crisply refreshing wine), Cabernet Sauvignon (balanced, polished, easy to drink when it is released), Colombard Blanc (well nigh the perfect summer sipper). Also, Chardonnay, Zinfandel. A second label, North Coast Cellars, covers 150,000 cases of non-vintage, somewhat lesser lots of the same spectrum of types at correspondingly lower prices, $2.35–$5.

Sparkling Burgundy
A generic term for red sparkling wines. Most are moderate to inexpensively priced transfer or Charmat process wines. (Their more expensive counterparts usually go by the name of Champagne Rouge.)

Spottswoode Vineyard & Winery Napa T nyr
The first vintage from Harmon and Mary Brown's historic restoration at the w. side of St. Helena was '82, when they made 1,500 cases of Cabernet Sauvignon and Sauvignon Blanc from their 40 acres. Prices, on release during 1985, $8–$16.

Spring Mountain Vineyards Napa T ***
With the '84s, Spring Mountain became an estate winery, producing all of its 25,000 cases from owner Michael Robbin's two vineyards, one at his showplace winery w. of St. Helena, the other e. of Rutherford. The main label goes back to '68. Prices $10.50–$15. The collateral Falcon Crest label (appearing on Cabernet Sauvignon and Chardonnay) arose after the dreary soap opera of that name was set at the winery property.
• Sauvignon Blanc. The welcome first impression is of proper vinosity, the second of subtle varietal character. Benefits from a year or two in bottle. '80 '81
• Cabernet Sauvignon. Starts out a bit lean and austere, but rounds into a complex, balanced wine with time in bottle. '78 '79 '80
Also: Chardonnay, Pinot Noir.

Stag's Leap Wine Cellars Napa T [****]
The winery of Warren and Barbara Winiarski became an instant success in the mid-70s with grand showings in tastings in the U. S. and France, especially with Cabernet Sauvignon from the affiliated 40-acre Stag's Leap Vineyard, which adjoins the cellar s. e. of Yountville. It has gone from strength to

strength since. Annual production is edging past 30,000 cases. Prices $5–$15, and to $35 for special lot Cask 23 Cabernet Sauvignon. A second label, Hawk's Crest, is used principally for Cabernet Sauvignon blended from lesser lots made at the winery plus bought-in wines. Other varietals appear from time to time. Price $5.

• Cabernet Sauvignon-Stag's Leap Vineyard. Perfect evocation of Winiarski's attempt to hide the most malleable of iron fists inside the stoutest of velvet gloves. This is a wine in which tannin counts, but is masked by full flavors of ripe fruit. '75 '78 '79

• Cabernet Sauvignon-Cask 23. A riper, headier wine than the Stag's Leap Vineyard, but essentially similar.

• Johannisberg Riesling-Birkmyer Vineyard. The elegance and durable structure have gone too little noticed in recent years. Sometimes available as a late-harvest wine.

Also: Merlot (a softer cousin to the Cabernets), Chardonnay (honed so smooth it can be enjoyed by the impatient), Petite Sirah (as polished as the other wines in the roster, and as such a real sleeper), Sauvignon Blanc, Gamay Beaujolais.

Stags' Leap Winery Napa T **

Carl Doumani, whose vineyards are just to the n. of the Winiarski holdings, makes about 13,000 cases a year under the primary label and a second one, Pedregal. The roster in both cases is Cabernet Sauvignon, Merlot, Petite Sirah, and Pinot Noir. To date, Chenin Blanc has appeared only as Stag's Leap, Chardonnay only as Pedregal. In all cases, the style tends toward burly and assertive. Prices for Stag's Leap, $4.75–$15, and to $37.50 for library wines back to a debut '73 Petite Sirah that suggests (correctly) the durability of Doumani's reds. Prices for Pedregal $3–$7.50.

Staiger, P & M Santa Cruz T **

Paul and Marjorie Staiger make only Chardonnay and Cabernet Sauvignon, and only from 5 shy-bearing acres of vines at their aerie-like vineyard above the resort village of Boulder Creek. The annual 400 cases sells mostly from the winery. Prices $10–$12.

Stearns Wharf Vintners Santa Barbara T nyr

All of the wines come from the Santa Ynez Valley, where the label's owners lease a 40-acre vineyard and contract for other grapes to fill a roster of six ably made varietals led—in the early going—by a well-received Chardonnay. The firm also makes wines for a label called Warner West, using both Santa Barbara and San Luis Obispo County grapes. The winemaking goes on in leased space for both. Annual volume is 14,000 cases, with the Stearns Wharf wines sold mostly in

California, the Warner West ones mainly in Michigan (the home of Warner East, as it were). Prices $5–$8.50.

Steltzner Vineyard Napa T nyr
Cabernet Sauvignon from owner Dick Steltzner's vineyard in the Stag's Leap district e. of Yountville is the only wine on the list. It is just beginning to appear in the marketplace, though the first vintage was '77. Volume has edged up to 4,000 cases, and is planned to go to 6,000 with the '85. A bit of Cabernet Franc or Merlot may go into the blend from '84 onward. Price $14.

Stemmler Winery, Robert Sonoma T **/***
Veteran winemaker Robert Stemmler (ex-Charles Krug, Simi) started his own label with a set of '77s. His wines have gained character steadily as he has homed in on vineyards that meet his sense of style. All are currently from Sonoma grapes. The cellars are in Dry Creek Valley w. of Healdsburg. Annual production is 8,000 cases on the way to a planned peak of 10,000. Prices $7.50–$15.
• Pinot Noir. Fat, supple, sunny-ripe in the best California tradition. '81
• Chardonnay. Appealing fruit flavors lightly spiced with wood.
Also: Cabernet Sauvignon, Sauvignon Blanc.

Sterling Vineyards Napa T **/***
Since its founding in '69, Sterling has undergone all sorts of changes at the top—while the founders still owned it, when they sold it to Coca-Cola in 1978, and again when Seagrams Co., Ltd., bought the dramatic winery and its 350 acres of vineyards in 1983. The main effects for bibbers have been to trim the size a bit at each change of hands—to a current 75,000 cases—and, with that, to narrow the roster from 10 wines to 6 (using only 4 grape varieties). The surviving wines have changed style some, but not much.
• Sauvignon Blanc. Lean, austere, understated for fruit flavors. '81 '83
• Merlot. Soft, supple, full of fruit. '82
• Cabernet Sauvignon. Has lost the old note of v. a. that was an intentional hallmark for a while. Now a fine, conventional Napa Cabernet. '80
Also: Chardonnay (recent vintages have been all bouquet, even early), Blanc de Cabernet (dry, crisp, cleansing).

Stevenot Winery Calaveras T **
Barden Stevenot's winery and 27 acres of vineyard hide away in a deep canyon outside the Gold Rush town of Murphys, but its annual 50,000 cases of wine are spreading the name

across the country. The projected increase to 65,000 cases will take care of the last few unenlightened corners. The prides of the house are sturdy estate Cabernet Sauvignon, Chardonnay, and Zinfandel (pleasingly berryish). Larger bottlings of these varietals come from coastal vineyards. Other Sierra Foothill vineyards in Calaveras, Amador, and El Dorado counties supply the grapes for Chenin Blanc and Zinfandel Blanc. Prices $4.75–$10.

Stonegate Winery Napa T **
The winery of the James Spaulding family has built patiently on small beginnings in '73 to its current level of 15,000 cases. Since '83 all of the grapes have been from Napa, some from a patch at the winery s. of Calistoga, some from a family vineyard in the w. hills, some purchased. The roster is Cabernet Sauvignon (dark, plummy, tannic), Merlot (Estate), Chardonnay (Estate and Napa bottlings, both well marked by oak), and Sauvignon Blanc (fresh, beautifully fruity '83 followed heavier earlier vintages). Prices $8–$15.

Stoneridge Amador T *
Gary and Loretta Porteous make an annual 1,000 cases of White Zinfandel, Zinfandel, and Ruby Cabernet from their two small patches of vines s. of the Gold Rush town of Sutter Creek. The tendency in reds is to be hefty and heady (as much as 16% alcohol). The first vintage was '75. Prices $4.75–$5.25, mostly in local markets.

Stony Hill Vineyards Napa T ****
One of the first (if not the first) Napa cellars devoted to doing grand things on a small scale. Since the mid-1950s, it has been a premier voice in producing Chardonnay of distinctive style and unsurpassed substance. It and smaller amounts of Gewürztraminer and White Riesling come from Eleanor McCrea's steeply sloping 42 acres of vines high in the hills n. w. of St. Helena. Winemaker Mike Chelini's 4,000-case annual production sells almost exclusively by subscription. Prices $6–$12.

• Chardonnay. Delicacy of fruit flavors and astounding durability are its hallmarks. Demands 5 years and more in bottle to develop to its fullest. '73 '75 '78 '81 '82
• White Riesling. Intensely fruity and just off-dry, maybe the quintessential evocation of the berry-tart flavors of its grape. Prospers with two years in bottle. '81 '82

Also: Gewürztraminer (just off-dry, uncommonly delicate for varietal aroma), Sémillon de Soleil (a fine *vin de paille* sold only through Sacramento wine merchant Corti Brothers).

Stony Ridge Winery Alameda T, S */**
Newly built cellars on a 300-acre vineyard near the Livermore Valley town of Pleasanton went into receivership in December 1984, but the annual volume of 100,000 cases will keep the label in the market for some time. The roster included Chardonnay-Santa Maria Valley, Chevrier-Estate, Sauvignon Blanc-Estate, Malvasia Bianca-Estate, Zinfandel-Estate, Cabernet Sauvignon (two bottlings, one from Monterey, one North Coast), White Zinfandel, and Carignane. The wines are sometimes a bit rustic, sometimes more polished than that, but almost always marked by faint earthy overtones. Prices $4.50–$7.75, and to $15 for the Monterey Cabernet.

Story Vineyard Amador T *
The cellar, dating from 1973, makes three wines from Amador grapes—Premier White (a curiously interesting blend of 80% White Zinfandel and 20% Mission), non-vintage Zinfandel, and, most impressive, a strongly flavored, vintage-dated estate Zinfandel (fine '80) from proprietor Anne Story's 27 acres of ancient vines e. of Plymouth in the Shenandoah Valley. Production is 25,000 cases. Prices $3.95–$6.

Storybook Mountain Vineyards Napa T nyr
The product is estate-bottled Zinfandel from a hilly 36-acre vineyard n. of Calistoga and hard against the Sonoma County line. Both the regular bottling and smaller lots separately labelled as Barrel Select are enveloping wines, redolent of ripe fruit and oak. Owner Bernard J. Seps launched his label with '80s. The site was the pre-Prohibition vineyard and winery of two non-writing brothers Grimm, hence the fanciful name. Annual production is 4,000 cases. Prices $8.50–$12.50.

Stratford Napa T nyr
The label was launched in leased space with a fine '82 Chardonnay that speaks well for partner Tony Cartlidge's belief that blending yields better results than single-vineyard or even single-appellation wines while nobody knows exactly where is best for which grape varieties. (The case in point comes mainly from Monterey and Mt. Veeder in the Napa Valley, with smaller dollops from Carneros, Santa Maria Valley, and Alexander Valley.) There is also a Sauvignon Blanc. A winery is under construction s. e. of Rutherford for the '85s. Annual production is 33,000 cases and growing. Prices $6–$9.

Strong Vineyards, Rodney Sonoma T **
The name changed from Sonoma Vineyards during 1984 as part of a general effort to signal a narrowed focus and raised overall quality of wines produced from several well-regarded vineyards in the Russian River, Chalk Hill, and Alexander

Valley areas of Sonoma. The top wines in the line are vineyard-designated, including Cabernet Sauvignon-Alexander's Crown (dark, tannic, at its best in cool vintages such as '75, '79), Chardonnay-Chalk Hill (understated, light), Chardonnay-River West (riper, fuller of fruit), Johannisberg Riesling-LeBaron, Pinot Noir-River East, and Zinfandel-River West. Also in the lists are the same types designated only by area. Annual production is 150,000 cases, with plans to increase to 200,000. Prices $5.50–$12.

Sullivan Vineyard and Winery Napa T nyr
Dry Chenin Blanc ('81 matured quickly), Chardonnay, Cabernet Sauvignon (dark, heady), Merlot, and Zinfandel come from proprietor James Sullivan's own vineyards—two pieces, one at the winery s. of St. Helena, the other s. of Rutherford. The first crush was '81. Production is halfway to a planned peak of 8,000 cases. Prices $9–$14.

Summerhill Vineyards Santa Clara T, D nyr
New in 1982 (though built on the bones of an old country jug winery in the Hecker Pass district w. of Gilroy), Summerhill offers a broad spectrum of varietal table wines, plus some dessert wines. They have been sound, relatively steady. A Cabernet Sauvignon is estate-grown; the rest are bought-in as grapes or wine. Volume approaches 30,000 cases. Prices $3.75 for the table wines, to $15 for a '73 Aleatico.

Summit
A label belonging to Geyser Peak.

Sunrise Winery Santa Clara T *
Since its beginnings in 1976, the winery has moved from a mountaintop above Boulder Creek to a low ridge w. of Cupertino, reorganized its ownership, changed winemakers, and otherwise refused to sit still long enough to have its picture taken. The current roster of proprietors and wines begins to look permanent. Ronald and Rolayne Stortz are offering 2,500 cases of Sauvignon Blanc-San Luis Obispo, Chardonnay-North Coast, Zinfandel-Sonoma, Pinot Noir-Sonoma, and Cabernet Sauvignon-Santa Cruz Mountains. Beginning with '84 there will be an estate Zinfandel from ancient vines. Prices $6–$7.50, mostly in California.

Susiné Cellars Solano T nyr
Launched with '81s, the 1,000-case winery of Charles O'Brien produces Cabernet Sauvignon, Sauvignon Blanc, and Gewürztraminer from purchased Napa grapes, plus an Amador Zinfandel. Most sales are from the cellar, on a side street in Fairfield; nearly all are in northern California. Prices are $5.50–$5.75.

Sutter Home T **
For all practical purposes, proprietor-winemaker Bob Trinchero invented White Zinfandel, and has ridden the resulting wave from a 20,000-case winery to a 600,000-case one. The cellars are s. of St. Helena, but the grapes come from the Sierra Foothills, mostly Amador, to some degree El Dorado County. The White Zinfandel is perfumey of its fruit, and noticeably sweet. New in '85: a sparkling White Zinfandel. Sutter Home's Red Zinfandel is hearty, heady, and ripe in the Amador tradition Trinchero did much to establish beginning in the late 1960s and early 1970s. The roster of Zinfandels rounds out with an El Dorado Dessert bottling in the high alcohol, sweet style others call late-harvest. Prices $4.50–$5.95, and to $8.75 for a Reserve. Also available, mainly at the winery: Moscato Amabile and Triple Cream Sherry.

Swan Vineyards, Joseph Sonoma T ***
Retired airline pilot Joseph Swan pursues an intensely personal style of winemaking in his 1,200-case cellar not far from Forestville in the Russian River Valley. The wines, all estate-grown from Swan's 10-acre vineyard, are Chardonnay, Pinot Noir, and a tiny bit Cabernet Sauvignon. Swan also makes small lots of Zinfandel from grapes purchased in Dry Creek Valley. Sales are almost entirely to a subscription list. Prices $9–$15.

Sycamore Creek Santa Clara T **
A one-time Hecker Pass jug winery was rebuilt by Walter and Mary Kaye Parks into a modern 5,000-case cellar producing increasingly well-regarded vintage-dated varietals from a range of Central Coast vineyards. Chardonnays (three bottlings from vineyards in Monterey, a fourth from the home property) dominate production. Also on the list: Johannisberg Riesling-Monterey, Gewürztraminer-Monterey, Cabernet Sauvignon-Central Coast (in fact Monterey; '81 very ripe, heady), Pinot Noir-Monterey, Carignane-Estate, and Zinfandel-Estate. The first vintage for the Parkses was '75. Prices $4–$12, and to $20 for a special lot of Cabernet.

Sylvaner
The grape and its wine. Both are alternatively known as Franken Riesling (see p. 20).

Syrah
The black grape and its wine (see p. 24).

t. a. (**total acid**)
Natural fruit acids give (or fail to give) wine its characteristic crispness or freshness. In California, they usually are measured as tartaric, and shown on labels either as percent or

grams per liter. The normal range is .4% to 1.0% (or .4 to 1 gram per liter). For reds the desired range is .5–.7% (or .5 to .7 grams per liter), for whites from .5% to 1%, depending on how much r. s. (residual sugar) there is to balance against the acid.

Taft Street Sonoma T nyr
The winery of Michael and John Tierney jumped up quickly from 825 cases in its first vintage, '82, to 7,000 in '84. The goal is 15,000 cases of just four wines: Chardonnay (from Santa Barbara and Sonoma), white house wine, Medallion (a blend of Napa Cabernet Sauvignon and Cabernet Franc with Sonoma Merlot, well made, though '82 was curiously soft and fleshy), and house red. Prices $4.50–$9.75.

tannins
Compounds (polyphenols) naturally concentrated in grape skins and seeds, which give esp. red wine its color and its puckering sensation in the mouth. Their primary function is to protect against oxidation, allowing wine a longer life. Tannins tend to be harsh in young wine, softening with age.

Tavola
A brand of Guild Wineries & Distilleries.

Taylor California Cellars Monterey T, S */**
Seagrams now owns a highly successful commercial label launched by the Coca-Cola Co. The wines (both generics and varietals) blend San Joaquin Valley fruit fermented under contract there with Central Coast grapes made at Taylor's own cellar or right next door in the sister Monterey Vineyard cellars. The wines styled to be affably appealing. Annual volume of about 7 million cases includes Chardonnay and Cabernet Sauvignon as well as French Colombard, Chenin Blanc, and generics. The sparklers are Charmat, in a range of styles from Brut to Pink. Prices $4–$6.

Temecula
An AVA in Riverside County, near its s. w. corner. See maps.

Tepusquet
A grower-owned label offering custom-made Claret (Cabernet Sauvignon and Merlot), Vin Blanc (Chardonnay and Sauvignon Blanc), and Hock (Riesling) from Tepusquet Vineyard. It is a 1,500-acre property in the Santa Maria Valley, near the n. boundary of Santa Barbara County. Production in 1984 was 60,000 cases after a startup in 1983. The thought is to grow to 80,000 in 1985, more after that. Prices $4.99, and to $8.75 for Vineyard Reserve Claret and Vin Blanc.

Thomas Vineyards
A label and sales outlet in Cucamonga belonging to J. Filippi.

Tijsseling Vineyard Mendocino T, S nyr
A family with 285 acres of grapes spread across several thousand acres of hilly country between Hopland and Ukiah makes 40,000 cases per year of Chardonnay (toasty and pineapple-ripe), Sauvignon Blanc (oaky, poor man's Chardonnay), Cabernet Sauvignon (strong varietal, '81 harsh in youth), Petite Sirah, and *méthode champenoise* Brut under the family name. The first vintage was '81. Prices $7–$12. In a separate winery on the same property, the Tijsselings produce another 8,000 cases of table and sparkling wines under the older (to '79) Tyland label. Prices $3.99–$8.

Tinta Madeira
The black grape and varietal Port-types made from it (see p. 24).

Tinta Port
Essentially a synonym for Ruby Port, though custom dictates the use of "Tinta Madeira" and other Portuguese grapes rather than non-Portuguese varieties.

T. K. C. Amador T *
The only wine is Zinfandel from grapes purchased from neighbors in the Shenandoah Valley e. of Plymouth. The wine is characteristically ripe, and rough-hewn in the tradition of the territory. Owner-winemaker Harold Nuffer commutes from a full-time job as an engineer at China Lake Naval Air Station to make about 1,000 cases a year. Price $5.

Topolos at Russian River Vineyards Sonoma T */**
Mike Topolos makes a range of sturdy, straightforward varietals from grapes purchased in several Sonoma districts. Reds are the particular focus, especially Petite Sirah, Pinot Noir, and Zinfandel. The label dates from '78. Annual production in an imitation Russian wooden fort near Forestville approaches 8,000 cases. Prices $4–$12.

Toyon Winery and Vineyards Sonoma T */**
Two Cabernet Sauvignons—one from a 6-acre estate vineyard, the other vineyard-identified—and two Sauvignon Blancs—one lot barrel-fermented—are the mainstays of Don Holm's 2,500-case winery in Healdsburg. These wines and small lots of Chardonnay are all from Sonoma County grapes. The first crush was '79. Prices $5.29–$10.

transfer process
Method of producing sparkling wine in which bottles are emptied into a pressurized tank after secondary fermentation

so filtering can remove sediments, rather than using the laborious *méthode champenoise* process of riddling. Such wines usually have the words "bottle fermented" or "fermented in the bottle" on their labels, rather than "*méthode champenoise*" or "fermented in this bottle," as traditionally riddled wines do.

Traulsen Vineyards Napa T nyr
Zinfandel is the only wine John Traulsen makes. One lot comes from his own 2-acre vineyard at Calistoga. The other is from purchased Dry Creek Valley grapes. Both were heavyweights in Traulsen's first vintage, '80. There are but 500 cases a year, all sold in California. Price $6.75.

Trefethen Vineyards Napa T [***]
Major grower Gene Trefethen and his family select small lots from their 600-acre vineyard at the n. limit of Napa city to make wine for the family label. The results have been consistently fine and stylish from their first vintage ('74) onward. Production has edged up to 60,000 cases. Prices $4.25–$13.50.
• Chardonnay. Silky textures harmonize perfectly with subtle but complex fruit flavors and a mere whisper of oak. '78 '80 '81 '82
• Johannisberg Riesling. Wonderfully lighthearted companion to cold cracked Dungeness crab. Best as young as possible, when varietal flavors are freshest.
• Cabernet Sauvignon. Balanced wines have aged well. Most vintages carry a distinct flavor of American oak. '75 '77 '78 '79
Also: Pinot Noir (rich, plummy, purely Californian), Eschol White (excellent value styled after Chardonnays), Eschol Red (another fine value with noticeable character from "Cabernet Sauvignon").

Trentadue Winery Sonoma T *
After a good start in the mid-70s, the winery has staggered in recent vintages, but appears to be righting itself with a new winemaker who had a first hand in the '83s. All the wines come from proprietor Leo Trentadue's 200-acre vineyard in Alexander Valley between Healdsburg and Geyserville. The roster includes Chardonnay, Sauvignon Blanc, White Zinfandel, Cabernet Sauvignon, Petite Sirah, and Zinfandel, plus tiny bits of such unusual varietals as Nebbiolo and Aleatico. Annual production is about 10,000 cases. Prices $4–$7.

Tudal Winery Napa T [**/***]
Arnold Tudal and family planted a small vineyard n. of St. Helena to "Cabernet Sauvignon" in 1974. They built a cellar

on the property in time to make an impressive '79, the first of a consistent series. A bit of Chardonnay (sometimes Napa, sometimes Edna Valley) fills the odd corner of a 3,000-case winery in vintages when there is room to spare. Prices $9–$11.

• Cabernet Sauvignon. Dark and full of flavor without being overripe, heavy, or tannic. '79 '80 '81

Tulocay Vineyards Napa T **/***

A family winery e. of Napa city attempts to do grand things on a small scale, and succeeds, notably in reds. Bill Cadman makes Pinot Noir, Cabernet Sauvignon, and Zinfandel, plus some Chardonnay, all from purchased Napa grapes. Annual production is 2,000 cases. Prices $6.50–$9. The first vintage was '75.

• Pinot Noir. Cadman seems to have a touch with this variety. The result is not Burgundian, but is deft, superior in varietal character, almost meaty in texture. Pleasing to drink young or after a few years. '79 '80

Turner Winery San Joaquin T *

Major growers in Lake County bought a sizable old winery n. of Lodi when they decided to open their own winery in 1979 (after operating in leased space since 1975). The 10 varietals are from their own 580 acres in the Clear Lake area. Generics are from grapes purchased in the Lodi area and nearby. The whole roster has been sound but plain. Annual production is 80,000 cases (plus double that amount of a wine cooler called Highland). Price $2.75–$7, and to $14 for a Proprietor's Reserve Cabernet Sauvignon.

Tyland Vineyards

A winery and label belonging to the proprietors of Tijsseling Vineyards.

v. a. (volatile acidity)

Mostly acetic acid, the basis of vinegar. Tiny amounts are inevitable in wine and—as a flavor complication—desirable. However, the level must be kept at a controlled minimum or wine will spoil. Normal concentrations at bottling are 0.025–0.040% in whites and 0.050–0.070% in reds. See also: t. a.

Valley of the Moon Sonoma T, D */**

A durable Sonoma Valley cellar n. w. of Sonoma town draws on the owning Parducci family's 200-acre vineyard for all of its long list of varietal and generic table wines. The old standbys are Zinfandel, a dry French Colombard, and the generics. Recent vintages of White Zinfandel, Pinot Noir, and Cabernet Sauvignon have been steadily appealing values. Sherries, Ports, and Charmat sparklers are also available under the label. Annual production nears 50,000 cases a year. Prices $2.95–$7.

varietal
Wine named for a predominating grape variety. See p. 13.

Vega Vineyards & Winery Santa Barbara T */**
Estate-bottled wines of the Mosby family's 7,500-case winery at Buellton are Johannisberg Riesling and Gewürztraminer, from 30 acres of vines in the Santa Ynez Valley. The roster rounds out with Chardonnay, Cabernet Sauvignon, and Pinot Noir, all from Santa Barbara County grapes, the Pinot Noir partly from family-owned vineyards. The wines have been sound if a bit plain since the label began with a '78 Johannisberg Riesling. Prices $6–$9.50.

Ventana Vineyards Monterey T **/***
A much-praised 350-acre vineyard supplies its own small winery and, it seems, scores of others. The Ventana winery has been trimmed back from a peak 15,000 cases in 1981 to 5,000 in 1984, at which time founder J. Douglas Meadow had the property for sale. Chardonnay is the flagship of both vineyard and winery. Other wines of particular interest on the roster: White Riesling, Pinot Noir, and a plethora of *Botrytis*-affected wines of several varieties. Prices $4–$14, and to $20 for botrytized specialties.

Vermouth
Wine-based apéritif flavored with patented formulas of herbs and spices. White vermouth usually is dry whereas red is sweet.

Viano Winery Contra Costa T *
An old-line family operation at one edge of the town of Martinez, Viano makes sound, sensible, country wines for modest prices ($2.25–$8), and sells most of them at the cellar door. Proprietor Clem Viano gets most of his grapes from his own 60-acre vineyard flanking the winery. Zinfandel is the mainstay.

Vichon Napa T nyr
After a brilliant start under other owners, the winery was purchased in 1985 by the Robert Mondavi family. Changes in direction, if any, remain to be seen.
All 50,000 cases of Vichon's consistently attractive wines come from purchased Napa grapes. The short roster is Chardonnay (subtle, bouquetish early after partial barrel fermentation and aging on the lees), Chevrignon (50:50 blend of Sauvignon Blanc and Sémillon was wonderfully tart and cleansing in '80 as "Chevrier Blanc" and again in '83 under its new name), and Cabernet Sauvignon (subtle, well balanced

for aging). Prices $9.50–$15, more for vineyard-designated Cabernet Sauvignons.

Villa Armando Alameda T *
An old-line winery in the Livermore Valley town of Pleasanton has recently outgrown those quarters and is moving into new ones e. of Livermore itself. Most of the new impetus has come from wine coolers (California Special, California Sunshine, Tropical). The roster of table wines has long been dominated by the heavy, off-dry style associated with the house wines of inexpensive Italian restaurants. There are varietals also (Chardonnay, Cabernet Sauvignon, Petite Sirah, Malvasia Bianca) from a 200-acre vineyard s. of Pleasanton. Annual volume is 800,000 cases including the coolers. Prices $3.29–$10 for the table wines.

Villa Mt. Eden Napa T **/***
Since his winery's first vintage, '74, owner Jim McWilliams has weeded varieties out of his vineyard e. of Oakville until he is down to the ones that have given him his best wines. Pinot Noir and Gewürztraminer are going out of the lists after the '82s, leaving only Chenin Blanc (dry, well marked by oak), Chardonnay (ditto), and Cabernet Sauvignon (probably to be blended with small, recently planted proportions of "Merlot" and "Cabernet Franc"). Production is at 18,000 cases of estate wines from 87 acres. Prices $5–$12, and to $25 for Reserve Cabernet.
• Cabernet Sauvignon. From the outset, has leaned toward the dark, tannic school. The hallmark is intense varietal character from ripe but not overripe fruit. '78 '79

Villa Paradiso Santa Clara T *
Hank and Judy Bogardus make less than 1,000 cases a year of Paso Robles Merlot and Hecker Pass Petite Sirah and Zinfandel at an old winery building w. of Morgan Hill, and sell from the winery. They launched the label with a '79, after several years of deepening involvement as home winemakers. Prices $4.25–$8.

Vinmark
Label belonging to Markham Vineyards.

Vose Vineyards Napa T **
From 35 acres of vineyard well up Mt. Veeder in Napa's w. hills, Hamilton Vose III makes estate Chardonnay, Cabernet Sauvignon, and Zinfandel. He buys grapes for Sonoma Sauvignon Blanc, Napa Gewürztraminer, and a California white Zinfandel called Zinblanca that round out production at 10,000 cases. The first vintage was '77. The wines have been ripe, and a bit weighty. Prices $4.50–$12.50.

Walker Winery Santa Cruz T **
Launched in 1979 by Russell Walker as a first step up from home winemaking. His tiny but well-equipped cellar at Felton in the Santa Cruz Mountains area produces slightly less than 1,000 cases of Chardonnay, Sauvignon Blanc, and Cabernet Sauvignon, from grapes purchased in varied parts of the Central Coast. Sales are local. Prices $6–$9.95.

Warnelius Vineyards Sonoma T nyr
Owner-winemaker Nils Warnelius started his label with '82 Petite Sirah and White Zinfandel from a block of old vines he owns, and, in '85, will add Sauvignon Blanc, Chardonnay, and one or more blends from traditional Bordeaux varieties he is growing in a 54-acre block of new vines. Both parcels and the winery are s. of Cloverdale in the northern Alexander Valley. His announced style is light and dry. Current production is 3,000 cases and growing toward 15,000. Price for the debut wines: $4.50.

Watson Vineyards San Luis Obispo T nyr
Chardonnay, Johannisberg Riesling, and Pinot Noir come from owner Bryan Watson's 10-acre vineyard—part of Ignace Paderewski's old estate toward the w. boundary of the Paso Robles area. (In the great pianist's day it was famous for Zinfandel.) A Chenin Blanc comes from another small vineyard nearby. Production approaches 1,800 cases on the way to a goal of 5,000. The first vintage was '82. Prices $6–$8.

Weibel Champagne Vineyards Alameda/Mendocino S, T, D */**
A well-established family firm continues a steady upgrading begun several years ago. The latest signal is the release of Special Reserve Cabernet Sauvignons (which have aged attractively) and Pinot Noirs that constitute the first release of ongoing six-year vertical selections from their 450 acres of Mendocino vineyards. Other varietals from the winery n. of Ukiah include Chardonnay and Zinfandel. However, the mainstay remains sparklers (mostly Charmat and transfer process) made from a variety of sources at their original winery directly s. of Mission San Jose, on the e. side of San Francisco Bay. The total volume (including second and private labels) is around 1 million cases. Prices $2.50–$9.50, and to $14 for older vintages.

Wente Bros. Alameda T, S [**]
One of California's grand old names for white wines changes with changing times, but stays in fine form. The winery and 1,300 acres of vines are where they began in 1883, in the Livermore Valley. However, there are another 600 acres of

Woodbrook
A label belonging to Gibson Wine Company.

Woodbury Winery Marin D **
One of several dedicated specialists working to renew public interest in Port-types, Russ Woodbury makes about 3,000 cases a year of "Old Vines" Vintage Port and Alexander Valley Reserve Dessert Wine, both from Alexander Valley grapes. His first declared vintage was '77. It has been followed by '78, '79, and '81. Prices $8.50–$10. There also is a bit of pot-still, 8-year-old brandy.

Wooden Valley Winery Solano T, S, D *
Proprietor Mario Lanza offers one of almost every wine-type known in California only through his tasting and sales room in Wooden Valley, a small agricultural enclave n. of Fairfield. Prices $1.20–$3.50.

Woodside Vineyards Santa Clara T **
Bob and Polly Mullen make 1,000 cases of wine a year at Woodside town—a local Cabernet Sauvignon from their surviving bit of the legendary LaQuesta Vineyard (one of California's most famous before Prohibition), and two Chardonnays, one from the home neighborhood, the other from Monterey. Both wines from the Woodside area (the northern tip of the Santa Cruz Mountains) are distinctive. Prices $10.50–$11.50.

York Mountain
A small AVA in hilly country w. of Templeton in San Luis Obispo County, at the w. flank of the far larger Paso Robles area.

York Mountain Winery San Luis Obispo T, S *
Max Goldman brought the historic property in 1970 with the intention of turning it into a *méthode champenoise* sparkling house. The notion has changed. Now a pair of sparkling wines is bought-in, and emphasis is on estate-grown Chardonnay, Pinot Noir, and Zinfandel bottled under the Ascension label. Those wines are joined by Cabernet Sauvignon, Merlot, generic table wines, and a Dry Sherry offered under the York Cellars brand. Annual production is 3,000 cases. Prices $1.95–$9.50.

Yverdon Vineyards Napa T */**
Though the winery high on Spring Mountain w. of St. Helena dates from 1970, it has had enough gaps in its production to remain more an unknown factor than a proven one. Current production is limited to small lots of Cabernet Sauvignon and Chardonnay from owner-winemaker Fred Aves's vineyards (one n. of Calistoga, the other at the winery). Price $8.

Zaca Mesa Santa Barbara T ***

One of the pioneers in Santa Ynez Valley grape growing and winemaking is also one of the most impressive. Owner Marshall Ream has 240 acres near the winery, another 110 a few miles n. in neighboring Santa Maria Valley. Other local grapes supplement these bases for his 80,000-case winery. Meanwhile, winemaker Ken Brown has produced an unbroken stream of attractive, consistently styled varietal wines. Prices $4.50–$6 for second-quality lots subtitled Toyon, $6–$9 for the basic list, and $6.75–$12 for prized bottlings subtitled American Reserve.

• Chardonnay. Regular and American Reserve both richly aromatic of ripe fruit. Nice touch of oak as a sort of obligato. Deftly balanced in a big style.

• Johannisberg Riesling. Spot-on varietal flavors in a luscious sipper (usually 2% r. s.).

• Pinot Noir, American Reserve. Like the Chardonnay, rich and ripe. Has a distinctive regional overtone to the basic varietal character. Seems best with 4 or 5 years in bottle.

Also: Sauvignon Blanc (stout presence of regional cooked asparagus flavors), Cabernet Sauvignon, Zinfandel, Toyon Blanc.

ZD Napa T **

Gino Zepponi and Norman De Leuze moved their winery from Sonoma to Napa in 1979 without changing their minds about style. Chardonnay (a blend of Napa, Sonoma, and Santa Barbara grapes), Pinot Noir (Napa, sometimes with a separate Santa Maria Valley bottling as a running mate), and Cabernet Sauvignon (Napa, again with a separate bottling from Santa Maria as occasional company) are the mainstay wines. All are husky. All share a hallmark smack of oak that many practiced tasters identify swiftly as American. Annual volume is 10,000 cases. Prices $10–$14.

Zellerbach Vineyard, Steven Sonoma T **

From the first, the reds from Zellerbach's 54-acre vineyard and 16,000-case winery at the southern tip of Alexander Valley have leaned toward the dark, tannic, and heady end of the stylistic stick, and been much admired as such. The whites have been ripe and full as well. Cabernet Sauvignon and Merlot come from the winery vineyard. Chardonnay comes from a neighbor on the opposite side of Chalk Hill Road. Prices $8–$9.95.

Zinfandel

The black grape and its wines (see p. 24).

Zinfandel Rosé

Varietal pink wine from "Zinfandel" grapes.

Wine and Food

The best part of drinking wine is discovering which ones fit best with favorite dishes. This is an altogether personal enterprise not subject to rules, and barely subject to suggestion. Still, the experience of others can make at least useful signposts.

Most of the combinations given in this section follow convention. They represent consensus to the extent that it exists. A few are personal choices tossed into the pot to help push against set habits. As California continues its explosive expansion with new wineries, new districts, even new grape varieties, there is much to be gained by exploring. It is a considerable hope that the recommendations here will serve only as departure points for more wide-ranging looks at what is available.

The use of stars follows the same rating system as is used throughout the alphabetic listing (see p. 11).

APPETIZERS

Caviar ***/**** Brut or Natural Champagne.

Cheeses See p. 206.

Cheese pastries Dry Sherry or any favorite white wine.

Clams, smoked Dry Sherry.

Cream molds Off-dry whites, esp. French Colombard.

Crêpes, mushroom **/*** Sauvignon Blanc or Johannisberg Riesling.

Fondue Chablis or dry Chenin Blanc.

Gougere Pinot Noir Blanc, Gamay, or modest Pinot Noir.

Liver pâté *** Gewürztraminer, Johannisberg Riesling, or Champagne.

Mushrooms
- **plain** Pinot Blanc or Chablis.
- **stuffed** Dry Sherry, dry rosé or Blanc de Noir, Gewürztraminer.
- **Morels, butter-sautéed** Champagne.

Oysters on the half shell ***/**** Brut Champagne or delicate Chardonnay.

Smoked salmon, trout, sturgeon Champagne.

Vegetables, raw (with dip) Dry rosé or Blanc de Noir.

FIRST COURSES OR LUNCHEONS

Artichokes
- **with lemon and butter** ** Dry to off-dry, full-bodied white.
- **bread crumb stuffing** Grignolino rosé or other dry rosé.

Asparagus ** Chardonnay for the echo of flavor, dry rosé for contrast, or dry Johannisberg Riesling as German classic.

Avocado with seafood stuffing *** Pinot Blanc or Sauvignon Blanc.

Clams, baked and seasoned *** Dry Chenin Blanc or Pinot Blanc.

Mushrooms, sautéed, on toast **/*** Off-dry, flowery Gewürztraminer or Extra Dry Champagne.

Pasta
- **cream sauce or creamy casserole** Dry Chenin Blanc or Pinot Blanc, Zinfandel, or quality Burgundy.
- **clam sauce** **/*** Chenin Blanc or Johannisberg Riesling.
- **herb sauce** Zinfandel or Grignolino.
- **lasagne** Any hearty red.
- **pesto sauce** Sauvignon Blanc.
- **polenta** Zinfandel, White Zinfandel, or modest Chardonnay.
- **raviolis** Sauvignon Blanc, Burgundy, or Zinfandel.
- **tomato sauce** */*** Generic red or Zinfandel, depending on how delicate the sauce and how fancy the dinner.
- **tomato and meat** Barbera.

Prosciutto with melon **/*** Johannisberg Riesling or Gewürztraminer sweet enough to play against the salty meat.

Quiche

Lorraine Johannisberg Riesling or dry rosé.

vegetable ** Off-dry Johannisberg Riesling to contrast fruit with vegetable, or Sauvignon Blanc to echo the vegetable.

shellfish *** Off-dry (to .9% r. s.) Johannisberg Riesling

Soups

carrot, puréed Johannisberg Riesling.

Chili con carne Mountain red, if one must, but beer is better.

cream of vegetable Chablis or dry Chenin Blanc.

meat and vegetable Blanc de Noir or light red (Grignolino, Gamay).

French onion Fruity white or Zinfandel Rosé.

seafood chowder or bisque Rhine, Johannisberg Riesling, Chablis, or, for Sunday best, Sonoma Chardonnay.

consommé Pale Dry Sherry.

Salads, greens

with blue cheese dressing Light, young red.

vinegar or lemon dressing Murderous to all wines.

ENTRÉES—Fish and Shellfish

Abalone *** Off-dry Johannisberg Riesling or Sauvignon Blanc.

Bass, perch, et al. ** Light, crisp, coast counties Chablis or Pinot Blanc.

Clams

steamed Off-dry Sylvaner, Emerald Riesling, or Gray Riesling.

fried French Colombard.

Cod, sea bass, rockfish, et al. Wide range of dry or off-dry whites.

Crab

Cioppino Zinfandel, or Barbera if sauce is thick.

Dungeness, cold cracked ***/**** Off-dry Johannisberg Riesling.

Eastern (or blue) Johannisberg Riesling.

King or Snow ** Chardonnay with little or no oak, or Dry Chenin Blanc.

Louis French Colombard or Johannisberg Riesling.

Crayfish, boiled Off-dry Johannisberg Riesling.

Halibut, grilled or poached, with lemon butter Sauvignon Blanc or Chardonnay

Lobster, whole or tails, with drawn butter **** Chardonnay of the richest flavors to be found, preferably with bottle age.

Monkfish, Sablefish Chardonnay, Pinot Blanc.

Mussels Sylvaner, Emerald Riesling, or understated ** Johannisberg Riesling.

Oysters
- **baked** *** Chardonnay of tart, delicate quality.
- **fried** Dry Chablis or Dry Chenin Blanc.

Salmon
- **baked** (plain or with cream or wine sauce) ***/**** Chardonnay typical of Napa.
- **baked with herbs** ***/**** Chardonnay or oaky Sauvignon Blanc.
- **barbecued** Surprise! Subtle Zinfandel, à la Louis M. Martini.
- **butter-sautéed steaks** Wide range of dry whites.
- **Gravlax or lox** **** Blanc de Noir Champagne. Or Pale Dry Sherry, Gewürztraminer, or other strongly flavored wine—to be taken alternately more than together.

Scallops Very difficult. Best hope is tart, understated white.

Shad roe Chardonnay with little or no oak.

Shrimp or prawns
- **fried in butter** Chardonnay.
- **Louis** French Colombard or other off-dry white.
- **plain** Wide range of off-dry whites.

Sole, petrale, sand dabs
- **baked** Dry Chenin Blanc, Chablis.
- **fried or grilled** Chablis, Sylvaner, Gray Riesling.
- **poached** Dry Chenin Blanc or Folle Blanche.

Squid or baby octopus
- **fried** French Colombard or other fruity white.
- **marinated** As above.
- **stewed with tomatoes and garlic** Grignolino or other bright, dry red or balanced Sauvignon Blanc.

Trout **/*** Chablis or barely off-dry Johannisberg Riesling.

Tuna steaks, broiled with bacon Chardonnay.

ENTRÉES—Poultry

Chicken

barbecued Any youthful, dry white or red, but especially Burgundy, Gamay, Chenin Blanc, or Riesling priced to fit the solemnity of the occasion.

fried Any dry or off-dry white.

whole roast Understated, bottle-aged Zinfandel or Cabernet Sauvignon, or dry Chenin Blanc or ** Chardonnay.

Duck, roasted ***/**** Cabernet Sauvignon, well aged, no matter which sauce, except cherry.

Goose, roasted ***/**** Cabernet Sauvignon or Petite Sirah with enough bottle age to be delicate but still some tannin to cut the fats.

Quail Blanc de Noir, aged Cabernet Sauvignon.

Rabbit

in wine stew Light, fruity Zinfandel or Gamay.

with prunes Pinot Noir.

Squab **** Chardonnay or Cabernet Sauvignon, depending on preference for white or red.

Turkey

roasted, with all the trimmings Chardonnay or well-aged Cabernet Sauvignon for fancy company, dry Chenin Blanc or Gamay for less stately occasions.

smoked *** Blanc de Noir or richly flavored Johannisberg Riesling.

ENTRÉES—Pork

Chops

baked Gamay or other fruity red.

fried Burgundy, dry rosé, or Blanc de Noir.

stuffed **/*** Zinfandel or Sauvignon Blanc.

Ham A ham is a ham is a ham. Drink rosé.

Loin, roasted **/*** Chardonnay or Pinot Noir with a year or two of bottle age.

with sage dressing *** Zinfandel with a bit of bottle age.

prune stuffing Dry Sauvignon Blanc of intense varietal character, or subtle Sonoma or Napa Zinfandel.

Sausages, baked, broiled, or barbecued Gamay, dry rosé, or Gewürztraminer.

Spareribs
baked, plain Frisky young red, esp. Zinfandel or Grignolino.
with sauce Tannic Petite Sirah or crisp Blanc de Noir.

ENTRÉES—Lamb

Chops ** Dry red, especially Zinfandel, perhaps Petite Sirah.

Crown roast *** Older Zinfandel or Cabernet Sauvignon.

Kebabs */** Burgundy or Zinfandel.

Leg, whole roasted, butterflied and grilled *** Petite Sirah, husky Zinfandel, young Cabernet Sauvignon.

Moussaka ** Soft red, especially Burgundy or Merlot.

Niçoise ** Zinfandel in its frisky youth.

Shanks, baked in wine Stout red, esp. Barbera or Petite Sirah.

ENTRÉES—Beef

Hamburger, meat loaf Burgundy, Gamay, lighter Zinfandel.

Liver ** Soft red, especially Merlot or a subtle Zinfandel.

Oxtail ** Zinfandel or Petite Sirah with some tannic backbone to help cut the fatty qualities.

Prime rib or roast ***/**** Pinot Noir. Beef and Pinot Noir fatten each other.

Steak **/**** Favorite red.

Stew (bourguignon or other) A red every bit as good as the one in the recipe.

Stroganoff Generic red, Gamay, or Zinfandel.

Tongue Red or white generic.

ENTRÉES—Veal

Kidneys *** Merlot or a less tannic Cabernet Sauvignon.

Osso bucco *** Zinfandel.

Parmigiana **/*** Zinfandel of character.

Roast *** Zinfandel of finesse and some age, or Merlot of similar qualities. Many prefer fine dry whites.

Scallopine *** Johannisberg Riesling, just off-dry, is a flawless match. Dry Sauvignon Blanc or Chenin Blanc is almost as good.

Stew, with mushrooms ** Coast counties red generic or Zinfandel.

Sweetbreads ***/**** Cabernet Sauvignon aged to maturity, especially if the sauce is Madeira.

ENTRÉES—Game

Duck, wild ***/**** Cabernet Sauvignon, preferably mature.

Frogs' legs **** Chardonnay, partly in tribute to the price.

Pheasant ***/**** Pinot Noir, preferably mature.

Venison **/*** Zinfandel is the middle ground. Seasonal flavors from forage and quality of cut suggest a wide range of wines, but dry and intensely flavorful are the common qualities.

ENTRÉES—Eggs

Omelets Depends entirely on amount and flavor of stuffing; best bets for seafood or herb omelets are off-dry generic whites, Sylvaner, or Gray Riesling.

Scrambled Choose wine at your own risk.

Soufflés Much the same as for omelets; Champagne for fancy occasions.

SAUCES

Brown Wide range of reds; choice depends largely on the meat.

Cheese Red or white from the lighter end of the spectrum.

Curry Gewürztraminer or off-dry Johannisberg Riesling, if no beer is to be found.

Garlic Sauvignon Blanc of the most intense varietal character for white meats, Merlot for red meats.

Herb Sauvignon Blanc for white meats, Zinfandel for reds.

Hollandaise Dry Chenin Blanc or other fruity white.

Lemon Uncommonly difficult to match. If not too citric, a French Colombard or Folle Blanche.

Mustard Gamay or other not-too-tannic red, or Johannisberg Riesling.

Onion Red or white depending on the meat, but intensely fruity in either case.

Red wine The same wine as in the sauce, or one shade finer.

Seafood Johannisberg Riesling, typically, or lighter Chardonnays.

Sweet and sour Gewürztraminer, Rosé, or Blanc de Noir.

Tomato-cream Dry Chenin Blanc, Pinot Blanc, or Chardonnay, depending on the elegance of the dish.

White Chenin Blanc, Johannisberg Riesling, or Sauvignon Blanc.

White wine The same wine as in the sauce, or one shade finer.

CHEESES

Blue cheeses

- **Oregon, Danablu, sweet gorgonzola** Pinot Noir or Tinta Port.
- **Roquefort, Stilton** Late-harvest or other heady Zinfandel, and better young than old.

Cheddar and cheddar types ** Zinfandel for milder-flavored ones to *** older Cabernet Sauvignon or Petite Sirah for sharper, aged types. Ports also do well. If as appetizer, Dry Sherry.

Goat cheese, fresh Gamay Beaujolais.

Firm, full-flavored cheeses: Port Salut, Esrom, Münster Wide range of young reds, or, possibly, Blanc de Noir or Johannisberg Riesling, the latter two esp. as appetizers.

Swiss, Gruyère, Samsoe **/*** Pinot Noir still in the flush of its youth.

Mild semi-softs: Edam, Gouda, Fontina, Jack Old red of quality, or old Port. If as appetizer, pale Dry Sherry.

Brie, Camembert Slightly underripe they go with almost any good wine, esp. Pinot Noir; ripe or overripe, they wipe out every wine.

DESSERTS

Rich desserts and sweet wines are almost impossible to balance, and sate too soon even if they can be brought into harmony. Better to choose one or the other especially where there's chocolate. If you choose wine, contrasting accompaniments can please.

Late-Harvest Johannisberg Riesling The sweeter they are the better they stand alone, but a simple butter cookie if you must.

Light, sweet Muscat Cashew or Macadamia nuts, pound cake, peaches or small melons, apple pie.

Sec Champagnes, sparkling Muscats Wafers, fresh strawberries, hazelnut torte, medium-sweet soufflés.

Port Plain butter or nut cookies, pears, apples, nut breads, pistachios, roasted chestnuts.

Cream Sherry Plain or nut cookies, toasted almonds or walnuts, apple-nut cake, apple pie or cobbler, zabaglione.

Angelica Pound cake, nut breads, baked apple, fruit cake, mince pie.